D0960790

No One
at the
Wheel

Driverless Cars and
the Road of the Future

SAMUEL I. SCHWARTZ

with **KAREN KELLY**

PUBLICAFFAIRS

NEW YORK

PublicAffairs
Hachette Book Group
1290 Avenue of the Americas
New York, NY 10104
www.publicaffairsbooks.com
@Public_Affairs

Printed in the United States of America
First Edition: November 2018
Published by PublicAffairs, an imprint of Perseus Books, LLC, a subsidiary of Hachette Book Group, Inc. The PublicAffairs name and logo is a trademark of the Hachette Book Group.

The Hachette Speakers Bureau provides a wide range of authors for speaking events. To find out more, go to www.hachettespeakersbureau.com or call (866) 376-6591.

The publisher is not responsible for websites (or their content) that are not owned by the publisher.

Print book interior design by Linda Mark.

Library of Congress Cataloging-in-Publication Data
Names: Schwartz, Samuel I., author. | Kelly, Karen, 1958– author.
Title: No one at the wheel: driverless cars and the road of the future / Samuel I. Schwartz
    with Karen Kelly.
Description: First edition. | New York, NY: PublicAffairs/Hachette Book Group,
    2018. | Includes bibliographical references and index.
Identifiers: LCCN 2018021594| ISBN 9781610398657 (hardcover) |
    ISBN 9781541724044 (ebook)
Subjects: LCSH: Automobiles—Automatic control. | Autonomous vehicles. |
    Autonomous vehicles—Social aspects. | Traffic safety—Technological innovations.
Classification: LCC TL152.8 .S35 2018 | DDC 629.2—dc23
LC record available at https://lccn.loc.gov/2018021594

ISBNs: 978-1-61039-865-7 (hardcover), 978-1-5417-2404-4 (ebook)

LSC-C

10 9 8 7 6 5 4 3 2 1

Dedicated proudly to Adam William Schwartz, my son

Contents

INTRODUCTION

You Can't Put This Car in Reverse

I guess I shoulda known
By the way you parked your car sideways
That it wouldn't last

—PRINCE, "LITTLE RED CORVETTE"

IN THE SECOND DECADE AFTER HENRY FORD'S MODEL T FIRST rolled off the assembly line, inventors were working to eliminate the weakest link in the chain—the driver. Nearly a century later, that effort is finally coming to fruition. With it could come either better and safer lives or a lifestyle change for the worse. This book explores both futures, as well as the shades of gray between them, and offers a recipe for the best outcome.

At the 1939 New York World's Fair, General Motors sponsored a "Futurama" exhibit called "Highways and Horizons." Visitors rode for a third of a mile in audio-equipped chairs through the 35,738-square-foot scale model of an imagined world of 1960, complete with automated highways connecting gleaming cities, sprawling suburbs, vast rural areas, and modern, efficient industrial districts.

The demonstration's architect, the industrial and theatrical designer Norman Bel Geddes, said of it in his book *Magic Motorways*: "Futurama is a large-scale model representing almost every type of terrain in America and illustrating how a motorway system may be laid down over the entire country—across mountains, over rivers and lakes, through cities and past towns—never deviating from a direct course and always adhering to the four basic principles of highway design: safety, comfort, speed and economy."[1] This vision must have seemed like a utopian dream to a population emerging from the Great Depression.

In 1960, I was twelve, and people were still driving conventional cars on non-automated highways and roads. On June 19 of that year, a short-lived amusement park billed as the world's largest opened in the Bronx, two boroughs away from where I lived. My next-door neighbor, a New York City Buildings Department official, gave the Schwartz family two free passes, and my twenty-two-year-old brother Brian took me. Freedomland, spread across 205 acres, boasted eight miles of navigable waterways for river rides, an 8,500-car parking lot, and 37 attractions, including, among other enticements, reenactments of the San Francisco earthquake of 1906, the Great Chicago Fire (gas jets ignited buildings every fifteen minutes and children ran to pump the fire hoses and douse the flames), and a western fort with daily shoot-outs.

One experience stood apart for me: a motor car traveling on a track that prevented riders from swaying and veering off the road—a form of today's autopilot. The idea that you could travel without steering a wheel (although I did pretend to steer) seemed more magical and powerful to my twelve-year-old imagination than any of the historical re-creations at the park.

By 1964, driverless cars for the masses were still just an aspiration, but especially after I rode on one of a line of automatic skyway cars at the World's Fair in the adjoining borough of Queens that year, the autonomous vehicle (or AV for short) became for me, as well as for many other people, an idea full of potential and promise.

My first car came the closest to being a self-propelled vehicle—at least in my mind. It was a used 1960 Chevy Impala I bought for $450 in 1966 from tip money I got delivering groceries by bike from my father's grocery store in south Brooklyn. It had wings (called fins) like an airplane. Each year all my friends and I would eagerly anticipate the fin changes and enlargements; as they got bigger, the feeling you were flying while driving got stronger. You could even believe you were a little airborne when accelerating on the highway.

Today, finally, mass automated transportation is clearly within reach, and the AV revolution is well under way. In October 2016, an autonomous truck from Uber's Otto division traveled 120 miles of Colorado highway hauling 200 cases of beer while a human driver relaxed in the sleeper berth.[2] Tesla owners can download an autopilot feature that allows drivers on highways to change lanes hands-free by just flipping the turn signal. Autonomous parking is already available on many different makes of cars. Swedish carmaker Volvo has introduced self-driving vehicles on the streets of Gothenburg. There are many more examples of AVs taking on roadways all over the globe. All major vehicle makers along with many private and public research organizations are focused on automating transportation.

Just as the horse and buggy became a quaint tourist attraction, the driven car will likewise become a charming relic as driverless cars, buses, and trucks are adopted by the general population worldwide. In the cult 1990 film *Total Recall*, Arnold Schwarzenegger jumps into a driverless taxi, one of a fleet of AVs that transports passengers around a nameless city, safely navigating traffic and pedestrians. The sci-fi film is set in 2084, but most transportation experts say that by 2075 driven cars will have been completely replaced. Others say the days of driven cars will come to an end even sooner—by midcentury.

By 2025, hands-free driving may be as common as E-ZPass tags became in the early 1990s. By 2035, we may find that the majority of driving miles are completed by machines, not humans. It actually doesn't matter when exactly the driven car will disappear—the lead-up to complete replacement will be a shock to our system, and we need to be prepared. Autonomous vehicles, or AVs, will be the most disruptive technology to hit society worldwide since the advent of the motorcar.

Some futurists and policy experts even talk about human driving being banned on some or all roads.

No One at the Wheel is about the impact of AVs and the choices that people, society, and government will need to make *before* the disruptions they cause reverberate through our daily lives—the good, the bad, and the ugly. These issues will affect family and work life, business, politics, ethics, the environment, travel, health, and, yes, our happiness. Some estimates say that one out of seven jobs in the United States are linked to transportation.[3] All over the world, people depend on drivers, from truckers and taxi operators to bus drivers and train conductors. Because everyone needs a way to get where they need to go and to acquire needed goods and services, no one's life will be unchanged by AVs. I equate the coming disruption to a volcano that's just spewing ash right now—when the lava starts to flow, we have to be ready for it.

Just about every city in the industrialized world was caught flat-footed by the invention and arrival of ride-on-demand services like Uber and other app-based companies, such as Lyft, Gett, and Via, and few cities are enthusiastic about them. In Paris, Toronto, and Brussels, as well as in the Netherlands, Germany, Spain, parts of Australia, Japan, Thailand, India, and dozens of other countries, Uber has been seriously curtailed or even partially or fully banned.[4] In London, taxi drivers have revolted. New York City attempted a short-lived slow-growth moratorium that nevertheless could be tried again after studies showing that a surge in vehicle-miles-traveled (VMT) by app-based cars has contributed to plummeting travel speeds.

It's hard to fault cities for not having sufficient foresight about app-based transportation, since no one had an inkling, including me, that people would change their travel habits so quickly and dramatically. We also have never seen such a rapid change in transportation in our lifetimes. Uber was launched in 2010, and by 2017 it had, according to reports, become a $70 billion company with a commanding social *and* political presence because of its enviable, if dubious, clout and market share.

When AVs become the norm, the reverberations will make app-based rides on demand seem like a minor blip on the transportation landscape. The AV industry is on its way to becoming a multi-*trillion-dollar* business—bigger than Amazon and Walmart combined as they exist today—and with that size will come an unprecedented amount of lobbying power. Impressive economic predictions are floating around from a variety of experts and stakeholders about the global AV market and its benefits to businesses and consumers from Europe to Africa to Asia. The Boston Consulting Group says the global AV market will reach $42 billion by 2025.[5] Infoholic Research LLP estimates that revenue from AVs could grow 39.6 percent annually through 2027, reaching $126.8 billion by that time worldwide.[6] Even more dramatically, the digital transformation of the auto industry will deliver $3.1 trillion in "societal benefits" to the world, according to the World Economic Forum, including the reduced costs of individual ownership, crashes, maintenance, and fuel, as well as lower carbon emissions and insurance premiums.[7] Intel says that the global AV market could create a $7 trillion "passenger economy" worldwide by 2050.[8] By comparison, the top ten car companies in the world today are worth about $650 billion.

There are two very different visions of a world with automated vehicles. One is the vision, based on the hype around AVs, of a utopia similar to Norman Bel Geddes's best-case scenario of driverless cars bringing "safety, comfort, speed, and economy" to society. The other view is a dystopian one. In the Disney movie *Wall-E*, spaceship-bound refugees from an Earth destroyed by environmental catastrophe are so well cared for by their robot transportation devices that hardly anyone has a reason to even stand up, with the result that the universe's entire remaining population of *Homo sapiens* is morbidly obese. This future—one in which fewer people die from vehicle crashes but more develop hypertension and diabetes at ever-younger ages—doesn't seem like much of a trade-off. I also fear that an AV-dominated society will direct transportation toward those with means. The lowest-income individuals will be shackled to low-performing, infrequent, unreliable, and overall odious transit options—if they have any options at all.

There are other potentially harmful outcomes of plunging ahead mindlessly with AVs, and these concerns are shared by some of the leading thinkers in transportation. Bern Grush, a transport futurist you will meet in this book, warns of the law of unintended consequences: "AVs will be like smart phones. After a few years, everyone will want the newer models. The number of cars worldwide will grow from just over one billion today to two billion, then four billion, in twenty-year jumps. This is akin to what we saw at the start of the last century— with just 8,000 cars in the United States in 1900 and 1.7 million by 1914—except a thousand times faster.

"We imagine an AV will cost the same as an average vehicle today, about $29,000," Grush continues. "In reality, in 2040 an AV may cost just $7,500. A number of reasons will bring the cost down—fewer moving parts, and advancements in manufacturing technology. [We] will be far more likely to print an AV. We could order a car from Amazon or the local 3D printing shop and have a vehicle the next day. I'm telling you it can happen," he cautions.

Moreover, since cars will be not just cheap but multifunctional— containers in which we can work and sleep and play—having an individual car might seem very appealing. And since AVs will be upgraded frequently, as cell phones are today, rapid improvement could lead to more frequent purchases. Most people own a car for about ten years and generally replace their cell phones after only a few years.[9] In the future, however, people may start replacing cars at the same rate as cell phones. If that happens, the roads are likely to be both littered with abandoned vehicles and overcrowded with operational vehicles.

Bill Ford, executive chairman of Ford Motor Company, warns of "global gridlock" by 2050 "if we continue on the path we're on." He adds, "Our infrastructure cannot support such a large volume of vehicles without creating massive congestion that would have serious consequences for our environment, health, economic progress and quality of life." The path that Grush and Ford warn about is one that continues to focus on the individually owned car—on private transportation carrying one person on a disproportionate number of trips.

AVs have the potential to bring both benefits and disadvantages. On the one hand, tens of thousands of lives will be saved as traveling becomes safer and more predictable. On the other hand, after drivers of trucks, taxis, Ubers, and buses lose their jobs, they will have to learn new skills to adapt to a changed transportation marketplace. Cities could be imperiled if autonomous vehicles destroy public transit systems. It doesn't help when innovators like Elon Musk put down public transit:

> I think public transport is painful. It sucks. Why do you want to get on something with a lot of other people, that doesn't leave where you want it to leave, doesn't start where you want it to start, doesn't end where you want it to end? And it doesn't go all the time. It's a pain in the ass. That's why everyone doesn't like it. And there's like a bunch of random strangers, one of who might be a serial killer. . . . And so that's why people like individualized transport, that goes where you want, when you want.[10]

This is a preposterous way to characterize public transit. The societal and environmental benefits of a well-run transit system are enormous. Any negative aspects of mass transit can be minimized, and in some cases avoided, if we act in the right ways. Showing how is the core premise of this book.

We shouldn't excuse our leaders and planners if they fail to plan for this next transportation revolution about to hit us. It can only hurt us if government sits back and waits to set policy—or worse, allows private business to completely control the narrative and public policy. We need to think now about how AVs will affect life, family, ethics, and the environment. To that end, I discuss many of the business issues, as well as some of the political and social policy issues. For example, unions need to prepare for AVs: if they enter the field early, they would have a lot to gain, but they could lose out entirely if they do not. City centers present distinct challenges for AVs. It's not so hard to imagine a businessperson going to a meeting in Midtown Manhattan and, instead of paying what will soon be fees in the triple digits for parking, telling his AV to drive around the block continually until he calls for it.

AVs have the potential to transform our existing highways as well. Since these cars can travel in very precise paths, we may not need 12-foot-wide lanes for 6-foot-wide cars. A 36-foot-wide, three-lane roadway could become four 9-foot lanes at the cost of no more than new lane striping. In the immediate future, we will likely see dedicated lanes for AVs only. In center cities, it would be a mistake to squeeze in more car lanes on city streets, but trimming down to skinny lanes could mean adding bus lanes, bikeways, pedestrian spaces, more outdoor cafés, rows of trees, and more. In many suburbs, AVs could link to existing transit lines, or new lines made up of autonomous transit vehicles could be designed.

All of these issues represent just a few of the ashes from the imminent transportation "volcano." We are at the dawn of a very new and different world that AVs will usher in before we know it. If you're not convinced yet, think about where young ambitious people in the recent past went when they sought their first jobs and careers. In the 1980s, many went to where they could move money around: Wall Street and its environs. In the 1990s and early 2000s, they went to companies that were moving data: the dot-coms, Silicon Valley, and other high-tech hot spots. Today many of the smartest young people are going to—and being courted by—companies and institutions focused on moving people and goods. That's where the money is today and into the near future: the AV industry.

***

ONE OF MY favorite books is Jack Finney's 1970 novel *Time and Again*, in which the protagonist, Simon Morley, travels back to 1882 as part of a government project. While living in the Dakota apartment building, sadly made famous as the home and site of the assassination of former Beatle John Lennon, he travels between 1970 Manhattan and 1880s Manhattan. Some forty years before my parents would emigrate to the United States from Poland, the 1880s were a gilded time in the city. Most people had never seen a motorcar, still barely in its infancy, much less ridden in one. It would be seventeen years, in 1899, before the first pedestrian, Henry Bliss, would be killed by one of these newfangled inventions. Coincidentally, the accident occurred just a block north of the Dakota.

I would like to be able to travel back to this time myself, to explain that I have news of the impact that motor vehicles will have in the future—that in the 2018 world nearly 1.3 million people will die in road crashes each year worldwide and an additional 50 million will be injured.[11] I'd be able to tell the people of 1880 that even though the century ahead will be one of world wars, motor vehicles will be responsible for killing and maiming more people than all twentieth-century wars combined. I would present the ethical argument that cars will improve the quality of life for many—by reducing travel time, allowing more people to prosper, and bringing city-dwellers to the country in less than an hour. But I would also warn that there is a good way to proceed and a bad way to proceed. That message is the essence of *No One at the Wheel*. In 2018, we should imagine a visit from a person from the year 2100. Will she look on our choices admiringly, or with her head in her hands at the chaos we are about to create? That is the moment we face.

ONE

Yesterday, Today, and Tomorrow: The Future Is Now

I think that cars today are almost the exact equivalent of the great Gothic cathedrals; I mean the supreme creation of an era, conceived with passion by unknown artists, and consumed in image if not in usage by a whole population which appropriates them as a purely magical object.

—ROLAND BARTHES, *MYTHOLOGIES*[1]

I N 2004, A SMALL AUTONOMOUS THREE-WHEEL VEHICLE DROVE itself around an open area in the middle of Florence, Italy, to the delight of onlookers.[2] Its designer had taken careful consideration of the ancient city's many narrow one-way streets and programmed its steering mechanism to go straight or turn right—no left turns allowed. No driver was needed to even sit in the cart to make sure it operated properly. The route was programmed into the vehicle, and the brakes could be operated remotely in case the vehicle had to be stopped quickly.

The vehicle was not the invention of twenty-first-century engineers testing out the latest in robotic cars. It was a demonstration of a third-scale working model of an autonomous cart designed by Leonardo da Vinci sometime around 1478. Historians say that the cart, which could travel just 40 meters (127 feet) before stopping, was probably designed for entertainment purposes. Still, Paolo Galluzzi, director of the Institute and Museum of the History of Science, who oversaw the building of the model, proved that da Vinci's previously unrealized plans worked as designed, and that his vision was centuries ahead of its time.

A BRIEF HISTORY OF THE AUTONOMOUS VEHICLE

Da Vinci's work also demonstrates just how long people have been dreaming about driverless cars. Indeed, autonomous technology (AT) existed long before the first gasoline-powered Model T was driven off the factory floor. AT got a boost in the early 1860s when English engineer Robert Whitehead invented the self-propelled torpedo, using an early guidance system for maintaining depth. Steamboats and trains were probably the earliest forms of self-guided vehicles, with trains using guided tracks to support not only their length and weight but their directional control as well. The earliest steamboats used various combinations of propulsive force, paddle wheels, and screw propellers.[3]

Airplanes were equipped with the first autopilot system when Sperry Corporation introduced it in 1912. The system allowed the aircraft to fly straight and level without a pilot's constant attention, greatly reducing the pilot's workload. That was just nine years after the Wright brothers took their first flight.

In 1925, the Houdina Radio Control Company demonstrated a radio-controlled car at the busy intersection of Manhattan's Fifth Avenue and Broadway. The new Chandler Motor Car was fitted with a transmitting antenna on its tonneau—the open passenger seat—so that a car following it could more easily operate it via a human driver with a transmitter in his hand. The radio signals operated a series of small electric motors in the car that directed its movement through traffic. Although we could think of this as an early driverless car, in reality the driver was simply outside the car, controlling it from another vehicle, much like a hobbyist controlling a remote-control car today.

This was the case with most of the driverless cars, often called "phantom cars," that were built and demonstrated throughout the 1920s and '30s. The Chandler followed a "wabbly [*sic*] course," wrote the *New York Times*, nearly struck a fire engine, and finally came to a stop after almost running down the press pack covering the event. Other driverless cars, similarly radio-controlled, were demonstrated throughout the country. In the fall of 1927, a former naval radio operator named R. L. Mack demonstrated such a car in Los Angeles and subsequently around the country. And despite its inauspicious debut, the Houdina Chandler was demonstrated in 1926 in Milwaukee and once more in June 1932 in Fredericksburg, Virginia.

In general, 1932 was a dramatic year for driverless technology. In August, a self-taught radio engineer named J. J. Lynch demonstrated a remote-controlled driverless vehicle in Hanover, Pennsylvania, before an enthusiastic crowd. According to journalist Brett Berk, Lynch had operated his automated car numerous times in front of large crowds, without incident. During this particular exposition, however, the autonomous Chrysler went rogue and headed directly into a crowd of 3,000 onlookers instead on staying on course. It hit at least twelve of them, including a sixteen-year-old boy who sustained a major head injury that may have been a factor in his death several years later in a sanatorium. Ironically, one of Lynch's purposes was to demonstrate the potential safety of driverless cars. Year later, in advance of another demonstration, Lynch told the now-defunct Yonkers-based *Herald-Statesman* that his "Magic Car never jumps a yellow light. It always takes the inside lane on a street when making a left turn. It stays way over on the right for a right turn. That's more than a lot of cars with drivers do."[4] Despite that crash—and others—the promise of the greatly increased safety of driverless cars has been an enduring hallmark of developers' enthusiasm for the vehicles.

Since that time, every world's fair and expo has showcased robo-cars of one kind or another, always underscoring their supposed benefits:

safety, convenience, and accessibility. In the 1950s, General Motors and RCA built a radio-controlled car that could only run on special highways embedded with steel cables tracked by magnets in the car. In 1977, the Tsukuba Mechanical Engineering Lab in Japan pioneered a driverless car that could travel at a maximum of about 20 miles per hour. Its computerized system tracked white street markers with machine vision. In the 1980s, the German pioneer of driverless cars Ernst Dickmanns figured out a way to retrofit a Mercedes van to drive hundreds of highway miles autonomously.

Autonomous technology is a full-scale reality today. The bread on our tables is likely to have been made from wheat gathered with a driverless harvesting machine like the Dutch Power Company's Greenbot; drones are a curse and a marvel, for they can kill from the air as well as deliver packages to our doorsteps; and unmanned ground vehicles (UGVs) are used in a variety of situations, many of them dangerous— for example, when explosives or other hazards must be handled.[5]

Yet until recently, the dream of a mass-produced driverless car has remained out of reach of the general public. Unlike a military UGV stationed in a far-off desert, a drone, a robotic vacuum cleaner, or even a sailboat with an auto-tiller, cars must navigate the complexities of urban streets and suburban avenues, roadwork on busy highways, and winding routes in rural landscapes, all of which contain people.

To meet these challenges, in 2004 the US Defense Advanced Research Projects Administration (DARPA) asked dozens of teams already working on autonomous vehicles to compete for a $1 million prize, in the hopes of automating one-third of all military vehicles by 2015. The expectation was that any successful resulting technology could be applied to vehicles for general use. That year's entries largely failed. The next year the competition produced several driverless cars and trucks that could cruise California's Mojave Desert without incident. In 2007, DARPA set up its "Urban Challenge" and asked developers to reach a new goal: develop AVs that could safely navigate city streets.[6] The 60-mile urban course had to be completed in less than six hours, and every entry had to obey traffic rules and negotiate traffic and other obstacles. The first prize was $2 million.

Advancements in computer technology—such as sophisticated software for road-following and collision avoidance, improved radar and laser sensors, and better mapping—made a significant difference between the outcome of the failed first contest and the results of the more successful Urban Challenge. "Tartan Racing," a collaborative effort by Carnegie Mellon University and General Motors, took first prize with the "Boss," a highly modified Chevy Tahoe. The Stanford Racing Team's "Junior," a 2006 Volkswagen Passat, took second place. A modified 2005 Ford Escape came in third.

One commercially available driverless shuttle, the "Navia," was introduced to the United States by the French company Induct in 2014.[7] It can travel only about 12.5 miles per hour, and it is powered by an electric motor. Essentially a very large golf cart, it cannot drive with other cars on highways and roads, but it can transport about ten people from point to point in more controlled environments, like a university campus or an airport parking lot. The vehicle knows when its battery is low, drives itself to a charging station, and plugs itself in. "It works like a horizontal elevator. You come in and choose your stop," says Max Lefevre, Induct's marketing director.[8]

By October 2016, Milton Keynes, a small city outside of London, had introduced small electric cars in the city.[9] The podlike vehicles travel at about 12 miles per hour and ferry passengers around on designated pathways (not roadways); they are able to travel alongside pedestrians.[10] To navigate around streets they use cameras and LiDAR (Light Detection and Ranging), a remote sensing technology that measures distance by illuminating a target with a laser and analyzing the reflected light. In Sweden, the first self-driving Volvos have appeared on the roads, and self-driving minibuses are operating in greater Stockholm.[11] A small fleet of AV Ubers (with an operator present if need be) were introduced in Pittsburgh in 2016 and in San Francisco in 2017.[12]

Japan has tested autonomous Nissans, Toyotas, and Hondas, but AV development in the country has been fairly low-profile (although Japan's technology is no less advanced than US, European, or Chinese advancements). The rollout of AVs in Japan stands in contrast to the United States, which seems focused on getting self-driven cars on the road faster than other types of AVs (like buses) in part because culturally the United States values individualism more than Japan, which is of course more homogeneous than the United States.[13] The United States also has a car culture that is missing in Japan.

In Tokyo, for instance, taxi use is less popular because the subway system is fast, efficient, and reliable. According to Yuki Saji, CEO of SB Drive, the driverless vehicle subsidiary of SoftBank, a telecommunications company, the rollout of AVs in Japan won't start with individually owned vehicles. "The first widespread commercial use we will see will be autonomous bus services in rural areas. This is a great market for two reasons. First, it is not as large of a technical challenge since these buses will always travel the same route, and rural roads are not as congested and confusing as city roads are. Second, a rural bus service can provide a huge economic gain for a community that cannot afford regular bus service now," he explained.[14] This is one example of the differences in how countries will incorporate autonomous transportation into the marketplace according to cultural norms, public interest, and legal and safety concerns.

Cities worldwide have also negotiated deals for autonomous car services like Uber, Lyft, and Via to augment or replace mass transit services. Some of these deals may be obsolete within the next few years, as the term "autonomous vehicle" may refer to a car that can, by itself, drive, fly, float, or leap over traffic—a vehicular Superman "faster than a speeding bullet, more powerful than a locomotive, and able to leap tall buildings in a single bound." The "Flying Cars" of Dubai and "Uber Elevate" are just two new AVs expected be in widespread use in the next decade. You may soon be able to travel from San Francisco's Marina to work in downtown San Jose in only fifteen minutes—a drive that would normally occupy the better part of two hours. The ninety-minute stop-and-go commutes from the suburbs to downtown Hong Kong could be reduced to ten minutes.

For the most part, current test cars look familiar—like streamlined versions of cars we see on roads today. Even a prototype of a fully autonomous BMW Level 5 AV is recognizable as a car.[15] However, the future of car design will be quite different. "Right now, all AV thinking is off existing vehicle design," says car designer Dan Sturges, adjunct professor of transportation design at the College for Creative Studies in Detroit. "Once you eliminate the need for a steering wheel and for a driver to be in a certain location in a vehicle, the design possibilities are wide open."[16]

That means a car could look more like a small house, or it could take on any shape, from tall and narrow to oval or round, and have a variety of wheel configurations. Vehicle materials will change too—a vehicle could be textured or eggshell-like. Cars will also become our personal assistants, understanding what music we like or what errands we need to run, how we like to sit or lie down in a vehicle, and accommodating those needs through flexible design features like fully reclining seating areas.

As you read this, scores of even more advanced AVs have been developed, and some may even be driving around your town. We can't know exactly what is happening this minute in research labs or assembly lines, but it is certain not only that there will be driverless cars, but that the dramatic social changes they usher in will in many ways be greater than those brought about by the invention of the motorcar.

Even though AV development continued unabated in the latter half of the twentieth century, most or many of the very best minds were focused during those decades on moving information around, not people. Once the ability to process millions of bits of information in a fraction of a second was attained, the reality of AVs became far simpler. There is now convergence between information and mobility. A driver may encounter hundreds of thousands of scenarios over the course of a year and have to make just as many quick decisions. Both are relatively easy tasks to deal with for today's microcomputers. Although various advances have been made since radio transmissions first allowed cars to move without a driver in the seat, it is information technology that has had the biggest impact on the advancement of driverless cars—and will continue to do so. It is information technology, not mechanics, that will most profoundly change the way we think about travel.

Decades before these advances in computer communication became a reality, popular culture was already predicting that information, not mechanics, would change the way we travel. "Sally," a 1953 short story by the science fiction giant Isaac Asimov, is about an "automatomobile" whose electronically charged motor guarantees that "there'd never been a human being behind her wheel."[17] With the automatomobile, "you got in, punched your destination and let it go its own way." Indeed, the cars in this story "can talk to one another," and "Sally" even predicts what will happen when AVs predominate: "We take it for granted now, but I remember when the first laws came out forcing the old machines off the highways and limiting travel to automatics. Lord, what a fuss. They called it everything from communism to fascism, but it emptied the highways and stopped the killing, and still more people get around more easily the new way."

Asimov was remarkably prescient: it is indeed likely that when AVs dominate, driven cars will be banned in many or perhaps even most places. Asimov's story takes a utopian view in part—the same view championed by early and current developers alike—although the tale takes a darker turn at its end when Raymond Gellhorn, an unscrupulous businessman, tries to steal some of the cars in order to recycle their sentient brains. Moreover, the main character, Jake, loses his confidence in his vehicles, fearing what will happen in the world if cars realize that they are effectively enslaved by humans and decide to revolt.

More dystopian visions see automated vehicles becoming destructive and evil. In novelist Stephen King's 1983 book *Christine*, the car anthropomorphizes into an uncontrollable killing machine. Stephen Spielberg's 2002 film *Minority Report* shows AVs as part of a complex and evil web of statist behavior control. Although it's true that there are real dystopian concerns about AVs, they have more to do with environmental and social inequities, health issues, and ethical problems than with the possibility of vicious-minded cars coming to get us.

WHAT DOES HISTORY TEACH US?

"By 2030, people will realize that the AV will stop for them, so they might be inclined to think, 'Hey, I don't have to worry about cars anymore, I can cross anywhere I like, anytime I like,'" says engineer and futurist Bern Grush. "Smart" cars that have been programmed to detect human beings of all shapes and sizes will halt throughout their journeys unless steps are taken to make blocking moving traffic illegal, with enforcement means set up. The AV will make so many starts and stops that it could become virtually useless in urban areas—as long as people are still allowed to walk around on the ground in cities, that is. As a result of the highly particular ways in which AVs interact with differing environments, they could usher in the end of uniform traffic laws, which have been largely unchanged for pedestrians since the first jaywalking laws were put on the books. We need to learn from automobile history how to avert some of the chaos and social ills that the coming dominance of AVs could bring.

It may seem counterintuitive, but in spite of great strides in the mechanics of mobility, the way we get from point A to point B hasn't changed that much since pre-car days. With the switch to driven cars, we simply went from one kind of fuel to another—from horses (and their manure) to oil and gas (and their emissions). We continue to link the two systems of propulsion by rating the power of car engines in terms of "horsepower." The shift from horses to cars was fairly slight compared to what we are undergoing now as we move from mechanical power to the power of communication and information.

History shows us how easily fooled we can be by hyped-up promises each time a new form of transit is developed. In the 1880s, bike riders joined with auto enthusiasts to create paved roads, and then drivers excluded bicyclists from those same roads. At that time, a variety of bicycles traversed urban and rural areas, and many of them were difficult and dangerous to operate, including high-wheelers—bikes with one very large wheel on the front and a much smaller one on the back. Men risked their necks (and backs) on these bikes, while women were much safer on adult-sized tricycles.

Mechanical innovations in the 1880s often associated with auto-mobiles were originally invented for tricycles, including rack and pinion steering, the differential gear, and band brakes. When bikes with two same-sized wheels became more stable and sophisticated—and afford-able—the tricycle diminished in popularity and standard bikes were adopted by men and women, boys and girls, alike.

The popularity of these more stable and affordable bikes led to more middle-class bike riders, and as a consequence to bicycle activism. An advocacy organization called the Good Roads Society was officially launched in May 1880 by the League of American Wheelmen (now called the League of American Bicyclists, or LAB), and it was this group that ultimately (although perhaps unintentionally) paved the way for the dominance of motor vehicles.

The group's political action was mainly focused on protecting rid-ers' interests from legislative discrimination, improving road condi-tions, and building new roads, particularly between rural and urban areas. The group was so popular that it went national in 1892 and began publishing *Good Roads* magazine. Regular contributions came from members of both the League of American Wheelmen and a newer organization, the American Road and Transportation Builders Association. In 1891, the Wheelmen had published and distributed a small book, *The Gospel of Good Roads*, which advocated the benefits of paved roadways in rural areas. The pamphlet was especially directed to farmers, since the group needed support from farmers if more roads were to be built to connect city to country. Nearly five million copies were distributed around the country.

In 1893, when horse-drawn buggies still prevailed, American en-gineer Charles Duryea produced the first American gasoline-powered buggy by installing a single-cylinder gasoline engine in it. The same year, Congress passed a law mandating Rural Free Delivery (RFD), a service that ensured the delivery of mail directly to rural farm families. Prior to RFD, residents of rural areas picked up their mail at postal depots that were often miles away from their homes. When gasoline-powered

Bicyclists worked side by side with autoists as part of the paved roads movement only to see themselves banned from roads for the first time (along with pedestrians and horses) as early as 1907 with the construction of the Bronx River Parkway. *Source:* Federal Highway Administration.

buggies became a popular way to deliver this mail, smoother, more uniform roads were needed to accommodate them safely.

Good Road Societies were making headway in getting roads built, with help from a growing number of auto advocates. As the English writer and bike expert Carlton Reid wrote in his 2015 book *Roads Were Not Built for Cars,* "Early motoring was highly reliant on the cyclists of the 1890s. Not only did motorists later benefit from improved roads first lobbied for by cyclists, but those motorists were often the same people who had done the lobbying. Cyclists and motorists of the late 1890s and early 1900s were not from separate tribes—they were often the exact same individuals."[18] Ironically, Reid says, the primary advocate for the Automobile Club of America (a precursor to AAA) was Amos G. Batchelder, who had earlier been an official with the Wheelmen.

New Jersey was the first state to pass a law providing state funds for road-building projects.[19] Other states quickly followed suit, with

Kansas being the last to form a state highway system, which it finally did in 1928. Kansas didn't have a Good Roads Society until 1900, at which time Kansas ranked tenth in the nation in number of automobiles on the road.[20] In the late 1890s, the Kansas secretary of agriculture, Foster Dwight Coburn, asked farmers and other land owners to drag the roads in front of their property to maintain them, often ten or twelve times a year.[21]

Bike riders were in for a rude awakening. The same people who had helped cyclists lobby for highway and road systems began to dominate the roads with cars, making road-sharing with bikes difficult and ultimately even illegal in some places, like highways (although to this day it remains legal—if dangerous—to ride on some interstate highways as long as there is no other accessible parallel route). In addition, walkers were being banned from many of these new limited-access roads, ending a tradition millions of years old of people being able to walk wherever they wanted to.

The automobile was invented somewhat simultaneously and independently in a number of locales in Europe and the United States in the late 1800s. Not surprisingly, most cars in the early 1900s were located in either the United States or Europe. In 1908, for example, there were only about 20 cars in Tokyo, Japan. Karl Benz created the first gas-powered car, the Benz Patent Motorwagon, in 1886. By 1895, his company, Benz & Cie., had sold 1,132 vehicles. At the start of the twentieth century, there were probably fewer than 25,000 cars worldwide and only about 8,000 cars in the United States. By 1903, about 63,000 cars had been manufactured worldwide, with half of them coming from France.[22] In the mid-1890s, there had been only about 15 motorcars on Britain's roads, making them quite a novelty. By 1900 there were about 800, by 1930 there were approximately one million, and by 1934 there were 1.5 million cars on English roads.[23]

American manufacturers like Ford quickly came to dominate the industry during the first half of the twentieth century. When automobiles were first introduced in the United States, they were a luxury and a rarity, but as mass-production technology lowered costs, more people could afford to buy a car—and they did. In 1900, Americans owned just 8,000 cars. By 1920, eight million cars were on the road. The increasing dominance of cars was also felt by railway companies, which by June 1894 had to start making pricing concessions for transporting goods, even including free transport.

As cars came into urban areas, crashes and car-pedestrian and car-bike fatalities happened more often than had been the case when horses were the most common form of transportation. Those killed were predominantly pedestrians, mainly the elderly and children.[24] In the earliest days of the automobile, streets were still for everyone. People were free to find the most convenient way to go from point A to point B, usually by crossing in the middle of a street instead of at corner intersections. There were still no stop signs, no traffic lights, and no traffic cops. Children played in the street, and cyclists went wherever they wanted—there were no defined "one-way" streets. "Pedestrians were walking in the streets anywhere they wanted, whenever they wanted, usually without looking," says Peter Norton, a historian at the University of Virginia and author of *Fighting Traffic: The Dawn of the Motor Age in the American City*. As fatalities climbed with the advent of automobiles, cities built memorials for children killed in traffic accidents, and newspapers covered traffic deaths in detail, usually blaming drivers.

According to car historians, the world's first auto crash is thought to have happened in Ohio City, Ohio, in 1891.[25] Automotive pioneer James William Lambert was driving a single-cylinder gasoline automobile with his friend James Swoveland when he hit a tree root and lost control of the car, then crashed into a hitching post. The men suffered minor injuries.

Densely populated cities like New York were at highest risk for crashes. New York City's first automobile-bike crash happened on May 30, 1896, when Henry Wells of Springfield, Massachusetts, struck cyclist Evelyn Thomas on the "Western Boulevard," today known as Broadway.[26] Wells was operating a "horseless wagon" in a "horseless wagon race" sponsored by *Cosmopolitan* magazine when, according to witnesses, Wells lost control of the wagon and confused the bicyclist. Thomas suffered a fractured leg, and Wells was briefly arrested.[27]

Mary Ward, Bridgett Driscoll, and Henry H. Bliss were not so lucky. On August 31, 1869, Ward, a young female scientist, was thrown from a steam car onto a road in Birr, Ireland, making her the first person in the world to be killed by a car. Ironically, a relative of Ward's built one of the world's first steam-powered automobiles.[28] Driscoll was the first pedestrian in the United Kingdom to die in a car crash, in 1896.[29] In the first recorded car-pedestrian fatality in the United States, on September 13, 1899, real estate agent Bliss was hit by a car after getting off a trolley on West Seventy-Fourth Street and Central Park West (already known as "the Dangerous Stretch"). According to the *Times* report, the car that hit Bliss veered after a truck blocked its path, "and the two wheels of the cab passed over [Bliss's] head and body. His skull and chest were crushed."[30]

By the early 1900s, auto crashes were becoming a real concern to city-dwellers. In a two-month span in 1908, 31 people were killed in car crashes in Detroit, Michigan. To put this in perspective, the city of Detroit had a population of between 300,000 and 400,000 people in 1908.[31] Today, New York City has a population of 8.5 million, or 21 times as many people.[32] That would be the equivalent of 651 people killed in two months, or more than 10 people killed daily! Today fewer than one person dies daily in a New York City traffic crash.

As the encroachment of cars became more of a burden on city life, local bureaucrats began introducing strategies and laws to prevent pedestrians and bikes from getting in the path of cars. In other words, they tried to control *people* to the benefit of cars, not the other way around. Despite valiant efforts by citizen groups, municipalities made several attempts to prevent people from going into the street, including putting up signs, lights, fences, and other obstacles.

In 1915, Detroit became the first city to use stop signs, lane markings, and traffic signals, all meant to control the movement of foot traffic.[33] Detroit and New York were also two of the first cities to employ a squad of police tasked with traffic control. Beginning as early as 1860, New York City's Police Department was given the task of regulating competitive and aggressive drivers of horse-drawn buses.[34]

Manhattan was the first city in the United States to create a judicial court for traffic violations. By 1969, the criminal courts had become so crowded that parking ticket defendants had to wait ten months for a trial.[35] The first synchronized traffic signals for motor vehicles were set to timers in 1926 in Chicago. More than ninety years later, city planners still argue about the best way to time traffic lights correctly. These sorts of controls would have been unthinkable and unimaginable to anyone in the nineteenth century, when roadways were viewed as an integral part of the community, meant for use by any and all. But it didn't take long after the car's arrival for the idea of limited-access roads (with no intersections, just on and off ramps) to emerge. The world's first limited-access roadway, called the Long Island Motor Parkway on Long Island, New York, opened in 1908 and was privately funded and built. The first limited-access publicly funded roadway in the United States was the Bronx River Parkway in New York, which opened in 1907.[36] Germany created the first automobile-only road in Europe, the Autobahn, in 1913.[37]

Jaywalking laws, which made crossing at the wrong part of a street a crime, were rare in the early 1900s. "In the early days of the automobile, it was drivers' job to avoid you, not your job to avoid them," says Peter Norton.[38] As more cars invaded cities, a new model appeared. "Streets became a place for cars—and as a pedestrian, it's your fault if you get hit," says Norton. Kansas City passed the first jaywalking ordinance in 1912, which limited the crossing of streets to designated crosswalks.[39]

As I travel back, in my mind, to Simon Morley's New York City of the 1880s, I imagine myself talking to a pedestrian and explaining to him that, within twenty years, we would shine a light in his face and he would stop, that he would "hug" buildings while he walked, and that he'd only cross at corners when the government said it was okay to proceed. If he failed to comply, he'd be charged with a criminal violation and subject to arrest. This pedestrian from the 1880s would laugh at me and say

Boy Scouts would hand out cards like this to people they targeted as jaywalkers. The cards were sponsored by the Kiwanis Club, a service organization. *Source:* "Boy Scouts and Kiwanis Club of Hartford Put on Anti Jay Walking Campaign," *National Safety News* 3 (February 7, 1921): 4; reprinted Peter Norton, *Fighting Traffic: The Dawn of the Motor Age in the American City (Cambridge, MA: MIT Press, 2008),* p. 76.

that no sane society would allow that to happen; it was inconceivable. Keep this conversation in mind as you go through this book—what outrageous, inconceivable concepts might we hear from a visitor from 2100 explaining the "traffic wars" of the twenty-first century?

In December 1913, a department store in Syracuse, New York, hired a Santa Claus to stand on the sidewalk outside its doors. He was equipped with a megaphone, which he used to shame people who weren't crossing the street at the proper places and times, specifically using the word "jaywalker."[40] Norton says that Boy Scouts were enlisted by local car dealers to hand out cards to pedestrians explaining jaywalking. When he saw someone starting to jaywalk, the Boy Scout would hand a card to the person explaining just how dangerous and old-fashioned it was to jaywalk. In the new era, streets had to be crossed differently.[41]

By the mid-1920s, the auto industry had begun advocating for jaywalking laws as a way to make more room for cars and eliminate a nuisance—people. Their vigorous campaigns to get jaywalking laws passed across the country would be successful. For instance, industry lobbyists were instrumental in getting the 1928 Model Municipal Traffic Ordinance passed during the Hoover administration.[42] "The crucial thing it said," according to Norton, "was that pedestrians would cross only at crosswalks, and only at right angles. Essentially, this is the traffic law that we're still living with today." Crossing against a red light was also considered jaywalking. For millions of years, humans had been walking on the earth and stopped only when they perceived danger or an obstacle. For the first time, humankind was asked to stop because a colored (red) light appeared.

I grew up in New York City in the 1950s. To this day, I can still fully sing the anti-jaywalking jingle that played endlessly over the airwaves starting in that decade and in the 1960s:

> *Don't cross the street in the middle in the middle*
> *In the middle in the middle in the middle of the block*
> *Teach your eyes to look up!*
> *Teach your ears to hear!*
> *Walk up to the corner where the coast is clear*
> *And wait*
> *And wait*
> *Until you see the light turn green*

The country was slow to adopt traffic regulations between the 1920s and 1940s, and only thirty-nine states required driver's licenses by 1935.[43] In the 1930s, some cities gave pedestrians the right-of-way under certain circumstances, while other installed barriers to stop them from crossing at undesignated areas of the street.[44] In 1941, about 38,000 Americans had died as a result of automobile crashes.[45] During World War II, car crashes declined, probably because gas, rubber, and metal rationing, among other reasons, reduced driving.[46] Even so, in 1943, 22,727 died in car crashes, and there were 23,165 fatalities in 1944.[47] The Federal-Aid Highway Act of 1944 provided federal funding to states for "modern traffic arteries, both rural and urban, which will incorporate maximum safety into their design and construction. Improvements of this kind in the highway plant will make a permanent and substantial contribution to accident prevention."[48]

After the war, crash levels spiked again. In 1946—a year when fatalities climbed to nearly 32,000—the first of a series of Presidential Highway Safety Conferences held in the United States created the framework for traffic safety work in the postwar years.[49] The May 8 conference was attended by 2,000 federal, state, and local officials, highway transportation and traffic experts, and leaders of national organizations. On its opening day, President Harry S. Truman addressed the conference:

> The problem before you is urgent. Since restrictions on highway travel were lifted at the end of the war, traffic accidents have been increasing steadily. With the 1946 automobile touring season still ahead, the toll of injury and death already has reached prewar conditions.
>
> At the present rate, someone in the United States will die and a score will be injured during the few minutes I am speaking to you here today. During the three days of this Conference, more than one hundred will be killed, and thousands injured.[50]

One result of the conference was an action program to fight highway deaths and injuries. A uniform vehicle code and model traffic ordinances were adopted to help end confusion over road rules, promote education in schools, increase the enforcement of traffic laws, and improve highway design. The conference also created vehicle licensing requirements and funded an aggressive public information campaign.[51]

Another result was Executive Order 9775, signed by President Truman on September 3, 1946. The Executive Order established the Federal Committee on Highway Safety, as recommended by the Presidential Highway Safety Conference. The Federal Committee included representatives of thirteen federal agencies and was given the following mission:

> The Committee shall promote highway safety and the reduction of highway traffic accidents and, to this end, shall encourage Federal agencies concerned with highway safety activities to cooperate with agencies

of State and local governments similarly concerned, with nationwide highway safety organizations of State and local officials, and with national non-official highway safety organizations, as the Committee may determine. The Committee shall also, to the extent permitted by law, coordinate the highway safety activities of Federal agencies.[52]

On June 29, 1956, President Dwight Eisenhower signed the Federal-Aid Highway Act of 1956, which created the 41,000-mile National System of Interstate and Defense Highways. According to President Eisenhower, the law would eliminate unsafe roads, inefficient routes, traffic jams, and everything else (especially pedestrians and bike riders) that interfered with "speedy, safe transcontinental travel."[53] As a result, pro–car traffic laws were now codified on a national level. Traffic regulation, however, did not become a national issue until 1966, when Congress passed legislation putting the federal government in charge of safety standards for cars and highways. Cities and states have remained in charge of enacting and enforcing local traffic laws, including speed limits and impaired driving laws. However, the federal government influences local traffic standards by placing minimum safety standard conditions on states if they are to receive federal funding for highway building, maintenance, and so forth.[54]

By the 1950s, driving safety had become an international issue. In 1958, the United Nations established the World Forum for Harmonization of Vehicle Regulations, which tried to introduce international standards for auto safety.[55] Many lifesaving safety innovations, like seat belts and roll cage construction, were brought to market under these standards. Also in 1958, a Volvo engineer named Nils Bohlin invented and patented the three-point lap and shoulder seat belt, which became standard equipment on all Volvo cars in 1959.[56] Seat belts became mandatory in the United States in 1968, but it took several decades before they were mandated in all vehicles throughout the industrialized world.[57]

Pedestrian activism has a lot of catching up to do to compete with car industry advocacy. If history warns us about anything, it's that pedestrians and cyclists have to be better organized, more vocal, and more vigilant if they are going to ensure that AVs will not completely eliminate walking on many streets, except in fenced-in locations or at different levels from the roadway. As outrageous as it sounds, the urban "modernists" of the 1920s and '30s, such as the Swiss-French architect and designer Le Corbusier, proposed eliminating pedestrians from car roads.[58]

In his "contemporary city" of 1925, Le Corbusier envisioned "sectors," or self-sufficient neighborhood units with pedestrian-only streets filled with shops, schools, health centers, and places of recreation and worship. The population of a sector would vary between 3,000 and 20,000, depending on the sizes of plots and the topography of the area in which they were located. The "shopping street" would run northwest to southeast across sectors. Every sector would permit only four vehicular entries into its interior. The shopping street of each sector would be linked to the shopping streets of adjoining districts to form a continuous, ribbonlike thoroughfare.[59]

After pedestrian rights groups were soundly defeated by the car in the first third of the twentieth century, it took another third of a century for a new nascent movement of citizens, fed up with being squeezed by the automobile, to rise up in a few places and challenge the concept of auto domination.

In 1949, Professor Carlos Maria della Paolera of the University of Buenos Aires founded World Urbanism Day, sometimes called World Town Planning Day.[60] It was an effort to engage citizens in town and city planning and to consider the human element in these efforts.

"Car-free" groups started to spring up in the mid-1960s and '70s in the United States as an outgrowth of the clean air movement. As a student activist in the 1960s and a bona-fide veteran of Woodstock, which symbolized music and a return to nature, I became a firm believer in a cleaner environment. I entered graduate school at the University of Pennsylvania in September 1969, just a few weeks after attending the huge concert and happening. At Penn, I soon learned that the way to transform cities like mine (New York City had been hemorrhaging population my entire life, and the words "cesspool" and "New York City" were often used interchangeably by those who had escaped to the suburbs, the South, or the West) was by improving transit, decreasing reliance on cars, and even taking pedestrian space back from the cars.

I returned to Brooklyn in 1971 and joined the Traffic Department as a junior engineer. The mayor, John Lindsay, was a big proponent of walking and biking. He closed Central and Prospect Parks to cars on weekends and opened them to walkers, bikers, and joggers. The New York City Marathon, by no accident, got its start in Central Park in 1970.[61] Lindsay made Fulton Street in Brooklyn a bus-only street, and Nassau Street in the Financial District became pedestrian-only for most of the day.

I was absolutely thrilled when one of my very first assignments in 1971 was "the Red Zone." This Lindsay plan would have banned cars from a huge chunk of Midtown Manhattan from 10:00 a.m. to 4:00 p.m. We were so far ahead of any other US city in planning for these new/old modes. My job was to do a before-and-after study, so in March 1971, I was busy collecting data on traffic volumes and speeds. Signs were manufactured that read RED ZONE, NO CARS 11 A.M.–4 P.M., MON.–FRI. The implementation date, April 22—Earth Day—was fast approaching. Two weeks before the start date, the mayor, bowing to pressure from the hotel and other business groups, abandoned the plan. The sole remnant of that plan is a Red Zone sign I managed to squirrel away; it hangs in my Chelsea office.

While my hopes for the first car-free plan in the United States were dashed, my enthusiasm was not. Without my bosses knowing, I quietly began to widen sidewalks, eliminate traffic lanes, and even close a car ramp in Prospect Park adjacent to the Prospect Lefferts Garden neighborhood where I was living at the time.

I was far from alone. Other movements to humanize cities ravaged by cars were forming across Europe. The Campaign for Better Transport was formed in the United Kingdom in 1972 in reaction to funding cuts to the country's railroad network.[62] Between 1978 and 1996, the Dutch more than doubled an already massive network of bike paths and lanes, and the Germans tripled theirs from 1976 to 1995. To this day, Germany and the Netherlands continue to increase the number of "bicycle streets" where cyclists have strict right-of-way.[63]

The "New Urbanism" movement, which first gained prominence in the 1980s, promotes urban development that views human interaction and community as hallmarks. Its principles are based on walkability, connectivity, mixed-use spaces, diversity, mixed housing, quality workmanship, good transit, and traditional neighborhood structures.[64]

An early pioneer of the New Urbanism concept, although she didn't use the term, was the late New York City community activist and writer Jane Jacobs, whose 1961 book *The Death and Life of Great American Cities* was groundbreaking in its influence on how we think about city planning. At a time when the conventional wisdom was centered on bulldozing so-called slums and run-down neighborhoods to make way for modern buildings and open spaces, Jacobs saw the dynamism and true community in the diversity and density of traditional urban neighborhoods. Her thought was that crowding people and activities together created a joyous, energetic, organic, and economically sustainable community. The book was in part a reaction to the urban decimation starting to take place in cities, which included the construction of roads that sliced neighborhoods in half and turned many urban landscapes into desolate, dangerous, and impoverished areas.

The Death and Life of Great American Cities makes four recommendations for creating a positive urban environment: (1) a street or district must serve several primary functions; (2) blocks must be short; (3) buildings must vary in age, condition, use, and include rentals; and (4) population must be dense. These are principles that smart urban planners still consider today—or should.

Cars were not a significant element of Jacobs's vision—in fact, they detracted from it. Her philosophy was inspired in part by study, but mainly by her own experience living in New York's Greenwich Village. As she observed life below her home above a candy store at 555 Hudson Street, Jacobs noted the rhythm of an urban neighborhood where children walked to school in the morning, shopkeepers opened up a bit later, sweeping their sidewalks and getting ready for customers, house-wives gossiped on the sidewalk, and laborers stopped into bars after work for a drink. One thing was evident: the neighborhood's activity and density made people feel safer, because there was always someone around.

Today we struggle with the same issues in urban planning, and I have the same concerns for the diminishment of bike riders and pedestrians as AVs come to dominate roadways. If pedestrians are going to have any hope of taking back turf from a car-dominated society, they will have to be organized and strategic about it, since AVs will be designed to be used anywhere and everywhere, eliminating the need for walking more than a few feet. Even as I write this, a battle continues to rage between pedestrians and city officials in Milton Keynes in the United Kingdom, where autonomous pods are allowed on walkways.

"How we behave is up to what we devise and regulate," says Bern Grush. "One possibility is creating large tracts of the city that do not have capacity for cars, with streets that have no motorized vehicles, which would include larger plaza areas that many European cities have had for centuries." History shows us that such plazas have provided a sense of inclusion and community that can't be experienced in a "drive-by" culture. The feeling that you are part of a neighborhood is difficult to achieve while sitting in a car. Sitting, standing, or walking around a pedestrian square or plaza—where it's easy to interact with people, have conversations, engage in friendly trade, and form bonds—gives you a feeling of being at home.

As the writer, farmer, and environmental activist Wendell Berry has observed, communities exist only where people know each other.[65] If cars are everywhere and humans are excluded from the places where cars go, cities and communities will be lost. History shows us how communities have been negatively disrupted by the introduction and subsequent dominance of cars—and AVs present an even bigger problem because they take the human out of the equation completely.

Yet if we can sharply reduce or even eliminate privately owned cars in some places and focus on ride-sharing and public transit—which can be improved and made easier with autonomous technology—we can save the interaction between people that is crucial for a humane, healthy, equitable, and economically sustainable civilization. The question we have to ask is: How do we become less dominated by cars while still using motorized conveyances when AVs dominate? Or, as Peter Norton asks, what kind of cities do we want? Do we still want places where people interact eye to eye, or do we want to stay in our pods, effortlessly gliding from one destination to another and picking up what we need without ever moving from our vehicles? Do we want everyone to own an AV, and is that even possible? Or do we want AV technology to embrace convenient, clean, and accessible-for-all mass transit?

We are mostly still besotted by the novelty of the technology: the idea of texting while you drive, or reading while driving, or sleeping or working, is enticing. Very few of us are thinking about the other outcomes AVs may bring. If we can make people understand how Peter Norton sees urban areas—that is, in terms of a "transportation solution" that puts access to both necessities and social engagement within reach—we can make smart decisions about how and where AVs are used to coordinate accessible, affordable transit for everyone without the unpleasant side effects of congestion.

For instance, in the twenty-eight-member European Union (EU), where people age fifty and older account for a far higher proportion of the overall population—about half in most cases—AVs could offer advantages for these and other older populations, allowing for expanded mobility options.[66] However, whether a stagnating and slow-to-recover European economy could support AVs—either as part of modern transit systems or as individually owned vehicles—is certainly debatable.[67] European birth rates are in severe, below-replacement-level declines, and millennials are a minority, at about 24 percent of the adult population in the EU.

It would also be a shame if the AV industry stopped the revitalization that is happening in many cities, especially the smaller American cities that have become magnets for millennials, knowledge workers, and entrepreneurs, such as Columbus, Ohio; Raleigh, North Carolina;

Des Moines, Iowa; Madison, Wisconsin; Boise, Idaho; Grand Rapids, Michigan; Fargo, North Dakota; and Beacon, New York.[68] US millennials will eventually overtake baby boomers as the majority adult population, so it makes sense to pay attention to their migration patterns—and to keep them attracted to downtown cores.

History shows us, as Jane Jacobs pointed out in her second book, *The Economies of Cities*, that dynamic cities are economic engines that offer opportunity and access to people from all strata of society, and to newcomers and established citizens alike.[69] Urban revitalization efforts and the people involved in so-called walkability activism have to work in coordinated ways to ensure that the progress they've made in improving downtown areas of any size is not stopped in its tracks by the money and power of the AV industry.

Ultimately, history urges us to question, if not abandon, the assumption that the only way anybody can go anywhere, or wants to go anywhere, is via car, driverless or not. This assumption is a fairly recent legacy, but an incredibly powerful one. AVs can and should be part of a better system of movement that takes the best from the past, the assumption that streets are for people, and avoids the worst—the idea, barely more than a century old, that streets are only for the car.

TWO

Infrastructure: Less Is More

The right to have access to every building in the city by private motorcar in an age when everyone possesses such a vehicle is the right to destroy the city.

—Louis Mumford, American historian and literary critic[1]

For decades, conventional thinking about national infrastructure—our roads, bridges, and tunnels—has been that constant expansion, renewal, and improvement are necessary to accommodate travel trends. "Better" is usually defined as "more." "Cars first, people second" is a mind-set that has been difficult to change—even today. The tax plan of 2017 took away a current federal provision that allows people to exclude $20 a month from taxable income for "expense related to regular bicycle commuting." Moreover, ever since car ownership became a middle-class rite of passage, it has been assumed that individuals should own cars, and the more cars the better.

I'll come back to the question of ownership, as it plays an important role in our thinking about infrastructure and, indeed, in all our thinking about AVs. For now, it's important to take a brief look at how the enthusiasm for building roads grew both in the United States and abroad as personal vehicles became more common.

In the United States during the nineteenth century, most roads and bridges were constructed by local associations to address a need. These associations, which were unique to this country, would eventually be superseded by nationalized interstate road-building efforts, starting in the twentieth century. A handful of men were responsible for establishing the idea that "good roads" specifically meant good roads *for vehicles*, and moreover, that good roads for cars were good for America and its people. These future-thinking men ultimately influenced what became the first government intervention in road-building, the Federal Aid Road Act of 1916, which provided $75 million in federal money in fifty-fifty matching funds to states over a five-year period. By 1917, every state had a highway agency to administer the money.

Virginian Logan Waller Page, a geologist and testing engineer for the Massachusetts Highway Commission, joined the US Office of Public Road Inquiries (OPRI) as chief of tests in 1900. In 1905, the OPRI was renamed the Office of Public Roads (OPR), and Page was named its director. With an expanded mission and funding, Page held great power to advance his belief that science and technology could solve society's problems, including the "road problem."[2] He worked to secure passage of the Federal Aid Road Act of 1916 and to get the new federally aided highway construction under way.

Motoring was a personal passion for President Woodrow Wilson, and it remained so for his entire life. Toward the end of his first term, on July 11, 1916, the president signed the Federal Aid Road Act of 1916. By providing access to education and jobs, roads were the key, in Wilson's view, to economic empowerment and national unity. The 1916 Democratic platform included Wilson's idea that "the happiness, comfort and prosperity of rural life, and the development of the city, are alike conserved by the construction of public highways. We, therefore, favor national aid in the construction of post roads and roads for like purposes."[3] Wilson believed that it was in the national interest for the United States to think in "big pieces" and "ultimately as a whole."

Binding communities together through roads was one way, the president believed, in which "freedom and facility" could flow most easily.[4]

The idea of social improvement via good roads was echoed by US Representative Thomas H. Tongue of Oregon. "Good roads do not concern our pockets only. They may become the instrumentalities for improved health, increased happiness and pleasure, for refining tastes, strengthening, broadening, and elevating the character," he wrote.[5] Without roads, he argued, the city-dweller would not be able to access the purity and healthfulness of nature.

The former Civil War general Roy Stone was also instrumental in pushing the Federal Aid Road Act. Stone was in demand as a speaker at "good roads" conventions and related events, including an event for farmers, whose support was necessary for large, federally sponsored highway construction projects that would build roads across farms and fields. He referred to the absence of good roads as the "last great stain upon our civilization," a "relic of barbarism," and a "disease" that needed to be cured by government intervention.[6]

Although there have been rapid periods of massive infrastructure-building during certain periods of American transportation history, these efforts have never been made in line with actual travel habits. World War I may have curbed Congress's ability to fund the act—as did its limit on federal funding to $10,000 per mile—but the next national road bill, the Federal Aid Highway Act of 1921 (otherwise known as the Phipps Act, after Republican senator Lawrence C. Phipps of Colorado) demonstrated that by then the enthusiasm for federalized road-building had become a nonpartisan exercise. By 1923, the roads authorized by the act had been completed.

The next substantial federal roads project was the Federal-Aid Highway Act, also known as the National Interstate and Defense Highways Act (Public Law 84-627), enacted on June 29, 1956, by President Dwight D. Eisenhower. In designating $25 billion for construction of 41,000 miles of interstate highways over a ten-year period, it was the largest public works project to that time. Part of the original funding was taken from the defense budget, and the highway design gave the US

Air Force a direct link to the road system. That one of the stated purposes of the 1956 act was to provide access for military vehicles in the event of an attack on the country is probably the origin of the 12-foot highway lane: tanks were 12 feet wide.[7] Money for the project was to be generated via new use taxes on fuel, cars, trucks, and tires.

When I first started studying transportation engineering at the University of Pennsylvania in 1969, it was clear that the United States was the world's leader in highway-building. Europe, having spent the postwar period rebuilding its cities, was only beginning to reconstruct its highway system. But with the exception of Germany, prewar roads were designed for local rather than long-distance travel. The concept of limited access highways—freeways free of intersections—was mostly a US concept.

In prewar Europe, there was no genuine equivalent of a "good roads" movement. Nonetheless, new roads were being built across Europe in response to a growing usage of cars. Throughout the nineteenth century, most road-building in Britain was administered and financed locally. The national government got involved in response to increased pressure from both cyclists and drivers, who demanded more consistent roadways. In 1909, a national road board was formed, and it authorized both construction of new roads and improvements to existing roads.[8]

For example, Dartford, an English town outside of London whose origins date back to the twelfth century, was constructing pedestrian crossings in its downtown core as early as 1905 in response to increased use of motor vehicles. By 1922, the town's bridge was widened to accommodate more cars. In 1934, when local authorities asked the UK Ministry of Transport to help the town build bigger and better crosswalks, similar projects were already under way throughout the United Kingdom.[9]

Meanwhile, Germany started to build the Bundesautobahn system, also known as the Autobahn, in 1913. Germany's first cars-only roads opened in 1929 between Düsseldorf and Opladen and in 1932 between Cologne and Bonn. In the early 1930s, more routes were planned. Adolf Hitler, seeing the propaganda and military benefits of creating a modern high-speed road system, accelerated construction projects. The Reichs-autobahn opened in May 1935 between Frankfurt and Darmstadt. The Bundesautobahn network totaled 1,322 miles (2,128 kilometers) at the end of World War II, and the Federal Republic expanded the highway system in 1953 and 1959.[10] There is a link between Germany's Autobahn and the US interstate system built during the Eisenhower administration. During World War II, General Eisenhower had been stationed in Germany and was very impressed with the network of interconnected highways there.

Freeways were being built in other places as well. In 1924 Italy began construction on a toll road between Venice and Turin. By the mid-1920s, local Australian governments had formed road-building commissions to address the difficulties of motorcar travel, which would soon prevail over train travel. With railroads long providing the dominant form of transit in the country at the time, Australian roads were often neglected or narrow and unpaved. One of the first tasks of the Main Roads Board in New South Wales was construction of a coastal road between Newcastle and Sydney, which facilitated construction of a system of roads joining other major Australian cities.[11]

In my first trip to Asia in 1973, I traveled across India to "find myself." I'm not sure I accomplished that, but I did find the absence (at the time) of wide interstate-type highways with grandiose cloverleafs in the dozen or so cities I visited, from Bombay to New Delhi. In the 1980s, I traveled in Japan, where they had already caught up to and surpassed the United States in highway construction despite the destruction of most major roads in World War II. China in the early 1990s had few "freeways," but today highways crisscross the country. When I visited Russia a couple of years after glasnost, I found the country devoid of fully controlled highways. A generation later, I was brought to Moscow to help solve the traffic problem. Despite my insistence that building new highways would provide only short-term benefits, if any, Moscow officials pressed me to recommend nine elevated highways over the rail tracks leading to the central business ring. Needless to say, I did not win them over.

I first visited South Korea in 2005. Seoul had just torn down a 1976 elevated highway built over the Cheonggyecheon stream and replaced it with an exciting stretch of green public space in the middle of the city. More recently, the city has converted another elevated highway with Seoullo 7017, a pedestrian oasis in its urban center.

After the highway-building epoch in the twentieth century, the "freeway-teardown" movement has arrived in the first decades of the twenty-first. Somewhat by accident, I was in the vanguard of the movement after a portion of Manhattan's elevated West Side Highway collapsed in the 1970s; in the 1980s, as New York City's chief engineer, I recommended tearing the entire viaduct down and replacing it with an at-grade boulevard. The removal of San Francisco's damaged Embarcadero Skyway after the 1989 Loma Prieta earthquake added momentum to this movement, which has now spread across the globe.

Still, road building, repair, and improvement remains a hot button issue in politics. Roads and rail lines connecting cities to suburbs and the countryside are still seen as vital to our economic engine, and to a great degree that is true. Today we're told that much of the US road infrastructure is reaching the end of its useful life. Bridges and roads are crumbling, according to the American Society of Civil Engineers (ASCE); the group's most recent "Infrastructure Report Card" gave transit a "D+" grade.[12]

The infrastructure debate often takes center stage in local, regional, and national political campaigns, but it remains an omnipresent promise that never seems to advance from the talking stage. In the 2016 election, both major candidates talked about investment in infrastructure, not just because we need to improve our transportation network but because such investments would also serve as a jobs program. However, neither US presidential candidate considered the effect that autonomous technology will have on infrastructure, which was unfortunate, since that impact will be profound. AVs will change everything about how infrastructure renewal, repair, and construction should be approached.

Before countries, states, cities, or towns anywhere spend billions or trillions of dollars on new roads, we should consider that AVs are likely to require less infrastructure—with narrower lanes and greater capacity per lane—and therefore less spending than conventionally driven vehicles, including both private cars and trucks and all forms of public transit. That means infrastructure costs (and budgets) should go *down* in the future, not up.

Some states are aware that having more roads doesn't necessarily improve life or the economy. In 2012, Rich Davey, then the transportation secretary of Massachusetts, said at a news conference, "I have news for you. We will build no more superhighways in this state. There is no room."[13] He had a point: Massachusetts has 76,200 lane-miles of roadway, yet the state is just 190 miles long. It has more roadway than Wyoming (60,454 lane-miles), an area several times larger than the Bay State.[14] Massachusetts was the first state to make such a declaration. As transit secretary, Davey also tried to encourage people to shift from single-car ridership to other modes of transit, including trains, buses, bikes, and walking.

Davey's goal of tripling the share of trips taken in those modes included efforts to improve mass transit and promote transportation amenities such as better lighting and more sidewalks, curb cuts, and rail-trails.[15] A rail trail is a disused railway converted into a multi-use path, typically for walking, cycling, and sometimes horse riding. Such conversions not only get people out of cars but also in the long run encourage more social interaction and physical exercise, with their attendant benefits. I must admit, however, that I'm torn by the rails-to-trails movement. I would hope to see some of these tracks returned to service instead.

California has made efforts to improve mass transit services that, if effective, should reduce the need for more roads. In 2012, Deputy Secretary for Environmental Policy and Housing Kate White told a legislative committee that 30 percent of all car trips in California were less than a mile. The agency has focused on four strategies, none of which includes building more roads: bicycling or walking as the default solution for short excursions; high-speed rail; local public transit for trips between 5 and 100 miles long; and the Active Transportation

Project (ATP), which would make walking and biking an alternative to driving, especially for errands that are less than a mile.[16]

Of course, large areas of California (and other states) are rural and remote from services, and people often live in these locations because they cannot afford to live in some of the most expensive real estate in the country—places like San Francisco, Los Angeles, and San Diego—or because they simply prefer these areas or they work there. Such pastoral regions often don't have sidewalks or nearby walkable amenities. Smart investment in infrastructure and AV technology, however, can solve transit and mobility issues in remote and rural areas. These solutions are not short-term, and they don't have to be expensive.

When envisioning a time when we'll have complete travel automation, some futurists talk about possibilities like traveling pop-up amenities, such as mobile libraries or convenience stores, that could serve as weekly meeting places within walking or biking distance for residents of rural areas; high-speed tracks that would efficiently transport people into business districts; and drones that would deliver needed goods to those who don't live close to retail areas. None of these futuristic facilities would require building more and wider conventional asphalt roads. At the very most, retrofitting existing roads to accommodate AVs might be all that is required.

AV INFRASTRUCTURE: CHEAPER AND BETTER

With the increase in a variety of vehicles that driverless technology will assuredly usher in, there may be an even more rapid period of infrastructure deterioration as existing travel routes become more and more stressed. As I discuss in Chapter 3, it is highly likely that vehicle miles traveled will increase at that point, making traffic worse on most roads. On top of that, the United States continues to shortchange public works maintenance, so count on more road and bridge closings. The Trump infrastructure plan of 2018 (still in concept as of this writing) will do little to address the situation—which nevertheless could be temporary, if we're smart.

Semi-automated driving (already available on some models) will come before fully automated driving, and as the driving experience trends toward greater convenience and affordability, more drivers will adapt to the technology. During what I estimate will be a twenty-year transition period, drivers' growing comfort with this technology may encourage more suburban growth, further stressing existing infrastructure as parking demand and traffic around larger urban areas increase as well, particularly at peak times.

There will be a bigger push to expand the number of lanes in roadways, and not only will it be tempting to do so, but it will remain difficult to convince people that lane widening or expansion is unnecessary. However, we should not let this challenging transition period determine how we approach the future or infrastructure-building. During the second phase of AV development, the mid-2030s to 2040s, the trend may very well reverse. As fully driverless systems expand, many experts believe, significantly fewer people will want to own a car. In this scenario, ride-sharing, automated public transit, and robo-shuttles will decrease demand for infrastructure. If no policy is in place to encourage ride-sharing over self-driving, however, I fear that the shift will be too small to realize significant reductions (if any with increased average trip lengths) in vehicle miles traveled or congestion.

We need to ask different questions about our roadways than we have been asking for the last fifty years. Infrastructure in the age of AVs will not and should not be the same as the infrastructure of the past. Instead of asking how many roads we should build, we should instead be working on how best to use the space formerly used for parking and driving that will inevitably be freed up by the full use of lighter and shared AVs over the next fifty years.

As mentioned already, one noticeable change related to infrastructure and AVs will be in the width of travel lanes on highways. We love wideness in the United States, but it's a misguided affection. While working with a city in the Southeast, I found it difficult to convince the state's DOT to think of redesigning a road with lanes less than 12 feet in width. Safety is always the trump card that traffic engineers use to reject narrower lanes, yet studies show that, on both urban and suburban roads, a 12-foot lane is not any safer than a narrower lane of 10 or 11 feet.

Today most major roadway lanes are 12 feet wide even though cars are only about six feet wide and most buses are 10 feet wide. A typical tractor-trailer is eight to nine feet wide, including mirrors. The extra width is to allow for the swaying of imperfect drivers and to accommodate buses and trucks. AVs will be similar to tracked vehicles; their paths can be so precise that there will be little or no swaying to account for. Imperfect driving in general will be greatly reduced by AV technology—drifting because of sleepiness, for example, will no longer be a concern. Drivers with poor peripheral vision (who are still allowed to drive today) won't have to worry about overcompensating to the left or right. Thus, car lanes could potentially be as narrow as seven feet.

A 36-foot-wide, three-lane roadway designed for today's cars could become four or five AV lanes at no more than the cost of a program of new lane striping. That's a 33 to 67 percent increase in capacity just from adding lanes. Because AVs can travel more closely together, effectively in platoons, vehicular capacity could increase by 50 to 100 percent, or even more. Such a capacity improvement per mile under today's standards would cost many tens of millions of dollars per mile, excluding land acquisition (even costlier in dense areas), and be extremely disruptive for years. Restriping a roadway can be done much more cheaply per mile and much more quickly—almost overnight—compared to constructing new roads. Larger vehicles like delivery trucks and flatbeds could be accommodated in narrow lanes because the vehicles around them could be programmed to stay clear of them, even if they overhang a portion of the lane.

Consequently, the cost to maintain and improve our road and bridge infrastructure, if we are smart, could drop dramatically. We should now scrutinize every highway project on the drafting boards. If it calls for widening—as many do—I'd say the default assessment should be to scrap it. During the next decade or so, opportunities will arise to designate narrower AV-only lanes on existing roadways, and that will increase the car-carrying capacity of those roads. Traffic engineers need to develop a new simulation model that takes into account the impact of AVs on both capacity and lane widths. We may find that one-third to one-half of the concrete devoted to our infrastructure system will no longer be necessary in twenty years.

To my knowledge, at present no new freeway roads are being built in narrower widths, at least not in the United States. However, some existing roads are being narrowed. Los Angeles and Seattle, for example, have restriped freeway pavement into narrower 11-foot lanes to create new HOV (high-occupancy vehicle) lanes, eliminating the need to widen those highways. Since 2007, Minneapolis has used the same strategy on stretches of I-94. Miami has done the same on I-95, whose existing five lanes and shoulders in the northbound direction, including an HOV lane, were restriped to create six lanes, two of which were designated as HOT (high-occupancy toll) lanes. The Wiles Road project in Coral Springs, Florida, has widened that roadway from four lanes to a divided six lanes; each lane is 11 feet wide, with five-foot-wide bicycle lanes and rebuilt sidewalks in each direction. Its capacity is 33,000 vehicles per day, but local planners predict that will increase to 40,000 by 2020.[17]

We also don't know how the transport of large goods will change in the future. In fact, we don't know whether manufacturing technology will still even require that large structures built in one place (for example, modular, factory-built housing) be moved to another place many miles away—it may not be. We may also find a reduction in trucking as 3D printing becomes more effective.

In 2018, there is no reason why we should consider widening highway lanes to increase capacity. Although politicians and others like to think that making more roads will reduce congestion, it is more often the case that if you build it they will come: more roads often lead to more cars on them (a phenomenon called "induced traffic"). More and wider lanes are unnecessary to accommodate more vehicles in the age of AVs. There is no point in building 100-year infrastructure now that we may need for only ten to twenty years.

With automated technology, the distribution and delivery of goods won't require more infrastructure. Transporting freight by truck is relatively expensive today simply because fewer goods can be carried at once and human drivers limit the distances that can be covered. Labor is also costly, but trucks today need the flexibility provided by human drivers so they can pull up next to their goods' final destination. In the future, AVs will greatly reduce the costs of truck driving, since far fewer if any human drivers will be necessary. Automated trucks will also be able to travel in close, regimented convoys, enabling the delivery of a greater number of goods at a time. A platoon of autonomous trucks has already made one successful journey. Traveling across Europe in April 2016, it demonstrated that more than a dozen trucks could travel in a pack, their speed efficiently controlled and connected via wireless technology.[18]

We may not need traffic signals and signs, crossing guards, and traffic police, or even sidewalks, because vehicles will be programmed to drive designated speeds and obey all laws (I hope) in populated areas. Scientists may work out technology that allows AV wheels to travel safely over ice and avoid locking up when gaining traction is difficult. That could extend the life of infrastructure because deicing salt—a major culprit in the destruction of roads, especially bridges, in more than half the country—may not be needed in the quantities required now. And with lighter vehicles that travel at speeds predetermined by the nature of the roadway, the need for heavy guardrails and other barriers will also decline, saving yet more money on infrastructure. In fact, at the highest levels of autonomy, no barriers may be needed at all. Just think of the absence of barriers on Chicago's El. In sum, connected, "smart" AVs may virtually eliminate the need for all the accoutrements of today's streets and roads and almost certainly make road-building and maintenance less expensive.

There will still be stressors on infrastructure despite the positive impacts of AVs, even if we approach the coming change in the right ways. For instance, AVs can be dramatically lighter than even the lightest and most efficient car made today, but no one has seriously studied how cars alone cause road damage; most road condition studies have looked at how heavy loads, and specifically trucking, cause roads to deteriorate. For example, a US General Accounting Office (GAO) study determined that the road damage caused by a single 18-wheeler is equivalent to the damage caused by 9,600 cars.[19]

We might assume that lighter vehicles, even those that carry cargo, will create less stress on infrastructure. For example, each stress on a bridge—whether it's the Williamsburg Bridge in Brooklyn or the wooden Dingmans Bridge that allows drivers to cross over the Delaware between New Jersey and Pennsylvania—could cause a microcrack, invisible to the eye. Lighter vehicles will reduce such damage somewhat, but because lighter vehicles will be able to drive closer together (as will heavy trucks), the weight on a bridge at any one time could also increase as the number of vehicles increases.

In general, North and South America and Europe have decent enough road infrastructure for AV intelligence needs and have a long history of mass car ownership. But what of those places that have poor infrastructure or are in the midst of the kind of private car revolution (largely Communist or post-Communist countries) that we experienced fifty to eighty years ago? Indeed, every concern we've discussed so far is an issue that every city and town across the globe will have to address, and in ways that suit their own unique culture, economy, infrastructure, laws, environment, and urban fabric. There is no one-size-fits-all infrastructure answer for incorporating AVs around the world.

While visiting the two Berlins in the 1980s, I found West Berlin to be a very exciting city that resembled any large city, complete with traffic jams. When I crossed the wall at "Checkpoint Charlie," I was immediately struck by the absence of cars in East Berlin. Will people who live in places where cars are rare, like many parts of Africa, end up skipping driving completely and go right to AVs? Will progressive countries like Finland and Sweden prohibit or severely disincentivize individual ownership or designate AV-only areas and lanes in city centers? Will other countries follow suit or continue on the path of mostly private ownership and increased congestion?

There will also be many organizations and people around the world, not just in the United States, who would like to get a piece of any potential business that comes from AVs. The European Concrete Paving Association, seeing the potential of AVs for its members' businesses, held a summit on road infrastructure for connected, autonomous, and electric vehicles in June 2017, attended by forty representatives from around the EU. Unsurprisingly, the paving association's conference concluded that concrete will remain the most durable material for roads traveled by these vehicles.[20]

While it may be true that AVs will need highly predictable roads and accurate signage to operate efficiently, some of Europe's infrastructure may not have to change as much as concrete manufacturers and others want to believe. Researchers at the Organization for Economic Cooperation and Development (OECD), an intergovernmental economic group with thirty-five member countries, found that Europe has more than enough roads and rails to meet the demand.[21] It's likely that many countries won't have to build new roads or replace wholesale existing technology to accommodate AVs, particularly in western Europe.[22]

However, ancient cities will have some obstacles to overcome. On holiday in Athens, Greece, in the summer of 2017, I was struck by how many pedestrian-unfriendly streets there were in the downtown area. After all, Athens is where walking and learning became famous with Aristotle's Peripatetic school. Many parts of the city's core do cater to people on foot—like the Plaka, which sits in the shadow of the Acropolis and where most streets are closed to cars. In other central areas, however, pedestrians are forced to walk for several gated blocks before coming to a corner without a metal fence where they can then cross the street. In these neighborhoods, sidewalks are cracked and desolate and few people are in evidence as cars zip by, typically at 30 to 50 miles per hour. There are few speed cameras in Athens, where drivers are known for their aggressiveness.[23]

Athens is ancient, and as in many European cities, its streets aren't based on the tidy grids characteristic of Hippodamus-style planning, as

Gated sidewalks in Athens force pedestrians to walk long distances to reach crosswalks. *Source:* Sam Schwartz.

are large parts of Manhattan. Instead, over the centuries, Athens developed outward from a web of irregular, narrow arteries. Like similar cities, Athens has built modern roadways that lead to the city core to serve commuters and residents just outside the center. The population of the city of Athens is about 665,000, and greater Athens has a population of more than three million. There are about two million cars in the greater area, or 667 cars registered for every 1,000 residents, the densest per capita car ownership in Europe.

Since there is limited space for parking, car owners often leave their vehicles wherever they can, which is not always convenient for pedestrians.[24] As a result, "car vaulting"—stepping on and over cars—has become a popular act of pedestrian protest (and navigation) in the city. Moreover, road signs are not always consistently placed or maintained, and some are erratically placed or missing, obscured, covered with graffiti, bent and twisted, or nailed high on the sides of buildings, where they are impossible to see.[25] A conundrum I've posed to my international traffic engineering colleagues to no avail is why, in Athens, there are so many stop signs atop traffic signals. So, when the signal is green, do you stop? What would an AV do in this circumstance?

Noticing all of this, I couldn't help but consider how competently tens of thousands of AVs would be able to traverse Athens's labyrinth of streets and thoroughfares. Will AVs impart some of those trillions of dollars' worth of societal benefits predicted by the World Economic Forum and the Rand Corporation, or will AVs contribute to the chaos and congestion already prevailing on many Athens roads? And will aggressive drivers here and the world over become so frustrated with slow-moving AVs that "road rage" will take on a new, even more destructive meaning?

INFRASTRUCTURE AND THE DEVELOPING WORLD

Human mobility enables economic betterment—it's our ticket to better social networking and better jobs. Anytime we can improve human mobility we contribute to our overall quality of life, so we have to look at opportunities to improve access to mobility. Places like Switzerland, Singapore, and Hong Kong have modern infrastructure (some of the best in the world, far outpacing the United States) and an educated, tech-savvy populace who may be able to accommodate AVs quickly and with little disruption to existing roadways.[26] Indeed, they welcome AV policies that spur economic growth and encourage social cohesion. But what impact will AVs have in those places where access to mobility is hard to come by? While every country and continent has unique infrastructure challenges, the developing world could be particularly challenged when it comes to AVs.

For example, it is surprising that a country like India, which has produced a tremendous amount of modern technology, might be one of the last to accept AVs. India, with over 130,000 road deaths annually, has overtaken China in having the worst road traffic crash rate worldwide, according to the Indian government. It also reported that in 2016 at least 410 people *a day* lost their lives in road crashes. Most incidents in India are due to driver error, such as drunk driving, jumping traffic lights, and sudden lane changes.[27] Although AVs could prevent many such crashes and resulting deaths and injuries, India is struggling with whether it should even adopt AV technology—and if it *can* adopt AV technology given the infrastructure problems that plague the country.

India's roads are chaotic and vary widely in condition, even in large cities. Fewer than half of India's roads, about 47 percent, are paved. For comparison, according to the Federal Highway Administration (FHWA), as of 2012 one-third of all roads in the United States were unpaved (defined as roads without a surface of crushed stone and hydrocarbon binder or bituminized agents, with either concrete or cobblestones).[28] Of course, a very tiny percentage of vehicle-miles-traveled (VMT) occur on such roads. For these reasons, the World Economic Forum ranks India eighty-seventh in infrastructure in the world.

"AVs depend on highly defined environments, lane markings, so jagged sidewalks, merging freeways, and road boundaries, they have to be clearly defined," says Venkat Sumantran, chair of Celeris Technologies and coauthor of the book *Faster, Smarter, Greener: The Future of the Car and Urban Mobility.* "The more ambiguous these things are, the more complicated and more expensive AV computers and sensors have to be in order to overcome even simple markings on unpredictable roadways. There is a wide spectrum of roadways, and every time you move down the spectrum, you make life difficult for AV," he says.[29]

An "unpredictable" and varied spectrum of conditions defines infrastructure in India. From cows, camels, and elephants traveling on rural routes and major thoroughfares alike to rickshaws, hard-carts, trucks, and bicycles, the traffic on Indian roads is also the most diverse in the world.[30] Maps often fail to comprehend the encroachments common on Indian roadways. Add to that very poor road maintenance, incredible potholes, and other road damage, and AVs don't really seem like a natural fit.[31] However, fully autonomous cars don't need road signs or markings to operate, and they could help bring needed services, jobs, and goods to remote areas of the country, as they could in other similarly developing countries.

There are champions of the technology in India. Sirish Batchu, general manager and head of infotronics technology at Mahindra & Mahindra, says that if infrastructure and network challenges could be overcome, autonomous cars in India could reduce driver stress, increase safety, reduce pollution, and increase capacity—moving more people on autonomous transit to and from jobs, services, and amenities. In other words, AVs could bring to India all the benefits they promise everywhere.

John Moavenzadeh, head of Mobility Industries and a member of the executive committee of the World Economic Forum, told a group of Indian suppliers that India would probably not be the best market for AVs specifically because of its poor infrastructure, its complicated traffic patterns, and the low cost of hiring drivers. On the other hand, he pointed out, India could benefit from AV technology via its human capital. "What I personally find really exciting about India," Moavenzadeh told the group, "is the skills and talent around software and certain technology and that to me seems like a great opportunity."[32] For instance, Ford is experimenting with smart mobility projects in Bengaluru, the capital of the state of Karnataka.

The chief information officer of Daimler, Jan Brecht, agrees with Moavenzadeh. He adds that India's biggest gain from AVs, at least in the short term, will come via the IT and analytics skills of its population; this expertise will "drive a big portion of the development of these services. . . . I think it is more challenging to have an autonomously driven vehicle here in India than in Europe or the US. But that is probably the ultimate test then to prove the technology."[33]

Despite India's infrastructure issues and the skepticism of many about AVs' chances on the subcontinent, Tata, the largest car manufacturer in India, is testing AVs in Bengaluru. It has so far reengineered two sedans with LiDAR radars, stereoscopic cameras, and ultrasonic sensors. An onboard computer receives inputs from the sensors and makes any necessary corrections.[34]

Japanese carmaker Nissan has also filed several patent applications related to self-driving technology in India.[35] Most of them are linked to systems that enable vehicles to sense traffic conditions and assist with navigation. These patents make sense in light of the government's plan to electrify the roads by 2030 in anticipation of more than seven million (human-driven) electric vehicles (EVs) on Indian roads within a decade.

Africa's infrastructure challenges are also well known. Rural Africa has only 34 percent access to roadways (or land covered by roads) compared to 90 percent in the rest of the world.[36] In addition, the state of the continent's infrastructure is generally quite weak. According to the UN, rural African women walk an average of six kilometers, or about four miles, each day to retrieve water from rivers and springs because they lack piped water and wells. Moreover, rural Africans often find it impossible to bring harvests to market or take sick children to the hospital because of poor or nonexistent roads.[37]

Africa's agricultural productivity is sluggish, and a major reason for the continent's inability to feed itself and its lack of meaningful rural entrepreneurship is its poor infrastructure, including roads and transportation. "Infrastructure in much of Africa is not ready for AVs; it's not even ready for conventional cars," says Freetown native Nyambé Séinya Harleston-Blake, a global immigration and mobility specialist for Koch Industries and formerly the United Nations high commissioner for refugees in Sierra Leone.[38]

"Governments are not adequately prepared either," she says. "We are still fifty years behind in terms of technology. In Freetown, for example, power shortages are common, as they are in other African cities, including neighboring Liberia. Most people, if they can afford it, have personal generators, which are costly to maintain. Without a reliable power source, there is [a] trickle-down effect that has an impact on how goods and services can be delivered." Africa's rural populations also don't live within range of all-season roads or any sort of public transit. In middle-income African countries, about 60 percent of rural people live within two kilometers of an all-season road. Those who lack transportation options are unable to participate in any meaningful way in entrepreneurial activities. Expanding rural road networks could be a strategic investment for rural development—but that takes money.[39]

Whether AVs will be developed to accommodate African roads in all their variations or Africa's roads will be improved enough to accommodate AVs is an open question—although it seems likely that the cars will have to be made to fit the roads. In September 2017, the Technical University of Munich debuted a prototype electric vehicle, the aCar, designed specifically for conditions in rural Africa.[40] It is a rugged, four-wheel-drive vehicle with large wheels and an angular, boxlike body that can handle the rigors of dirt roads and off-road driving. It has a range of about fifty miles and enough torque to clear obstacles. The vehicle is also modular, in that it can switch between carrying passengers and transporting cargo, and would retail for about $10,000.[41] That's not a small sum for many rural Africans, but it's far below the price of what is now considered an inexpensive EV: the Nissan Leaf, for instance, is about three times that price.[42]

If more AVs like the tough little electric aCar are developed in ways that allow them to navigate over rough terrain, and if, like other technology, they follow Moore's Law (the number of transistors you can fit on a chip will double every eighteen months) and become cheaper, will they enjoy the same success that cell phones have had on the continent?[43] Africans across the continent basically skipped the landline stage and jumped right into using cell phones, which are now as common in South Africa and Nigeria as they are in the United States, according to an April 2015 study from the Pew Research Center.[44]

Yet Venkat Sumantran doesn't think the cell-phone analogy works and argues that AV technology probably will not be embraced in Africa in the same way that cell phones were. It's not just that the continent has a huge number of drivers who don't charge as much for a trip as taxi drivers do in developed countries, nor that its inconsistent roadways will slow the adoption of AV technology. "Cell phones can rely on lumpy, sparse infrastructure," he points out. "You need one cell tower every fifteen miles, and beyond that you can move to wireless and isolated routers. Cell-phone services can serve a lot of people with targeted investment and very little infrastructure. AVs require very predictable infrastructure and highly accurate mapping."

Sumantran doesn't see such infrastructure and mapping coming to Africa anytime soon. And even though cell-phone usage has grown in Africa, it still lags behind Europe and the United States in the population's use of digital technology. Of America's 319 million people, close to 90 percent use the internet daily, compared with only about 55 percent of people in South Africa.[45] Harleston-Blake agrees. "Existing cell-phone networks would not be adequate to accommodate networked driverless cars. The technological infrastructure required for networked vehicles would be prohibitively expensive for most African governments," she says.

Sumantran says that rural Africans would probably be better served by autonomous drones, which could bring them needed supplies, than by driverless cars. Nevertheless, and despite the difficulties faced by African nations in getting AVs on the road, there are those who hype AVs in Africa, especially the continent's modern cities with better infrastructure, like cities in South Africa. Ruckus Wireless, Inc., a global supplier of advanced wireless systems for the mobile internet infrastructure market, is expanding in South Africa with an eye toward enabling AVs. Riaan Graham, sales director at Ruckus Sub-Saharan Africa, admits that the human-driven taxi industry will be around for a while in Africa. He also believes that a total mass uptake of AVs would require legislation enabling the testing and use of AVs on the road.[46]

CURB THE PARKING

Most of the time cars are parked, either in a driveway, on a street, in a garage, or at an office or shopping center. According to some estimates, a typical car is parked about 95 percent of the time.[47] Yet during busy periods, as town planners and consumers often complain, there is not enough parking. Some studies have found that on average some 30 percent of the cars you see driving around a downtown core are circling around looking for a place to park.[48] In the United Kingdom, it takes on average six minutes and forty-five seconds to find a parking space; for Londoners, it takes twenty minutes, thanks largely to parking restrictions, yellow lines, and meters.[49] In July 2017, the traffic data company INRIX Research issued a report detailing the economic cost of "parking pain." In the United States, that price tag is estimated at $95.7 billion a year from fines, time wasted looking for a space, parking fees, fuel costs, and running out of time (i.e., time spent "feeding the meter" or being late for work). For UK drivers, the cost is £31.2 billion ($39 billion), and German drivers' parking pain runs to €45.2 billion ($56 billion) a year.[50]

A survey by IBM found that worldwide, urban drivers spend an average of twenty minutes per trip looking for parking.[51] The journal *Transportation Science* has shown that drivers who park at the first available spot and then walk to their destination on average save considerable time (never mind savings in fuel and stress) over those who cruise around until a "better" spot opens. Searching for parking closer to the destination creates a perception that parking spots are scarce, but in reality spaces are simply not always available at the exact times a driver wants one.

Don't be fooled. There *are* parking spaces: In *Rethinking a Lot*, Eran Ben-Joseph, a professor of urban planning at MIT, contends that "in some US cities, parking lots cover more than a third of the land area, becoming the single most salient landscape feature of our built environment."[52] Donald Shoup, a professor of urban planning at UCLA, argues that free parking has contributed to auto dependence, rapid urban sprawl, extravagant energy use, and a host of other problems. In *The High Cost of Free Parking*, Shoup contends that when planners mandate free parking as a way to alleviate congestion, they actually end up distorting transportation choices, debasing urban design, damaging the economy, and degrading the environment.[53]

There are no hard numbers on parking lots and available spaces, but Ben-Joseph estimates that about 500 million parking spaces are available in the United States at any given time, taking up about 3,590 square miles, an area larger than Delaware and Rhode Island combined. About 268 million registered cars are in use, meaning that there are about two parking spaces per car in this country.[54]

The bottom line is that when AVs on-demand become ubiquitous, the emphasis will be on shared vehicles and we shouldn't need more parking infrastructure—in fact, we will need far fewer parking spaces and better planning. The huge area of land devoted to parking could be freed up for more attractive and beneficial uses than housing cars, such as recreational areas, parks, running or biking tracks, housing, retail and mixed-use facilities, and so much more.

Parking can also destroy downtown areas. The *New York Times* architecture critic Michael Kimmelman coined the term "Pensacola Parking Syndrome" to describe a city that tears down old buildings to make way for parking spaces as a way of enticing more people to come into downtown areas. Yet if too many buildings are torn down, no one will visit downtown because places worth visiting will have been replaced by parking lots.

In 1973, Boston instituted a successful parking freeze in concert with the Environmental Protection Agency (EPA). Since then, Cambridge, Massachusetts, has set its own limit on parking spaces, and more cities should follow suit. As car ownership decreases with the growing dominance of AVs, ride-sharing increases, and urban areas become less vehicle-friendly and more pedestrian-friendly, demand for parking, even during peak commuting times, will certainly decline.

Reinventing existing parking lots as outdoor market stalls and recreational areas and relocating parking outside of city and retail centers makes sense. Like many experts working, studying, and planning around a future with AVs, Stelios Rodoulis, a development transport planner in London who specializes in AVs, says that driverless vehicles will drop off and then collect passengers when and where required. Many of them will operate continuously and either won't park at all or will return to depots in less expensive and less densely populated areas. Moreover, because cars without human drivers can park much more closely together than they do now, parking areas could be much smaller than they are now, while fitting more cars.[55] That's because passengers won't enter and exit cars in such parking lots. Metro trains, light rail, streetcars, and buses would also help meet the demand for peak travel times into business districts. These demands can be filled with existing infrastructure or less invasive infrastructure.

In *Rethinking a Lot*, Ben-Joseph says that the most profound advances in modern parking lot designs provide for mixed use and take people into consideration. This is an important point to consider for any municipality interested in extending parking options. He cites Renzo Plaza in Turin, Italy, as an example. Planners transformed part of the area around Fiat's Lingotto factory by extending a grid of trees from the parking lot, creating a canopy of soft shade and a place for people to walk or rest. At Dia:Beacon, the Minimalist museum of contemporary art along the Hudson River about an hour outside of New York City, a parking lot designed by the artist Robert Irwin in collaboration with the firm OpenOffice has trees planted in such a way that they rise gently toward the museum's front door, making the parking lot part of the building's entry.

One of the leading global architecture firms, San Francisco–based Gensler, sees private car usage peaking by the end of the 2010s (if conventional demographic predictions hold true, and we have already talked about why they may not) and ride-sharing becoming dominant by 2025. One of the firm's parking concepts features a modular garage floor section that can be easily moved or removed to let in light and facilitate circulation. Built-in utility hookups also help make conversion to other uses easier. Gensler has already designed a building in Ohio with three parking levels made to be changed into offices over time, with easily added facades and details similar to those found on other floors. Mixed-use areas in communities are important in promoting equitable access to new jobs and services to disadvantaged populations, who may have few alternatives to access jobs and services.

Andy Cohen, cochair of Gensler and an evangelist for flexible parking garage design, says that, in all cities, 25 to 35 percent of the land area is taken up by streets and parking. "Municipalities have an opportunity to design future parking projects so they are adaptable," he argues. "That can be accomplished through flat plate design and exterior ramps that can be removed, leaving the facade of the structure looking like a conventional office or apartment building." The height of each floor has to be at least eleven to twelve feet to accommodate other uses, such as offices, retail, and housing. Most existing above-grade parking lots are eight or nine feet, according to Cohen. "We see such modifications as adding between 10 to 15 percent to the cost of the structure," he notes, but that additional cost pales in comparison to the costs involved in destroying an obsolete building and constructing a brand-new one.[56]

Cohen predicts that even airport and retail parking will become obsolete in the next fifteen to thirty years as ride-sharing and mobility services overtake private ownership of vehicles. "I am talking to airports about consolidated parking and car rental facilities and creating better ways for people to be picked up and dropped off at their destinations," he says.

Below-grade lots, which Cohen does not advise building in the future, can also be modified into tech spaces and data storage areas and other windowless uses, such as fitness centers. The problem is the loss of revenue to office buildings when parking goes away. "Between 10 and 15 percent of a building's revenue can come from parking, so how do you make that up?" Cohen says he gets that question frequently when talking to developers. "You can make up a lot of that revenue by charging for access VIP drop-off areas." If you want to get dropped off in front of a building in a specific place or at a specific time, you would pay a premium, he contends.

Zurich, Switzerland, has addressed the parking issue in a forward-thinking way that accounts for the sheer number of cars that private ownership of AVs could represent. In 1996, parking was capped in the core of the city at a 1990 level. Any new parking would have to replace the surface parking that blighted most city squares at the time. Today most of these squares are free of parking and have been converted to public parks. What is instructive about Zurich's approach is that it turns the conventional "parking minimum requirements" on their head; instead, the city has set a "parking maximum" that protects it from having too much parking, which can often erode the character and foot traffic of downtown areas. By making parking space numbers even more restrictive, the 1996 law increased the number of walkers and cyclers in the downtown core and decreased the number of cars.[57] In other words, if you don't build it, they won't come.

As the traditional parking lot becomes less necessary for cars in the future, Zurich's idea of putting restrictions on parking areas makes even more sense. Moreover, new construction should be designed in a way that makes it easier to reinvent the space as a human-scale recreational area. The message sent by Dia:Beacon and similar projects is that if you build a garage today, in twenty years it may be obsolete. Any parking facilities built today should be designed to be modifiable for other uses. I've been recommending to clients that insist on building parking garages to increase floor heights from eight feet to ten feet, or more, to allow for conversion to housing or commercial offices in twenty years or so, when the garage may no longer be needed.

THE IMPACT OF OWNERSHIP ON INFRASTRUCTURE

As I mentioned earlier, ownership of personal AVs may also be less desirable as transportation as a service becomes more widely accessible, inexpensive, and convenient. With fewer driven cars, the need for roads, bridges, tunnels, viaducts, road signs, traffic signals, and traffic personnel will also decrease. As self-driving cars become ubiquitous, one likely consequence in some countries will be either a de facto ban or an outright governmental prohibition on traditional driven cars.

While I don't advocate a ban on driving *or* on AVs, I do believe that just as you can no longer take a horse and buggy on the interstate today, you will probably not be able to take your 2018 Ford Fiesta on many, if not most, roadways of tomorrow. This shift away from driven cars will change the number and size of needed roadways in significant ways. While cities may be unlikely to ban the operation of AVs (and I do not advocate that either), some may want to keep them out. For example, Paris has suggested a ban on the use of private AVs in the future to prevent congestion. "In say 2025 you will have mayors, not only in

Paris, [insist] that we don't want to have privately owned vehicles in the city. They will be forbidden. The idea is not to get rid of all vehicles, but making sure that what we call 'zombie cars' [autonomous vehicles with nobody inside] are not driving in Paris," says Jean-Louis Missika, who is responsible for architecture, urbanism, and economic development in the French capital. Instead, he says, Paris will work with AV makers and fleet managers to make sure that only vehicles that provide a public service are allowed in the city's center.[58]

Moreover, people are already driving less today, and most industry experts and analysts say the trend toward less driving per capita will continue. Since 1983, the percentage of people with a driver's license has steadily decreased among sixteen- to forty-four-year-olds. According to research done by Julia Fiore, a Theodore Kheel Fellow at Hunter College, in 2005 vehicle-miles-traveled in the United States per capita began to decline. In 2017, it was 5.4 percent below the 2005 level, mainly because of the shift in millennials' travel and living habits. They are choosing to live in urban areas where they do not have to depend on a car to access amenities, jobs, and entertainment. Simultaneously, reliance on public transportation and ride-sharing services is on the rise.[59]

For several years, opting out of driving has been popular among millennials and members of Generation Z. About 69 percent of nineteen-year-olds had a driver's license in 2014, compared with almost 90 percent in 1983.[60] Following suit are middle-aged people and baby boomers, declining numbers of whom are choosing to renew their licenses. Like younger people, older drivers—especially those who, like younger cohorts, are moving back into urban areas and walkable small towns and suburbs—say that the cost of insurance and the availability of ride-sharing and transit services make owning a car less appealing. One survey found that 10 percent of Americans who trade in cars do not purchase a new one and opt instead to use ride-sharing services.[61]

Across generational and socioeconomic demographics, people are looking for communities that offer street life. The Dutch concept of *woonerf*, for instance, refers to a pedestrian-friendly area where pedestrians rule the street and cars, considered intruders, are controlled through traffic calming or slow speed limits; cars and traffic must accommodate people, not the other way around. With mixed-use buildings and walkable amenities, street life in these areas is lively, and goods and services are within close proximity to residential areas. On many streets of Barcelona's historic district, cars must move slowly enough to allow pedestrians to be kings and queens of the road.

With the advancement of AVs, I recommend that traffic speeds be controlled by governments—no car would be able to travel faster than the posted speed limit. (There could be exceptions for emergency vehicles.) For instance, no vehicle would go faster than five miles per hour on a street found in areas set up like a woonerf or the Barcelona historic district. With the role of the car dramatically diminished, we could just as easily walk where we're going—and may prefer to. How annoying would it be to hop in your AV and then crawl a couple of blocks while stopping for every passing pedestrian compared to a simpler and more pleasant stroll to the supermarket for a carton of milk? The demands on infrastructure by pedestrians are far less than those on roads and bridges under constant stress from vehicles.

The harmonization of transportation and harmonization managers (an app, not a person) will make seamless travel as close as your smartphone. The idea behind harmonization is to be able to plug in where you want to go and see immediately how to get there. Finland is already offering a form of harmonization that tells you the best ways to get where you are going by suggesting the best combination of rides—for example, a bus plus a train plus a short walk. Harmonization is far more powerful than Google Maps (for example), and will be a critical service in cities when they make areas either enabled for AVs or available only to pedestrian traffic. Cities may close some pedestrian-only neighborhoods to AVs of any kind (or for that matter conventional cars), and AV buses and other shared vehicles will stop within walking distance. Anyone who tries to take a vehicle into such places will be frustrated when wireless programming and communication stop vehicles in their tracks. In still other dense urban areas with lots of pedestrians and bike riders, vehicles will go quite slowly, perhaps ten miles per hour.

At this level of automation, some people will see car ownership as onerous and inconvenient. It will be easier to summon rides, often shared, when needed. This change in travel habits will also reduce the need for heavy investment in more roads in cities and could amplify the need for different kinds of roads that connect city to country, including retrofitted railways and some expansion of tracks. In a way, we will return to the cities of the early twentieth century, when walking and mass transit were the main modes of transport.

Car designer Dan Sturges says that in the future cars and roads may look quite different than they do now, and how they look will have an effect on infrastructure needs and the redesign of roads. He describes a futuristic system called "Double Street"—vehicles and foot traffic are kept separate but enable each other as vehicles run at high speeds on roads underneath pedestrian streets. Double Street is reminiscent of what Le Corbusier suggested for the "contemporary city" in 1925. A living example of this concept can be found in downtown Chicago, which has some double-decked and even a few triple-decked streets. If adopted, such a system would demand a far different kind of infrastructure than we have now.[62]

I maintain that urban transport does not need to be complicated. For short distances—say, under a mile—walking is the most efficient and healthiest form of transit. Bikes, buses, and ride-sharing work well for going more than a mile and up to five to ten miles. Rail works best for greater distances. Cars (including AVs) have a place too for the 20 to 25 percent of central urban trips taken by those with limited physical mobility, be they the elderly, children, or people carrying heavy loads.

Naturally, AVs are central to the kind of future roadways we'll have. More nimble fleets of various-sized vehicles sensitive to peak travel times, working in tandem with transit, along with more pedestrian-friendly streets and communities, will not just reduce the need for conventional infrastructure but also change traffic patterns and gridlock. To that end, we now look at how traffic and gridlock will be transformed by the widespread adoption of AVs and increasing popularity of transportation as a service.

THREE

Traffic and the Future of Land Use

Americans will put up with anything provided it doesn't block traffic.

—DAN RATHER, AMERICAN JOURNALIST[1]

I HATE SITTING IN TRAFFIC. I HATE IT SO MUCH THAT IN 1986 I implemented a computer program that could determine the best way to beat rush hour so I could work a full day (I was traffic commissioner of New York City at the time) and still make it to Shea Stadium for the World Series. When it was time to go, my unmarked Plymouth Fury would glide effortlessly through the traffic signals on the Northern Boulevard as they turned green in sequence. (I'm exaggerating a bit here: travel patterns made my signal plan useful for many other fans as well.) My dislike of bottlenecks and gridlock also inspired my 1993 book *Shadow Traffic's New York Shortcuts and Traffic Tips*. It was specifically about avoiding and outsmarting the notoriously gnarly traffic in New York City in the pre-Waze days. The year 1993, let alone 1986, seems a lifetime ago, but traffic hasn't gotten any better.

In fact, it's gotten worse. Bill Ford, executive chairman of Ford Motor Company, warns of "global gridlock" by 2050 "if we continue on the path we're on." He adds, "Our infrastructure cannot support such a large volume of vehicles without creating massive congestion that would have serious consequences for our environment, health, economic progress and quality of life."[2]

According to a report from the Texas Transportation Institute (TTI), congestion levels in eighty-five of the largest metropolitan areas, including Manhattan, have all increased nearly every year since at least 1986.[3] INRIX Research ranks Los Angeles as having the worst traffic in the United States, and Houston and Dallas aren't far behind.[4] Most astonishingly to me, Beijing, the capital of China, is the tenth-most-congested city in the world, with a congestion rate of 46 percent. In 1980, New York mayor Edward Koch, upon returning from a visit to Beijing, urged me to build bike lanes in the city because he'd seen people in China getting around their center cities so easily without cars. Tainan, Taiwan, despite the fact that it is not the most populated city in the country, is one of its most congested, at 46 percent, mainly owing to a crush of mopeds.[5] Rio de Janeiro, Istanbul, Bucharest, and Jakarta also suffer from crushing congestion, topping global lists of most congested cities.

The Amsterdam-based GPS and travel service company TomTom estimates that traffic has increased by 13 percent globally since 2008.[6] Whatever their size, cities that have little or no control over vehicles are often those that don't use methods like congestion pricing, odd-even travel days, and other techniques. As a result, their traffic congestion continues to increase because of growing populations and lower fuel prices. Other factors have contributed too.

In New York City, one such factor is app-based services like Uber and Lyft. Between 2014 and 2017, traffic in the densest parts of the city increased by 7 percent and traffic speeds dropped by 28 percent in Midtown Manhattan, to a devastating average of 4.7 miles per hour. According to Bruce Schaller, a recognized transportation wonk with expertise in taxicab and vehicle-for-hire operations and regulation, the combined mileage of yellow cabs, black cars, and car services increased from 14 percent to 19 percent of total citywide mileage from 2013 to 2016.[7]

The American Highway Users Alliance found that the top thirty bottlenecks in the country are each responsible for more than one million hours of lost time annually.[8] Drivers stuck on roads with bottlenecks experience delays of about 91 million hours every year, the equivalent of 45,500 person-work-years. The lost value of time to the economy from congestion just in this handful of locations is upward of $2.4 billion annually. If the economy continues to improve, the 2015 Urban Mobility Scorecard predicts that by 2020 annual delays per commuter will grow from 42 hours to 47 hours (more than a full week's work lost); total delays nationwide will grow from 6.9 billion hours to 8.3 billion hours; and the total cost of congestion will jump from $160 billion to $192 billion.[9] To put this in perspective, even in a "recovering" 2014 housing market, Americans lost $192.6 billion to foreclosures.[10]

With the stakes and costs this high, the enthusiasm around the belief that autonomous technology can end global gridlock is understandable. "A Single Autonomous Car Has a Huge Impact on Alleviating Traffic" is a provocative headline that refers to a 2017 study done at the University of Illinois at Urbana-Champaign.[11] The research, led by assistant professor and engineer Daniel Work, demonstrated that placing a single autonomous car in a real-life circular traffic simulation greatly reduces the chance of a "phantom" traffic jam.[12] An autonomous vehicle with "intelligently" controlled speed reduced the standard deviations of speed in all twenty cars in the circle experiment by about 50 percent. The number of times brakes were hit by drivers in the circle was reduced from nine hits per vehicle for every kilometer traveled to about two and a half, and sometimes the rate went down to zero.

Although there is some truth to Work's finding that a speed-controlled car can influence standard deviations in speed, it's the kind of research that easily can be hyped as supporting the "miracle" of AV technology. It would be great if the solution to congestion really was as simple as setting a single AV into a stream of commuters. But it's not that easy.

The slowest vehicle on a road always has the biggest impact on other drivers, so Work's study isn't saying anything particularly new. In 2016,

I demonstrated for the TV news magazine *Inside Edition* how a phantom jam occurs even when we have one vehicle traveling at a constant speed—contrary to Work's finding.[13] The drivers following a vehicle going at a constant speed just don't have the ability to travel at a perfectly consistent speed themselves, so the spacing between cars begins to vary, with some getting too close to the car in front of them and some farther away. The close-in vehicles eventually tap their brakes, which sets a "shock wave" flowing through the line of trailing cars.

Nonetheless, I have little doubt that AVs in sufficient numbers on a freeway will sharply reduce the number of phantom jams. I also believe that the carrying capacity of freeways will increase with very high percentages of AVs. But I am less optimistic that we will see such improvements on city streets, where an increase in the sheer number of vehicles, made worse by the attractiveness of AVs, may actually worsen traffic flow.

Imperfect drivers are not the only cause of bottlenecks. Some other reasons are obvious, such as three lanes merging into two. Other bottlenecks occur near highway entrances and exits as traffic merges and weaves. Some bottlenecks are so subtle that only a professional traffic engineer can spot them. One example is what happens on a gradually inclining road as gravity causes vehicles, especially trucks, to slow down a few miles per hour: the spacing between vehicles shortens, drivers begin to tap on their brakes, and a jam begins. Other less noticeable bottlenecks are caused by slight changes in lane widths, loss of shoulders, bends in roads, signs with too much information, and sun glare. The US Department of Transportation's "2012 Urban Congestion Trends" report showed that 40 percent of congestion is the result of bottlenecks.[14]

Many of these bottlenecks could be reduced, or even eliminated in some cases, with increasing communication between AV cars on the road and connectivity with the road itself. The programming of AVs to talk to each other and anticipate and respond to changes in traffic flows, combined with traffic management systems, will get more cars through longer stretches of road without jamming. This already happens on a comparatively low-tech level with apps (like Waze) that tell drivers about police activities, potholes, or crashes on their route and help them avoid these potential slowdowns by suggesting alternate routes.

Car companies are creating their own Waze-like systems as well. In Europe, Honda has introduced connected car service platforms on its new vehicles.[15] While drivers are delighted with these apps, local communities are often up in arms over the traffic being diverted onto their streets. In January 2018, the city of Leonia, New Jersey, reserved sixty of its streets to residents only during peak hours; violators will now risk a $200 fine. It's not a perfect solution—local businesses have lost customers during these hours, for instance—so congestion rerouting and other fixes must continue to evolve.[16]

Some cities are going beyond reliance on apps and building systems that allow vehicles not only to "talk" to each other but also to communicate with the infrastructure, such as traffic signals or roadside appurtenances. New York City has already established connected vehicle (CV) technology; these applications deliver traffic alerts to drivers so that they can take steps to avoid a crash or reduce injuries or damage to vehicles and infrastructure.[17]

AVs could reduce congestion, as the argument goes, because there will be fewer collisions with AVs on the road. It is true that one of the clear advantages of AVs is that they won't crash as often as human-driven cars. But we may not need the driverless component of AV technology to achieve most of the reduction in crashes. The Insurance Institute for Highway Safety (IIHS) has found a 7 percent reduction in crashes for vehicles with a basic forward-collision warning system, and a 14 to 15 percent reduction for those with automatic braking.[18] Alain Kornhauser of Princeton University has made this point repeatedly: "The safety objective can be fully obtained with Safe-driving (automated collision avoidance and lane keeping) and doesn't need Self-driving (automated with a ready and able driver just waiting to 'save the day' and take control and drive conventionally) or Driverless (no one is there to take control and/or there are no controls to take control of and . . . no steering wheel or pedals)."[19]

Thirty-five percent of congestion happens simply because there are too many cars on the road. The finite amount of space in cities, with roads going in a variety of directions, both straight and circular, limits capacity no matter how efficient and "smart" cars become, and no matter how many lanes are added to roadways. The physics of this is not hard: vehicles cannot occupy the same space (that's called a crash) and keep moving. There is no such thing as infinite capacity, and we have to come to grips with that.

Unfortunately, actual traffic doesn't always work the way it does in a controlled experiment in a lone circle of traffic, nor do drivers always respond with common sense to mobile warnings about commuting tie-ups. Moreover, the mix of AVs and human-driven vehicles that will be common during the transition period between now and when AVs represent the majority of cars on the road may create types of congestion we have yet to anticipate.

We must plan for an AV future in the right ways and include both public and private stakeholders in the search for transport solutions. If we get it wrong, today's traffic jam on the Cross Bronx Expressway or the commute home on Fridays at 6:00 p.m. on I-405 in Los Angeles will seem like Sunday drives in the country compared to what the roads will look like in twenty years.[20]

DEMOGRAPHICS IS DESTINY: THE FUTURE OF TRAFFIC HINGES ON OWNERSHIP

In 2015, researchers at the OECD's International Transport Forum wanted to find out how AVs might change congestion patterns.[21] They created a model that replaced human-driven cars, taxis, and buses with virtual self-driving vehicles while using real traffic data from Lisbon, Portugal. The other difference between real life and the model was that all trips in the virtual Lisbon were shared (more than one person per vehicle) and were made in AutoVots and TaxiBots. TaxiBots are self-driving cars that can be shared by several passengers.

AutoVots pick up and drop off single passengers sequentially. Crucially for the study's outcome, no buses or private cars driven by humans were allowed. The subway system's usage remained the same as in the real Lisbon.

AutoVots and TaxiBots were set to pick up and drop off one passenger at a time in a car-sharing system (similar to Zipcar). A central "mobility dispatcher" decided whether an AutoVot or a TaxiBot would be more efficient for each journey. It took 90 percent fewer autonomous cars to accomplish the same number of trips as human-piloted vehicles on the road in the real Lisbon. The study found that 80 percent of Lisbon's off-street parking could be removed and streets could be about 20 percent narrower. A great deal of paved space could be freed up and exploited for other uses, including pedestrian recreation areas and even housing or work areas.

It is crucial that this experiment was not based on individually owned cars but on a fleet of AVs dispatched in a way to make shared trips most efficient. How we see car ownership—whether as something to be prized or as a hassle—is probably the single greatest determining factor in whether congestion improves or deteriorates. If people can embrace ride-sharing, and if we can coordinate it with public transit, congestion could be dramatically reduced. I have long argued that I could make congestion disappear overnight in New York City if we could just put two people in every private car instead of one.

In the near term—the next thirty years—there are three groups that will have the most influence over car or AV ownership: baby boomers, millennials, and members of Generation Z. Car ownership *seems* to be on a downward trend in general. But there are conflicting opinions from researchers and planners about what is happening now and, of course, about where we are headed. We have to look at both what has happened recently in the market and what people in these age groups are saying and doing about cars to envision the kinds of ownership scenarios we may be headed for and get a picture of the outcome—whether it's the good, the bad, or the ugly.

Baby Boomers

"For the first time in history, older people are going to be the lifestyle leaders of a new technology," Joseph Coughlin, director of the Massachusetts Institute of Technology's AgeLab in Cambridge, told *Bloomberg Business*. "Younger people may have had smartphones in their hands first, but it's the 50-plus consumers who will be first with smart cars." The article features ninety-seven-year-old Florence Swanson—way past boomerdom of course—who participated in Google's 2016 self-driving car demonstration. She loved it. "You haven't lived until you get in one of those cars," Swanson said after a half-hour ride in a Google self-driving Lexus SUV. "I felt completely safe."[22]

Today boomers seem to be the strongest buying market for human-driven cars, and their desire to have a personal vehicle may not change with the transition to AVs. People between fifty-five and sixty-four are the most likely to buy a new car, according to a study by the University of Michigan's Transportation Research Institute.[23] However, the number of boomers who have a driver's license has decreased. Boomers are not renewing their licenses at the same rate they once did. The Transportation Research Institute found that the percentage of persons with a driver's license who were age forty-five to sixty-nine increased from 1983 to 2008, followed by a continuous decrease from 2008 to 2014. The percentages for sixty- to sixty-four-year-olds in 1983, 2008, 2011, and 2014 were 83.8, 95.9, 92.7, and 92.1 percent, respectively.[24] While fewer boomers seem to be renewing their licenses, those who do are buying new cars.

According to Aaron Renn, senior fellow at the Manhattan Institute for Policy Research, evidence suggests that boomers are not moving into downtowns and other urban areas, as was once predicted, and so they continue to need access to transportation. "Boomers will likely age in place, wherever that place happens to be," says Renn.[25] Research from the Harvard Joint Center for Housing Studies backs him up: two-thirds of this study's respondents said that they had no plans to move into an urban area, either because they preferred where they were living or couldn't afford to move from their current suburban or exurban home into a pricier urban area.[26] They didn't seem to be willing to adjust their lifestyle to live in an affordable, but much smaller, urban space.

"These people may want to keep their cars," says Renn. "If services are not available to them, the temptation to have an AV will be great for people who previously would not have access to a car, either because of their age and failing abilities, including people with physical challenges (of any age) that prevent them from driving a conventional car." According to the US Census Bureau, about 28 million people in the United States say that they have a severe disability that could prevent them from getting behind the wheel today.[27] Indeed, disability levels are rising among middle-aged Americans (ages forty to sixty-four, a group that includes some baby boomers).[28]

"AVs could allow people like this, and others, to own a car," says Renn, "leading to thousands and thousands of additional vehicles on the road—and a great deal more congestion than we have now." In California, for example, the more than 700,000 people over age eighteen who are blind or have vision loss that makes seeing difficult even when wearing glasses or contact lenses will view AVs as wonderfully liberating—and they will be, but the impact of adding perhaps a million more cars to Golden State roads (I'm adding in others with disabilities that affect their ability to drive alone) on a state road system with some of the worst traffic jams in the nation could be devastating if the transportation policy status quo is maintained.

Millennials

North American millennials (those born between the early 1980s and the early-2000s, who are now ages eighteen to thirty-four and make up about 30 percent of the population) are not buying cars at the same rate previous generations did. "Millennials are demonstrating significantly different lifestyle and transportation preferences than older generations," says a report from the US Public Interest Research Group (PIRG).[29] The report concludes that "the driving boom is over." The University of Michigan's Transportation Research Institute has numbers backing this up: there was a continuous decrease in the percentage of sixteen- to forty-four-year-olds with a driver's license for the years examined. The percentages for twenty- to twenty-four-year-olds in 1983, 2008, 2011, and 2014 were 91.8, 82.0, 79.7, and 76.7 percent, respectively.[30]

The cultural view of cars and car ownership is different in Europe, where vehicles are used more for transit and less for leisure and sport, as they are in the United States. A survey of 2,500 millennials from the United Kingdom, France, Italy, and Germany shows that 77 percent have a license and own a car.[31] While about 53 percent of US households have at least one bike, 80 percent of German households, 63 percent of Italian households, and 59 percent of French households have a bike.[32] Moreover, research into European millennials found that a majority would rather give up their car than their smartphone, indicating an interest in information and connectivity over individual mobility.[33]

These trends are not applicable worldwide, of course. The Asian city-states of Macao, Singapore, and Hong Kong have lower rates of car ownership overall because consumption of cars is tightly regulated to keep traffic levels down.[34] Car ownership per capita remains low in China compared to other emerging economies with similar income levels.[35] This low rate could stem from tight vehicle registration regulations and the low share of household consumption in China's GDP (among the lowest in the world at 36 percent).[36]

However, those Chinese who do own cars are young: about 23 percent of all Chinese car owners are millennials ages twenty-five to twenty-nine, the highest percentage of any car owner age group.[37] Chinese millennials who can afford to buy a vehicle also often opt for a large SUV to signal wealth and success, in contrast to American millennials, who lived through the 2008 American recession and are more conservative in their vehicle choice, more often choosing a smaller, more efficient car.[38] Environmental concerns may also inform the choices of North American millennials, concerns that may not be important yet to Chinese young people.

Car ownership in India is depressed overall, a reminder that economic progress there, while growing, has yet to create a large consumer culture. Most people in India, including young people, still depend on public transit, bicycles, and two-wheelers for transportation. In India, the difference could be explained in part by both high import tariffs on passenger vehicles and the popularity and affordability of domestically produced two-wheel vehicles.[39] In urban areas, car ownership is still less than 10 percent, and in more rural areas, car ownership remains in its nascent stage as well.[40]

However, North American millennial driving trends are instructive when it comes to the ways in which land will be used if the future of mobility is more about walking, cycling, and ride-sharing and less about individually owned cars that take multiple unique trips. That said, some believe that as they age millennials are likely to behave more like past generations as they became older. They argue that young adults today don't prefer cities to suburbs and rural areas any more than previous generations did. Increasingly, urban planners are cautioning us to be careful not to confuse millennials' presence in cities with a preference for them. Understanding this could have a crucial impact on traffic and AVs, especially since, like everyone else, millennials are aging and their lifestyles are evolving.

Dowell Myers, an urban planning professor at the University of Southern California, said in a talk, citing research by CityLab, that the twenty-fifth birthdays in 2015 of millennials born in 1990 mark a moment in time that could be called "Peak Millennials."[41] He argues that we will soon start to see both the youngest and oldest millennials moving from cities to suburbs in the conventional pattern shown by previous generations. As they age, Myers points out, millennials' presence in cities could evaporate as they start families and become more established in their careers.

Demographer William Frey has long argued that millennials are just stuck in cities for economic reasons, from declining wages and uneven job prospects to difficulty in getting mortgages. These factors make it harder for millennials to buy houses in suburbs or rural areas—places they may prefer over small apartments in crowded cities.[42]

There's no end to the chorus of planners who almost gleefully pronounce that millennials are just like other age groups, basing many of their conclusions on the most recent two- to three-year period when driving rose. They seem to overlook that this increase coincided with a dramatic drop in gas prices, a record amount of credit available for car buying, and the lowest unemployment level we've seen this century. Furthermore, two or three years does not a trend make. I'm in a different camp (and admittedly have my own prejudices) and would argue, to borrow from Mark Twain, that "the reports of the death of the millennial revolution are greatly exaggerated."

For instance, millennials are living not just in big cities like New York, Chicago, and Boston, but also in smaller cities, like Des Moines, Austin, and Cleveland, that are attracting young, educated professionals and entrepreneurs. In Europe, young educated people are leaving suburbs in greater numbers than they're leaving the cities (and again, even if they cannot afford to live in Paris, London, or Rome, there are smaller European cities that do attract them). Compared to rural areas, European towns and suburbs have experienced a net gain of young people, particularly those with college or professional degrees. In 2016, only 9.7 percent of young people left European cities.[43]

Recently, driving in the United States, western Europe, and some other well-developed countries (but not the former Soviet bloc or China) declined for a sustained period of time, nearly a decade, for the first time in 115 years. The decrease in driving was most pronounced among millennials, and it preceded the Great Recession of 2008, accelerated through it, and continued for years afterward. The many reasons that underlie the decline are well covered in my book *Street Smart: The Rise of Cities and the Fall of Cars*.

In addition, a number of suburban cities and towns, recognizing that millennials are seeking a different lifestyle than their predecessors', have created more walkable communities, with more mixed-use neighborhoods and main streets that feature cafés and outdoor restaurants.

This is a smart move, and I believe it is working, both for these cities and towns and the people who live in them. It's not working so well, however, for automakers, who have managed their panic about the decade-long reduction in driving by pouring a record amount of money into car loans and leases.

Still, it may be premature to pronounce Peak Driving a thing of the past. I watch traffic volume statistics monthly and have been bothered for the past couple of years by the rise in traffic in some places. I don't know whether this is a trend or just what I like to call the "pendulum effect"—that is, people moved to cities in such large numbers from 2000 to about 2015 that the demand now far exceeds the supply of housing and thus prices have soared, forcing people to move out of city centers to more affordable outer areas. Falling gas prices have also changed the equation. These are just a few of the reasons why suburban communities and driving could become relatively more attractive.

Still, driving habits haven't changed as much as many proclaim. Julia Fiore, one of my students at Hunter College, looked at travel patterns over several decades and, with the Harvard-trained transportation economist Charles Komanoff, created a regression model correlating VMT and parameters such as GDP, gas prices, and demographic patterns. Their conclusion is that something different happened with millennials: they deviated from the model by driving less than predicted. Fiore also points out that "the recent increase in auto sales is likely a bubble caused by loosening credit. Due to low interest rates and the loosening of credit requirements, US auto debt is at an all-time high of $1.2 trillion. In 2016 alone, total auto credit increased by 13 percent."[44] And in response to those who say that millennials, as they age, will follow past generations and move to the suburbs, she emphasizes that "millennials are moving to suburbs at a slower rate than past generations." Joe Cortright of City Observatory states that twenty-five years ago people ages twenty-five to twenty-nine were twice as likely to move from a city to a suburb as to move from a suburb to a city. Today that same age group is only 25 percent more likely to move from a city to a suburb than vice versa.[45]

An analysis by Pete Saunders in *Forbes* looks at where educated millennials, those with a bachelor's degree, are moving. He finds that cities are growing at a stronger rate than their suburban areas. Educated millennials in particular are moving to core cities at a greater rate than to the suburbs. For every one millennial who moves to a suburb, 1.52 educated millennials move to a core city. In Chicago, around 50 percent of millennials are choosing to live in the core city rather than in the suburbs or the metro area.[46]

These developments are important because a balanced mix of strong cities and strong suburbs is good for society. It sounds simplistic, but in post–World War II America, the US government did just about everything it could to hollow out cities and expand suburbs, not just by building highways while ignoring transit, but also by financing new housing over rehabbing existing housing stock. Not surprisingly then, from the 1950s until the late 1990s many older cities across America seemed to be in a near-death spiral. Populations plummeted while crime soared. Budgets were slashed, leading to the closure of libraries, schools, and firehouses. Transit systems eliminated lines, cut service, and raised fares. Even in New York City, the transit capital of America, elevated subway lines were torn down, streetcars were eliminated, and stations were closed.

Approaching 2020, we face a major decision point: do we repeat the mistakes we made in the past when we accommodated the internal combustion engine, or do we move ahead smartly with AVs, seeking the best possible outcome for all?

One fear I have is that AVs will encourage more sprawl. Many people may find that removing the driving part of commuting from cars will be transformative: what is now a barely tolerable experience could become enjoyable and productive as people view the car as an extension of their living room or office. About forty years ago, a former boss of mine, the brilliant urban planner David Gurin, said that he thought New Yorkers were smarter than many others because of all the reading they got done while traveling on the subway. Car commuters have had no such option. In an AV, though, you can read—even if you are stuck in traffic—so there is a real concern that AVs will foster sprawl by extending "painless" commutes into the farthest reaches of exurbs and rural areas. In fact, that is already happening now, though to a very small extent.

Generation Z

Today the percentage of Gen Zers—sixteen- to twenty-three-year-olds—who have a driver's license has also dropped sharply since 1997. For the first time since 1963, fewer than 70 percent of people in this age group have a license. This suggests that the millennial revolution in transportation is spreading to the younger generation. Zs are also the first generation of "digital natives"—people who grew up with computers, videos, video games, social media, and other sites on the internet (the rest of us being "digital immigrants"). They will, in my opinion, have more faith than their elders in a "black box" being able to solve just about anything. Therefore, they will be far more willing, to paraphrase a Greyhound Bus ad, to "leave the driving to AVs." But that openness to technology doesn't necessarily preclude their desire to *own* cars. About 92 percent of Gen Zers surveyed in a study from Autotrader and Kelley Blue Book said they were excited about owning a car, primarily because of the freedom it provides.[47]

Gen Zers are technically proficient, but are also curious, driven, and entrepreneurial; they prefer in-person connections over online interaction, according to business consultant Alexandra Levit.[48] Thanks to social media, she says, they are comfortable engaging with friends all over the world, so they are well prepared for a global business environment. But will they want to (or need to, or be able to afford to) live in big urban centers like New York or Chicago? There is still limited research on this large group, but what does exist shows that Gen Zers may be slightly less interested in city living than millennials. According to Nielsen, just 52 percent of Generation Zers say they want to live in urban areas, compared to 54 percent of millennials who said the same thing.[49] As these young people enter the workforce, how they work and what kinds of work they want to do will influence their lifestyle choices, as well as their decision whether or not to own an

AV—which in turn will influence how much traffic they either create or help reduce.

MAKE IT CHEAP AND THEY WILL BUY IT

The economics of AVs will inevitably have an impact on ownership. Technology usually gets cheaper, not more expensive, as it evolves, along with advances in manufacturing.[50] The Foundation for Economic Freedom (FEE) recently did an exercise in which it calculated what an iPhone 7—with its computing power of 128 gigabytes of flash memory, A10 processor (which includes a CPU and GPU), and 3.3 billion transistors running at 2.34 gigahertz and delivering roughly 120 billion instructions per second—would have cost a consumer in 1991: about $3.6 million.[51]

Why will AV price trends be any different? They won't. As car manufacturing itself becomes more automated and cars less expensive to produce—in part because of decline in the labor costs associated with manufacturing them—AVs will become very affordable. This will be especially true of small, lightweight personal vehicles. What will be at first a luxury item will quickly become available in a cheap and practical format.

One example of the price drop comes from John Krafcik, CEO of Waymo, the company that spun out of Google's X division in 2016 as a new enterprise and is now developing autonomous driving technology. Krafcik says that one of Waymo's goals is to make AV technology very inexpensive. "Designing our own LIDAR ("Light Detection and Ranging") system has not only given us a more reliable product than what we can get off the shelf, but it's enabled us to do it at a fraction of the cost," he told reporters. "Just a few years ago, a single top-of-the-range LIDAR unit would have cost about $75,000. Today, we've brought that cost down by more than 90 percent. That's nine-zero. As we scale, we'll take that cost down even further, with the goal of making this technology accessible to millions of people."[52]

Because of lower price points, transport futurist Bern Grush warns, the spread of AV ownership could easily resemble the adoption of mobile phones in developing and emerging countries, where landlines never gained traction but mobile technology did. According to the Pew Research Center, only 2 percent of households in Nigeria and South Africa have a landline, but about 90 percent of adults in these regions own a mobile phone.[53] When AV technology becomes ubiquitous and cheap, you can bet that people who never dreamed of affording a human-driven car will want an AV. But having millions of new personal vehicles on the road will only add to traffic and related problems, including environmental problems.

In wealthier countries, people will be tempted to upgrade their AV after only a few years, just as today we want the latest smartphone as soon as possible. As a result, the number of cars worldwide may grow exponentially from just over one billion today to two billion, then four billion, in twenty-year jumps. This growth would be akin to the increase in the number of conventional cars on US roads—from just 8,000 cars in 1900 to 1.7 million by 1914—except that the growth in AVs would be even more accelerated. We used to keep cars for about ten years, but we'll be trading in our new cars after just a few years. I see this in myself. I own a 2017 Volvo and am eager to get the next model because it will have more safety features, its mapping system will be better, its voice activation system will better understand a Brooklyn accent, and its engine will be more efficient.

We can't discount the natural affinity that many people have for their cars, which will make it challenging to get drivers to rethink ownership. Michele Bertoncello, an AV expert with the consulting firm McKinsey and Company, expects private ownership to remain the dominant model, though Todd Litman at the Victoria Transport Policy Institute think tank says that it will become "cost-effective for a family to give up one of their cars if they're driving it fewer than 10,000 kilometers a year." Nevertheless, many families will still have a reason to own at least one car. Noah Goodall, a research scientist studying AVs for the Virginia Center for Transportation Innovation and Research, expects that ownership will continue among certain demographics and that single ownership will still make sense for people living in rural areas.[54] And let's face it: boomers and millennials may not be driving as much as they once were, but there are still a lot of cars in the world. The number of registered passenger vehicles in the United States has increased steadily since 1960 and was estimated at 263.5 million in 2015.[55]

However, Americans are not the biggest car consumers in the world. A Carnegie Endowment study ranked the United States twenty-fifth in the world by number of passenger cars per person, above Ireland and below Bahrain.[56] Other research ranks the United States number four in the world in car ownership. Whatever the reality, cars are coveted by and useful to people all around the globe.

Those who have cars seem attached to them for a host of reasons. Cars can serve as an extended storage unit or as a place to get away from family and grab some private time to listen to music as loud as we want or indulge in the rants of radio talk show hosts. In my day, and for decades before and after, the car was the place where teens could explore sex away from the watchful eyes of adults.

Some cars signify status or personality. They take us to places we want to go and to places there is no other way to get to. Anecdotal research from Tesla drivers using that car's autopilot technology shows that they take longer, more leisurely rides than those not using autopilot. Tesla models with free "Superchargers" allow drivers to take long-distance journeys.

Totally autonomous cars could allow owners to indulge more frequently in long, relaxing rides. Can a new technology like self-driving radically change the way people think about driving? Even if ownership levels remain steady—and certainly if they increase to include people who cannot drive conventional autos—the total number of miles driven is certain to increase—and with it, congestion.

MILES TO GO . . .

Congestion is directly related to total miles driven by cars. (AVs may change efficiency, but the mathematical relationship will still be direct.)[57] So even if, as Todd Litman predicts, two-car families become one-car families, congestion may not necessarily be eased. People may be willing to live farther from work or amenities because AVs relieve them of driving obligations. Also, overall trips could increase. For example, say there is an extended family of two parents, two school-aged children, and an aunt living in the home. One spouse works full-time in the city center, one works part-time at a local retail establishment, the children are in middle school and high school, and the aunt does housekeeping at home but is also responsible for shopping and errands that can't be accomplished via drone or delivery services. She has a wide social network, and she likes to connect with it. Today they get by with three cars.

Let's see what happens if they replace the conventional cars with one AV. The AV drops off one spouse early in the morning, and along the way drops off the children at their schools. The AV comes back to bring spouse two to a part-time job near the family home and then swings back to take the aunt on her rounds, including a water aerobics class at the local gym and lunch with her friends. At the end of the day, the children and spouses are picked up and dropped off at home. All of this could be accomplished in a one-AV household, but it doubles and even triples the number of miles driven because of all the trips back and forth transporting family members to work, to school, and on errands. Note, *the individually owned car is empty on up to half of the trips it makes—it's not taking anyone anywhere.*

A study by the University of Leeds predicts that, with autonomous vehicles, VMT will increase by as much as 60 percent because AVs will help productivity rise and reduce the cost of sitting in traffic, allowing people who rarely take a car today to start doing it much more in the future.[58] Another study done by the Atlanta Regional Commission predicts that by the year 2040 both the number of daily trips and the average trip length will increase owing to the better commuting experience. And in its most extreme projection—total market penetration of AVs and myriad benefits, such as reduced parking costs and travel times (which is questionable)—the commission predicts a decrease in public transit trips by as much as 42 percent over the baseline (reminiscent of the postwar decline in subway usage last century).[59]

Just about every study I've looked at (not the hype put out by AV proponents) predicts an increase, not a decrease, in vehicle-miles-traveled in central business districts. The only plausible solution is to require all vehicles, except for transit, to pay a premium for the right to travel through a city's most precious resource—its space—through congestion pricing. If we do not charge vehicle owners extra fees to come into city centers and business districts during peak hours, they (and we) will be overwhelmed even worse than we are today by traffic congestion.

Some advocates argue that an AV could drop someone off in the city center and then leave to park someplace else, thereby reducing congestion. However, a car owner can quickly access a car parked nearby, which is also driven fewer miles than a car that drops off its owner and then cruises away to a parking lot outside the city limits. And if many empty cars, what I call zombie cars, drive away from business districts at the same time every morning and then return there at the same time later in the day for pickup, the result is a congestion problem.

One way to solve this problem is to ensure that AVs coordinate efficiently with public transit. That might mean autonomous shuttles that pick passengers up at park-and-ride centers housed outside of business districts—of course, the traffic getting to these parking lots would likely become congested as well. Better yet, AV minibuses could be routed near people's homes for pickups and then could drop them off at transit stations. This solves the "last-mile" problem that transport professionals have struggled with for many decades. Many car commuters say that they have no good transit alternative because they live a mile or more from the nearest transit stop. AV transit could easily solve this problem.

A study by Scott Le Vine, a professor in the Department of Civil and Environmental Engineering of the Imperial College London, says that one reason why trains are so conducive to commuting is that they offer a relatively smooth ride to work compared to a car, which often stops and jerks more frequently.[60] And with no required restraints like seat belts, riding on a train is more comfortable than sitting strapped into a car. It's predicted that AVs, being able to travel at more consistent speeds on highways, will mimic the smoothness of a train ride. Comfort will also be increased if safety improvements make seat belt laws a thing of the past. You will be able to get work done in an AV as you do on a train today—so why wouldn't people choose the privacy of a personal vehicle in this scenario over a train filled with fellow commuters?

Le Vine's "smoothness" study found that rail-like quality can be achieved, but with a serious drawback once a vehicle leaves the highway. His researchers simulated traffic at a four-way urban intersection. They stipulated that AVs make up 25 percent of the vehicles, with 75 percent driven cars (as will be common during a portion of the transition period before we reach full autonomy). In some scenarios, AVs accelerated and decelerated more effectively and comfortably than a driven car, but with some jerking. In other scenarios, the AVs started and stopped with the elegant smoothness of high-speed rail.

The researchers also tested alternatives that reduce speeds but improve smoothness, such as longer yellow lights and larger following distances. They tested sixteen scenarios against a baseline with all human-driven cars. In every single test scenario, driverless cars designed to create a comfortable, rail-style ride made congestion worse than it would have been in a baseline scenario with people behind every wheel.

In the baseline situation, without any driverless cars, each vehicle experienced a delay of twenty seconds at the intersection. When driverless cars accelerated and decelerated in the style of light rail, congestion worsened from 4 percent (twenty-one seconds) to 50 percent (thirty seconds) compared to driven cars. The number of cars traveling through the intersection—at 1,793 in the baseline scenario—also fell between 4 percent (1,724 cars) and 21 percent (1,415 cars). Le Vine's study concluded that there is "a tension in the short run between these two anticipated benefits (more productive use of travel time and increased network capacity), at least in certain circumstances."[61]

Le Vine does say that congestion could be reduced if fleets dominate over private ownership and every vehicle in a fleet is autonomous.[62] None of Le Vine's models, however, incorporate pedestrians into any of the scenarios. One of my pet peeves with transportation engineers and researchers—and this goes back many decades—is that they almost always solve the vehicular problem first and then try to deal with those pesky pedestrians. Certainly, foot traffic, if it is allowed in proximity to cars, will be an additional cause of vehicle stopping and starting, jerking, delays, and congestion.

I was reminded of this when I was in Barcelona not long ago. While in a car, I observed pedestrians as they came out of buildings and maneuvered on the very narrow sidewalk flanking a very narrow side street where we were traveling. Any pedestrian trying to move past another pedestrian would see that their trajectory had to extend into the path of the cars on the road. My colleague, Xavier, was driving, and he did not hesitate. Since he was a local, he knew the pedestrian would turn and not enter the street. How would an AV react? It seemed to me that an AV, unable to predict the movements of pedestrians, would have had to stop or slow repeatedly, creating a very uncomfortable and jerky ride. The result? Congestion, as overall travel time increases and overall speeds decrease, at least in many walkable areas.

Will foot traffic outsmart AVs, knowing they can never hit walkers? Will this trigger an AV traffic rules movement that "fences in pedestrians," as in the 1900s through the 1930s, when pedestrians suddenly couldn't walk any way they wanted (as people had been doing for millions of years) but were relegated to walking only adjacent to buildings and only allowed to make perpendicular movements at corners? Prior to about 1915, the streets allowed the intermingling of both pedestrians and vehicles. After 1915, fast-moving cars threatened the status quo and were responsible for numerous pedestrian deaths. Public officials originally sided with the pedestrians but eventually capitulated as the auto industry successfully propagated the belief that automobiles belonged on the streets and that sidewalks were the place for pedestrians—who were "criminalized" if they didn't follow the rules.

In his book *Fighting Traffic*, Peter Norton argues that to accommodate automobiles, the American city required not only a physical change but also a social one: before the city could be reconstructed to serve the interests of motorists, its streets had to be socially reconstructed as places where motorists belonged—and people didn't. I fear that something similar will happen this century as AVs, towns and cities, and pedestrians renegotiate common space.

With AVs, antipedestrian laws could become even more draconian, and a new excuse to hassle citizens. Jaywalking laws can be applied inequitably to target minority groups and the homeless, disproportionately affecting the poor. Stricter jaywalking laws could also shift the way people view walking and turn potential pedestrians into drivers—causing more congestion in the process.

The Honolulu City Council introduced a bill in 2017 that outlaws looking at a mobile device while crossing the street on foot.[63] However, it is still lawful for a driver to look at his or her dash-mounted phone while crossing an intersection. Research on pedestrian distraction that expects to confirm the conventional wisdom that distracted walking is dangerous nevertheless has concluded that such laws are unnecessary and, again, inequitable. The blog Systemic Failure demonstrates the hype over this concern.[64]

The mass hysteria over distracted walking originated with a paper published in 2013 by Jack Nasar of Ohio State University and his student Derek Troyer.[65] Arguing that the increasing use of cell phones had caused a spike in pedestrian injuries, they were featured in major newspapers, such as the *New York Times*.[66] Cell phones, it was reported, were causing over 1,000 serious injuries per year. And that was just the "tip of the iceberg," they argued, because many injuries didn't require hospitalization. In absolute terms, those numbers may seem catastrophic. But in relative terms, they are insignificant. In 2010, 1,506 pedestrians were injured while using a mobile phone, but that accounts for any kind of injury, not just ones involving motor vehicles, and covers injuries that occurred while using a cell phone in any kind of public space, not just on sidewalks or in roadways.[67]

Systemic Failure points out that laws like the one in Hawaii could *increase* traffic risks by creating a more permissive atmosphere for driving behaviors that pose a greater threat to everyone. Meanwhile, however, towns in New Jersey and other places have also suggested additional laws criminalizing pedestrians.[68]

The separation of pedestrians from streets to "improve" traffic—which really means privileging cars over people in downtown areas—could become a reality if we allow city planners to be seduced by carmakers. The architecture and engineering firm EDG proposed a new traffic grid that would do just that for Manhattan. Its LoopNYC would supposedly create a safe environment for pedestrians when AVs come along. But it's really just a way to remove people from streets and force them into cattle-chute-type walkways. EDG's plan would optimize the traffic flow into and out of the city by creating AV-only lanes on major parkways like the FDR Drive and West Side Highway that would connect to selected exclusive crosstown lanes at 14th, 23rd, 42nd, 57th, 86th, and 110th Streets. Once inside Manhattan, driverless vehicles would use these as designated expressway loops.

Pedestrian overpasses and underpasses would keep pedestrians *separated from driverless vehicles*, ostensibly to increase pedestrian safety. With the proposed auto-grid in place, a route that currently takes a car forty minutes to cover, Grand Central Station to Lower Manhattan and back, would take eleven minutes—saving thirty minutes a day for the average commuter, according to the plan.[69] That plan doesn't say how much time would be added to a walk along the same route, or how many people might be dissuaded from walking, as they were by similar plans in the twentieth century. What the plan really does is remove people from streets in favor of cars. The argument is nearly identical to those used by interstate highway builders fifty years ago when they planned two elevated highways across Manhattan's Central Business District, one just south of Madison Square Garden in Midtown (where my New York office is today) and one barreling through Soho (there was no Soho yet in the 1950s when Robert Moses first proposed the Lower-Manhattan Expressway). Solutions like these have shown time and time again that far from reducing congestion, they induce more traffic and end up increasing congestion.

WHAT CAN GO RIGHT IF WE'RE SMART

Clearly, AVs are not a cure-all for traffic problems, and as I've detailed here, they could very well make things worse, especially if individual ownership becomes the norm. Certainly, carmakers want to sell as many AVs as possible, but congestion disaster will happen if we continue to emphasize the car as private transportation carrying one person on a disproportionate number of individual trips. The concept of ownership is mentioned often in this book because it is so critical to whether AVs turn out to be a social enhancement or a detriment. The consequences of increased traffic congestion could be disastrous if we shortsightedly allow the AV industry to dictate the terms of travel, as the auto industry did throughout most of the twentieth century.

If we're smart and insist on a variety of stakeholders having a say in how traffic laws and policies pertaining to AVs are written, we can cut down on lost time and money and decrease congestion while enhancing transportation. The right way to introduce AVs so as to reduce gridlock is to integrate them into our transit systems. The role of transit will evolve as AVs and ride-sharing become more common. Transit agencies should focus on high-frequency, high-capacity services in dense urban corridors and provide first- and last-mile connections through lower-capacity on-demand driverless shuttles as well as expanded mobility hubs.

City-operated robo-buses, whether Chariot, Via, or some other multipassenger next-generation form of micro-transit, could deliver much more service for the same amount of money. Smaller buses, operating at a lower cost per mile with less labor, would provide more frequent service at lower fares. Airports, notably London's Heathrow, are already doing this with people-movers, as are other services in cities from tiny Morgantown, West Virginia (which figured this out forty years ago) to Abu Dhabi. In many suburbs, AVs could link to existing transit lines or to new transit lines that will link trains to buses.

Cities can also work with transit agencies and private companies alike to design and adopt smartcards, open data, and universal apps that will allow riders to find, compare, book, and pay for trips that combine buses, trains, bikes, and ride-sharing vehicles. Such services will match customers with the most efficient (and healthiest) travel choices.

AVs could also help ease congestion if we create policies around them that limit their negative aspects and reinforce the positive. Dynamic road-charging—whether on a real-time basis or in an arrangement that varies by time, day, season, origin, destination, number of passengers, and household income—can be done through a combination of congestion pricing, zone pricing, variable tolls, and VMT (vehicle-miles-traveled) and VHT (vehicle-hours-traveled) fees. For instance, if you want to show your family the Christmas tree at Rockefeller Center in Manhattan while sitting in your vehicle as it slowly rolls by, that trip should cost a heavy premium—say, $25 per block. Traveling on an outer Manhattan avenue will cost far less, while travel outside the borough might cost very little or nothing at all.

If center cities can control the number of private vehicles coming in through congestion pricing, mobility for those remaining in motor vehicles would improve. Cars, trucks, taxis, Ubers, and buses would all move faster. That's why Uber, in late 2017, began airing ads supporting congestion pricing for Manhattan, which would also reduce air and noise pollution and our carbon footprint. Congestion pricing could create a wonderful opportunity for cities to add bike lanes, widen and add pedestrian paths and spaces, license outdoor cafés, plants rows of trees, and create parks, all to the benefit of residents and visitors alike. To me, this would be a win-win-win all around.

On-demand real-time mass transit is another benefit of smart traffic planning. Imagine a transit system that knows when a high school football game is ending, a concert will be over, or how many people are likely to be at a particular stop. Smart mass transit will also reduce the need for fleets of large buses; instead, a variety of passenger-capacity vehicles will be configured to respond to the needs to travelers. A forty-person bus would not need to be dispatched to pick up a handful of people.

AVs can help meet the demand for living and working in proximity to amenities through mixed-use neighborhoods, whether in urban areas or small towns and suburbs. To do this, communities would have to incentivize mixed-use development, overhaul parking requirements (I'd expect a greater than 50 percent reduction, and maybe much higher), and reevaluate new public transit projects. When shopping and work zones are easy to access and close by, the need for personal cars is greatly reduced.

If ride-sharing becomes mainstream—and more convenient, efficient, and pleasant and cheaper than owning a personal vehicle—we may see a dramatic decrease in congestion everywhere. Commuters may be more willing to forgo using their own cars if ride-sharing has been able to customize destinations. I proved the congestion-busting payoff of ride-sharing in 1980 during the New York City transit strike. We imposed an occupancy restriction, the temporary rule during the strike that cars could use the capacity-challenged Long Island Expressway (LIE) only if they had a minimum of three passengers. To get a report on conditions during the strike, I had traffic engineers in helicopters (in those days we didn't have Waze, INRIX, or drone technology) reporting back to the command center via walkie-talkies on traffic flow. The media's predictions were dire, and frankly, so were my own as a representative of the city: the LIE would be a parking lot! If so, traffic would receive a grade of F on the level of service.

What happened? Traffic on the LIE got an A during the morning rush hour of day one of the transit strike—traffic was free-flowing and moving as fast as if it were 3:00 a.m.—because we had tripled per-vehicle occupancy on the highway. Clearly, we now have a similar chance to free our cities of congestion if we get occupancy close to two per vehicle instead of a little more than one. There *is* an antidote to congestion, and I witnessed it firsthand in April 1980.

If we are smart—if we dramatically increase car occupancy to at least two per car and maintain other modes of transit, privilege pedestrians over cars, and increase walking, biking, and train use—we will solve the problem of congestion. We will put an end to the argument that "we can't do nothing about the weather and the traffic." But the politics is not easy. After the strike, I tried to require two or more people per car crossing the East River bridges during peak hours. The city was promptly sued by car interests and lost.

Several players in the field—and they will most certainly be joined by others—are even now working on providing a convenient, inexpensive, and pleasant ride-sharing experience. The Israeli-based company Via and its cofounder and CEO, Daniel Ramot, launched its US services in New York and have since expanded to Chicago and Washington. Using a mobile app, Via guides commuters to a "virtual bus stop" nearest to where they are located. There they hop into a Via-owned SUV with other riders who are going in the same direction. One by one, passengers are dropped off for a much more affordable fee than a taxi would charge. Once these vehicles are autonomous, the cost of ride-sharing will go down from the already affordable $6 it costs in New York, since the cost of drivers will be eliminated.

Uber has integrated with the Transit app in more than fifty US cities to show commuters how they can combine an Uber ride with public transit more efficiently to get to their destinations.[70] This is part of Uber's effort to position itself as a complement, rather than an alternative, to public transportation.[71] Ford Motor Company has invested $1 billion in a joint venture with the artificial intelligence firm Argo AI to completely outfit Ford vehicles with self-driving technology. In 2016, Ford paid $65 million for Chariot, a San Francisco-based shuttle bus service.[72] Chariot's routes are customizable because they are crowd-sourced based on rider demand. Ford says that these routes will operate using algorithms to map the most efficient routes to best serve people's real-time mobility needs.

In October 2016, the Finnish company MaaS Global launched an app called Whim, which serves as a portal to a wide array of transportation services.[73] For a flat fee, riders get unlimited access to transit and receive points that can be spent on taxi rides or car rentals. The app is part of an effort by the Finnish Ministry of Transport and Communications to get a head start on the mobility-as-a-service (MaaS) model. Its goal is not just to get people to the places they need to go more cheaply and faster—its core mission is to minimize car ownership.

Ride-sharing was also popular during World War II and en-
thusiastically encouraged by the government. *Source:* Labor-
Management War Production Drive Committee.

In order to work, ride-sharing has to not only be convenient and
affordable but also meet the near-instant availability of a car. If the average wait-time for a ride is ten minutes or more, people will be far less
likely to give up their vehicles. In cities, lengthy wait-times aren't going
to be much of a problem: population density and city-dwellers' access to
amenities make it more convenient for them to hitch a ride on a shuttle
bus than to walk to a car housed in a garage, get it out of the garage, and
drive to their destination. In this scenario, a shuttle bus already on the
road is nimbler than a private car could be. However, an autonomous
shuttle is likely to take longer to reach those who live in the suburbs or
in rural areas.

We have to determine the maximum amount of time the majority
of people are willing to wait for a ride before being unwilling to give up
at least one car. It's a sensible question, but no one knows the answer
yet. It could be a very short time. When a friend of mine stood for eight
minutes on a street corner in the city waiting for an Uber to pick him
up, he canceled the car and flagged down a street cab. Eight minutes is a
short time—can AV shuttles meet that demand?

If eight minutes is too long to wait for a ride, would up to five minutes of wait-time be sufficient to service people—and encourage them
to ditch their cars? To achieve wait-times of no more than five minutes,
vehicles would have to be strategically placed in and around towns and
cities. MIT researchers found that all 13,000 taxis in New York City

could be replaced by a fleet of 3,000 ride-sharing cars if used exclusively for carpooling. Ride-sharing services for carpooling may reduce traffic congestion, pollution, and fuel use if they replace taxis. The study calculated that the average wait-time for the ride-sharing service would be just 2.7 minutes. The scheme would include a "dynamic repositioning of vehicles based on real-time demand, which makes the system 20 percent faster."[74] Clearly, we can do more with less.

Managed fleets of AVs could reduce wait-times and shuttle more people in fewer vehicles, while also preventing empty vehicles from roaming the streets. These fleets could be incentivized depending on who they serve and how. For instance, if a fleet meets certain service targets—for example, running full 80 percent of the time—or exceeds its target—running full 90 percent of the time—it could earn a reduction in its operating fees. A fleet that serves disabled persons or people living in so-called last-mile transit areas could earn a subsidy. At the same time, there would be no incentives rewarding a fleet that runs below capacity more than 50 percent of the time or has no capacity to serve disadvantaged populations, and costs might even be imposed on such underperforming fleets.

It is hard to predict what sort of problems with fake riders and other means of "beating the system" this system might lead to, but by and large well-designed regulations and incentives would motivate fleets and mobility management systems to figure out how to reach goals and serve users at peak demand times. In fact, one of the biggest challenges for these new systems is peak demand. When I studied traffic engineering almost a half-century ago, we accepted the fact that we could solve (or at least thought we could solve) congestion and demand by identifying something called the thirtieth highest hour. For example, a shopping district might be able to accommodate demand 99 percent of the time (say, 2,000 cars), but for thirty hours a year it would have to deal with greater demand (say as high as 2,500 cars). Infrastructure (roads, parking, and so on) was built to accommodate the routine 99 percent of demand, not the 1 percent of demand that occurred during the thirtieth highest hour, since that would have been prohibitively expensive and would have required a wasteful use of land and resources. Sadly, this commonsense approach has fallen by the wayside, as many communities now demand capacity for the 1 percent of peak usage.

If we take a thirtieth highest hour approach in a midsized city, we may need 1,000 vehicles to ensure that passenger wait-times are usually no more than five minutes. But if we want to guarantee that wait-times will be no more than five minutes 100 percent of the time, we may need an extra 300 or 400 cars, which would be idle most of the time. I worry that my fellow Americans would be as demanding as they've been with parking issues and want that five-minute response 100 percent of the time. Anything less would be met by consumers demanding that their own AVs be available to them at all times.

——

THE ONLY WAY to truly reduce congestion and encourage people to use more environmentally friendly alternatives, including mass transit, ride-sharing, biking, and walking, is to make these alternatives more appealing to more people. In a city, suburb, or exurb, transit has to be accessible, fast, convenient, and comfortable. Ride-sharing in AVs has to be quick and convenient, and access to rural areas and nature has to be available equitably. Walking can be a widespread and attractive alternative only if the walking environment is safe, pleasant, and offers benefits and amenities.

We also need to show both the political and personal will to make the relative cost of individual ownership more expensive than riding transit and sharing multipassenger AVs. Reducing congestion via financial disincentives can also help raise the money that is likely to be needed to create and maintain attractive alternatives.

There are so many positive side effects of reduced congestion: less pollution and fewer greenhouse gas emissions, increased safety, more livable communities, and a far better business environment as delivery costs plummet. Businesses both big and small, however, including labor unions, need to get ready to meet some unexpected demands that will disrupt the world they live in now.

FOUR

Business and Consumerism

Money may not buy happiness, but I'd rather cry in a Jaguar than on a bus.

—Françoise Sagan, French novelist

W HEN I WAS GROWING UP, MY FATHER HAD A TINY GRO-cery store in Brooklyn that served our immediate community. Around 1960, something relatively uncommon in Bensonhurst at the time opened about 100 feet away: a supermarket. In our densely popu-lated neighborhood of multifamily houses and apartment buildings, it was the equivalent of Walmart opening in the middle of Main Street in a small town: disruptive, unusual, looming, but still somewhat enticing. Because of the chain supermarket's buying power and financial backing, it could undersell my father on some (but not all) products and absorb losing money on these items in order to entice customers into the store to buy other, higher-priced products.

Uber and similar ride-hailing services are doing exactly what su-permarkets did regarding pricing. These companies are willing to lose money in exchange for market share. They will charge less than a taxi to be competitive and gain riders. (Amazon did the same thing to become a leading e-tailer.)[1] For instance, Uber lost $4.5 billion in 2017; it had lost $2.8 billion in 2016. One analysis suggests that Uber may be covering as little as 41 percent of the cost of its fares.[2] However, Uber stated that in the first three months of 2018, it made $2.45 billion because it sold some assets.[3]

Uber also spends big on lobbying efforts. It employs 250 lobbyists at 49 lobbying firms—a lobbying troop that is larger than Walmart's.[4] Financing this effort doesn't come cheap. In Texas, Uber spent upward of $945,000 on lobbying costs in 2015. In 2014, the company spent $684,000 in California, $600,000 in Seattle, and $314,000 in Washington, DC, and these figures don't include the cost of advertising and public relations campaigns.[5] In the first half of 2017, the company spent $1.2 million on lobbying the New York legislature, making it one of the most aggressive lobbyists right as the state was considering legislation to allow ride-hailing companies to operate in upstate New York and on Long Island. The legislation passed.[6] That's chicken feed compared to the amount Uber spent in New York City on its "scorched earth" campaign to promote and advertise a petition calling on New York mayor Bill de Blasio and New York's city council to reverse their plan capping the number of Ubers allowed in the city.[7]

I believe that the AV industry will follow Uber's model and engage in pricing wars and aggressive lobbying because of the huge potential profits involved. General Motors president Daniel Ammann says that AVs represent "the biggest business opportunity since the creation of the internet."[8] Carmakers and tech companies are not going to let that slip through their fingers. The AV industry, as history indicates, will try to undercut every other form of transportation until it controls the sector. Then it will raise prices. The many people who work in and around the transportation business—drivers, conductors, machine operators, even insurers and law enforcement—will feel the same way my father did, the way horse breeders felt when the Model T rolled off assembly lines, and how postal workers felt when people started sending e-mail and paying bills online. When an acceleration of autonomous technology takes over jobs and makes competition on price next to impossible, economic battles will ensue. And it won't be a fair fight. Supermarket chains had some clout in the 1960s, but that was nothing compared to the money and lobbying power of the AV industry in the twenty-first century.

My father's grocery business was killed by bigger businesses, malls came along and killed Main Streets, and then internet shopping and home delivery made malls into desolate and often dangerous ghost towns.[9] AVs will have an impact like this on all kinds of transit if we let the AV industry call the shots on regulation, the market, and community planning.

No one I know of has done a comprehensive objective study of the economic impacts of AVs, and there is little to no funding available for such research because the AV industry is trying very hard to make it a non-issue. But make no mistake—the economic consequences of AVs will be huge. Some jobs will fall by the wayside, and new jobs, still unimagined, will emerge. AV proponents like to say that there could be a $7 trillion—yes, that's "trillion"—boost to the economy.[10] Change will be rapid. By contrast, it took nearly a quarter-century for all toll collectors within New York City to disappear after the E-ZPass electronic toll collection system was introduced in the 1990s. The technology led to fewer jobs for toll collectors, but the impact was spread out over a long period of time. Thus, many collectors avoided being replaced during their vital working years and had a chance to either "age out" of the system or learn other skills within the same agency.

The transition still took a toll, so to speak, on workers who lost their jobs. Bill Mullins was a New Jersey Turnpike toll collector who was forced to retire and give up a $66,000-a-year job he had done for more than thirty years. "I was 55 years old. When you get a reduction that big in your salary, how do you make up that difference? It's sad. It was a part of my life for a long time," Mullins told *Governing* magazine.[11]

As Dr. Barry Devlin, an expert in business intelligence, sees it, "The rise of the automobile swept away the horse dung but raised new fears about the livelihoods of stable boys, farriers, and coachmen. These fears also turned out to be unfounded; new jobs as valets, mechanics, and drivers easily took up the slack."[12]

Grayson Brulte, writing at futurism.com, agrees. In an article enti-
tled "Autonomous Cars Are Coming, but Not for Your Job," he says that
"autonomous vehicles will create new jobs, job sectors and economic
models." He reminds us that, "in 2006, the technical breakthrough of
cloud computing came from Amazon with the introduction of Elastic
Compute Cloud (EC2) as a commercial web service. IT professionals
and industry analytics predicted large job losses as companies would
outsource their computing needs. The opposite ended up being true, as
cloud computing directly and indirectly created millions of jobs across
the globe and tens of billions of dollars in wealth."[13]

WINNERS AND LOSERS

Some regions of the world will embrace the idea of connected smart
mobility and driverless technology. Switzerland, Singapore, and Hong
Kong have modern infrastructure in place (some of the best in the
world, far outpacing US infrastructure) and an educated, tech-savvy
populace who may welcome AV policies that spur economic growth
and encourage social cohesion.[14] Other winners from AVs will be
countries and cities keen to foster technological innovation for their
economic benefits, like Bangalore, Seoul, and Stockholm, three cities
that experts say are likely to become centers of AV and other related
high-tech innovation.[15]

Other areas of the world may resist AVs. Will there ever be driverless cars in car-free places like Venice, Italy, or Hydra, Greece? Do they
need them? Emerging economic powerhouse China may well pull ahead
of the United States and Europe in the manufacture of AVs, since such
innovation has the backing of the country's powerful Ministry of Industry and Information Technology.[16]

A great deal of the US economy rides on the car. Peter Drucker
called the car business the "industry of industries," in part because it has
a stake in both the fossil fuel (petroleum, oil) economy and the technology industry.[17] Advances in technology may displace certain types of

work, but historically technology has been a net creator of jobs. People and companies adapt to changes either by inventing entirely new types of work or by taking advantage of and capitalizing on uniquely human capabilities. Highly skilled workers will see tremendous success in this new environment, particularly those with computer and other technical skills and those with artistic skills that technology will not be able to mimic successfully for many more years.

Workers from drivers to assembly-line workers, unions, and industries from airbag manufacturers to the hospitality business (as people sleep in their cars instead of hotels) could lose out if they aren't agile, careful, and smart. Other workers could be displaced into lower-paying service industry jobs at best, or permanent unemployment at worst. Other industries, like the liquor business (drinking and driving will no longer be an issue), food delivery services, and entertainment, could win big.

Public and Private Transit

As of this writing the Taxi and Limousine Commission (TLC) of New York says there are 156,000 active taxi and black car drivers in New York City. Will AV technology give them a chance to age out of employment? Or will they be displaced almost overnight? If so, what will they do? What does this technology transition really mean? Can the same people who drive buses become attendants or fleet monitors when autonomy eliminates driving? If transit systems and their unions were forward-looking, they would start retraining people to manage and maintain fleets because people will still be needed for this work even if all transit is automated.

If individual car ownership does indeed decline as AVs are efficiently shared via Uber-style models, fleets will pop up and could grow to mammoth size. They would need people to manage and maintain them. According to Bern Grush's study on public fleets and how they would be managed in a city of 10 million, total employment for the first 30 billion kilometers (18.6 billion miles) of travel, which is predicted to happen by 2030, would not drop, even if automated trips largely replace labor-intensive taxi and bus trips, because the ratio of human support-to-robo-vehicle would initially be high.

Employment could drop during the second 20 billion kilometers (12.4 billion miles) of travel, but overall or "absolute" employment would increase as owner/drivers were increasingly replaced by the service staffs of fleet operators. "No matter how advanced the technology, these fleets will require human staff far into the future. Certainly, by the time 75 per cent robo-vehicle penetration would be achieved in public service vehicles, aggregate job rates for public transportation (including taxi), will be equal to or higher than current average employment rates even as the staff-to-vehicle ratio declines," says Grush.[18]

This net positive job stability is only possible if we do it right. Cost-efficient self-driving cars that deliver point-to-point transportation, whether owned or hailed, could shift commuter preferences away from public transit, and such a shift would affect government revenues. Moreover, reducing monies spent on public transit and underfunding badly maintained systems would have a negative impact on transport for those not lucky enough to have access to personal vehicles or rides, devastating both people who are already lower on the social and economic equity scales and the cities where they live.

If we get autonomous transit right and communities do not orient themselves around single-rider modes of transport (whether owned cars or hailed rides), strong networks of well-funded, affordable automated buses and train services could be developed and commuters and communities would win. Intelligent transportation systems (ITS) can meet these challenges as they incorporate connected and autonomous vehicles, alternative fuels, management of AV fleets, and analysis of traffic patterns, as well as local zoning and planning policies that support transit-oriented development. If communities can create a robust network of mobility options based on ride-sharing, car ownership could be reduced and use of public transit increased. Even if automated, these systems can't be implemented without people—perhaps not drivers, but transit managers, on-board attendants, maintenance crews, and back-office workers.

Trucking and Delivery

AVs won't move just people—they'll also move things. While autonomy may lower the cost of goods, because labor is one of the big three costs associated with the delivery of goods (fuel and maintenance are the other two), employment will change for many drivers. Autonomous delivery will have a huge impact on not just employment but trade and labor unions, including the Teamsters. Years ago, the elevator operators' union fought and fought against the self-operated (self-driving) elevator, which enabled passengers to press a button themselves and get delivered to the floor of their choice. Union members resisted, but they lost the battle as well as the war. Elevator operators have gone the way of the horse-drawn buggy driver. A few buildings in Manhattan and a smattering of them around the country still use elevator operators, but more for show (in a high-end building) than for utility.

Trucking is a huge economic driver in the United States. In 2014, 7.3 million people were employed throughout the economy in jobs related to trucking activity, excluding the self-employed. Over 70 percent of all the freight tonnage moved in the United States is transported on trucks. To move 10.5 billion tons of freight annually requires over 3.4 million heavy-duty Class 8 (large semitrailer) trucks and over 3.5 million truck drivers. Moving all of that freight also takes over 38 billion gallons of diesel fuel, according to the American Trucking Associations.[19]

A Goldman Sachs report says that when AVs are the norm, US delivery and truck drivers could see job losses at a rate of 25,000 a month, or 300,000 jobs per year.[20] Steven Greenhouse, author of *The Big Squeeze: Tough Times for the American Worker*, maintains that "driverless vehicles could play out much like trade agreements: a boon for corporations and consumers, a bane for many workers."[21] He believes that full automation could hemorrhage as many as five million jobs for drivers, including those who make their living driving taxis, buses, vans, trucks, and ride-sharing vehicles. Greenhouse further points out that "most of these drivers belong to the same demographic cohort as many factory workers—men without college degrees—who've already been hit hard by the loss of 5 million manufacturing jobs since 2000."[22]

That number could double to ten million if we take into account the ancillary industries associated with transportation.[23] According to the US Bureau of Labor Statistics, 884,000 people are employed in motor vehicles and parts manufacturing, and 3.02 million others work in the dealer and maintenance categories.[24] As more vehicles become automated and technologically advanced, it is believed that, finding it harder to fix their own cars, consumers will instead use professional repair services, which are increasingly offered through dealerships. The result will be fewer individual sales of auto parts at the retail level. Moreover, with AVs reducing the number of crashes, fewer trips to the repair shop will be required.[25] AVs themselves will also eventually require fewer working parts, so the manufacturing of numerous parts may decline. Parts may also become interchangeable across manufacturers, requiring fewer unique parts.

Truck, bus, delivery, taxi, and Uber-style drivers account for nearly six million professional driving jobs. Ironically, given that today there is a severe shortage of truck drivers, virtually all of these ten million jobs could be eliminated within ten to fifteen years. In the absence of driverless trucks, it's projected that around 6.4 million truckers will be needed across the United States and Europe by 2030, while fewer than 5.6 million are expected to be willing to work under what the International Transport Forum report "Managing the Transition to Driverless Road Freight Transport" describes as "current trucking conditions."[26]

Autonomous vehicles are not being developed in a vacuum. Simultaneous advancements in other kinds of transportation and in manufacturing applications of autonomous technology may also reduce the number of trucks needed to deliver items. For example, with floating warehouses—essentially blimps that hold goods that will be delivered directly to your doorstep via onboard drones—the storage and transportation of goods could overlap.[27] Walmart has applied for a US patent for the equipment to do exactly that. The machines, flying at heights between 500 and 1,000 feet, would contain multiple launching bays to disperse drones throughout a neighborhood. Each floating warehouse would be operated autonomously or by a remote human pilot. Amazon was granted a patent for a similar vessel in April 2016.

These self-driven airborne warehouses laden with drones would help retailers lower the costs of fulfilling online orders, particularly the costs incurred in the "last mile"—deliveries to customers' houses, particularly those in exurban and rural areas. Today doorstep deliveries are usually handled by local or national shippers—the US Post Office, FedEx, UPS, and others—that could lose out when delivery becomes automated or new jobs, like warehouse and logistics managers, surpass drivers as the primary jobs. "The core challenge of traffic and driving distance in any major city or in a very rural location can be helped by a floating warehouse," Brandon Fletcher, an analyst at Sanford C. Bernstein, told *Bloomberg*. "Movable warehouses are a really nice idea because any flexible part of a logistics system allows it to be more efficient when demand varies wildly. The e-commerce world suffers from highly variable demand and more creative solutions are needed."[28]

Kevin Gillette, whose father and grandfather, like him, were both independent big rig truckers in northeastern Pennsylvania, transports produce and also works on construction sites hauling heavy materials. He doesn't like to think too much about how autonomy will change his prospects, and his views echo those of many other drivers who make up the grass roots of the industry. But when he does think about the changing trucking landscape, he says, he knows he won't be part of an automated trucking industry, nor will he encourage his ten-year-old son, Chase, to join the family business when he comes of age. "Honestly, I don't know if I want to be out there sharing the road with autonomous trucks. I am not going to wait for one of them to crash into me, or for some guy who is getting $10 an hour to watch the truck to let it crash into me because he forgot to trip the brake. I can't believe a trucking company will pay someone a fair wage to just sit in the truck and mind it."[29]

Gillette is also skeptical about how safe a large autonomous truck can really be without a driver who knows how to operate it in all kinds of driving conditions. "Freight liners have a braking feature and anti-roll control that applies brakes when going around a curve if it is winter-time. In certain driving conditions, you cannot replace a human being with a computer that says, 'Oh, slam the brakes because of X, Y, or Z.' I don't give a shit what your truck is equipped with—if you slam on your brakes because of weather conditions or an obstacle, you will crash. No good will come out of that," he says. "There are many maneuvers a truck has to make that require a human brain to calculate and implement. Until the time that AV technology can figure out how to execute all those maneuvers, I'll have a job."

When those maneuvers are figured out, how do we help smooth the transition away from driving jobs for those employed in them today? MIT economist Erik Brynjolfsson believes in aggressive new job retraining programs for displaced drivers. Such an effort could be funded by per-mile taxes for driverless cars.[30] Additions to infrastructure and adaptations could require many new jobs, and unemployed and underemployed workers, somewhat like the factory workers who lose their jobs to imports receiving trade adjustment assistance, could be redirected into them. A Harvard labor economist, Lawrence Katz, offers suggestions, including wage subsidies, an increased Earned Income Tax Credit (EITC), and even a government-backed public jobs program (an idea that proponents of small government and free markets would reject).[31]

The AV industry could be a source of funds for such initiatives. Uber, Ford, Google, and other companies that see the billions to be earned from driverless cars will also be eager to pressure Congress to give AVs a green light and to set consistent national regulations that will help keep smaller upstart competitors at bay, at least temporarily.[32] In exchange for enacting such laws, Congress could levy a tax on each driverless mile traveled to finance programs for retraining, adjustment assistance, unemployment insurance, and perhaps jobs, at least for an interim period. I also support the industry's efforts to pay for the infrastructure it sorely needs to operate safely and reliably.

However, retraining and employing truckers may not be as big a challenge as we might think. According to the International Transport Forum's report, the majority of truckers working today "are in the later stages of their careers," and few women and younger men are choosing trucking as a profession. Young people are not attracted to what can be a very grueling, lonely, often dangerous, and labor-intensive profession. It is also likely, according to the report, that human drivers will still be required to operate large trucks in dense urban areas for last-mile deliveries. So, while many truck drivers will simply age out as autonomy takes over, some highly trained and skilled drivers will still be in demand and may be able to command very good wages for their work.[33]

As in the States, Europeans are thinking about the impact that driverless trucks will have on employment. In March 2016, the Dutch Ministry of Infrastructure and the Environment conducted an experiment called the "European Truck Platooning Challenge," which involved semi-autonomous trucks from six different European manufacturers (DAF Trucks, Daimler, IVECO, MAN, Scania, and Volvo). It was the first cross-border initiative with smart trucks, the precursor to fully automated trucks, both in Europe and worldwide. All the trucks were connected to each other via Wi-Fi, and each had a driver on board. The trucks from each company traveled in platoons to the Dutch port of Rotterdam, operating as close to autonomously as today's technology allows (and giving an indication of how autonomous fleets might operate in the future). Through networking-enabled synchronization, the vehicles could be driven much closer to each other than is possible with an "unconnected" human driver, and they were also equipped with radar and optical sensors, making them as smart as semi-autonomous Teslas.

The EU sees advantages in networked platooned trucks (and autonomous trucks). Reaction time within the platoon is cut way back if, for example, the lead truck needs to slow down or brake for any reason and the trucks behind it respond at once; this capability should cut back on drive times. By driving more closely together, trucks benefit from decreased wind resistance and thus fuel economy improves—up to 10 percent, according to the organizers of the Platooning Challenge.

Although drivers may lose out, AV technology could represent economic opportunities for skilled workers across Europe. Since car manufacturing will be less about physical design and engines and more about software development and data analytics, European manufacturers, including Audi, BMW, Volkswagen, Daimler, Mercedes-Benz, and Volvo, will need people with strong artificial intelligence skills and an aptitude for big data, high-definition mapping, and high-performance computing.[34] Companies and governments will have to either cultivate indigenous talent or import it, or both. Vivek Krishnamurthy, a Harvard-based cyber-law expert, says that smart manufacturers and developers should "enlist the help of good guys [with] strong science and computer backgrounds who want to do the right thing" to build secure software that AVs will run on. These are people who look for and identify software problems, make improvements, and allow public access, and many of them, he says, can be found in the open-source community.[35]

According to the tech investment bank GP Bullhound, there are about forty-seven private technology companies valued at more than $1 billion and based in Europe, more than one-third of them in Great Britain. They won't all service the AV industry, but many will.[36] AVs could present a competitive opportunity for these and other new and established firms to cultivate new, highly skilled workers. Ireland, for example, has emerged as a leader in supplying technological talent, innovation, and collaborative tech ecosystems to AV and AI development, and all of the Fortune Top 10 technology firms have a significant presence in the country.[37]

Legacy companies are ramping up their AV potential through partnerships and strategic hiring, which also represents opportunity to skilled workers. In July 2016, Audi announced that it had set up a subsidiary company devoted to advancing its self-driving technology.[38] According to reports, Audi partnered with Nvidia, the chipmaker that supplies the computer powering Tesla's Autopilot, to accelerate its efforts to bring self-driving vehicles to market by 2020. Volvo announced Zenuity, a joint venture with the Swedish auto supplier Autoliv specifically to develop the software that controls vehicles when in self-driving mode.[39] Both companies have also formed ties to Nvidia to develop AV systems.[40]

BMW has joined forced with Mobileye to create an open standards–based platform for bringing self-driving cars to market by 2021.[41] Bosch, one of the world's largest automotive suppliers, has reportedly dedicated more than 2,000 engineers to developing driver-assistance systems, and the company is partnering with the GPS maker TomTom for the necessary mapping data.[42] Continental, a German auto parts and tire maker, has taken a minority stake in the French autonomous driving company EasyMile. They plan to work together on developing environmental sensors, braking systems, and driving safety technologies.[43]

Major losses in driving jobs will not be seen in places like India and Africa, where driving is an occupation held by many low-paid, unskilled workers. In July 2017, Nitin Gadkari, the minister for road transport and highways in India, said that driverless cars will not be allowed in his country because it will cost thousands of jobs. "No driverless cars will be allowed in India. The government is not going to promote any technology or policy that will make people jobless," he told reporters. Despite this strong language, Tata Elxsi, the Tata car group's technology wing, has been working on driverless cars for India. Moreover, many experts feel that Gadkari's promise can't or won't be fulfilled since it's at odds with the Motor Vehicles (Amendment) Bill of 2017 (still pending as of this writing).

The same is true in Africa and other developing countries where hiring a driver is affordable. The absence of AVs on the road may have benefits for the large number of unskilled workers in those countries as well. India is not like the United States, where truck and taxi drivers can more easily find other related jobs. Because of the sheer numbers and logistics involved, it could be more difficult to train people in India who have low skills, or none at all, than it is in the United States and other developed nations. Less than 5 percent of the Indian population is vocationally skilled, so the high-tech jobs in the AV industry are available only to a

handful of people.[44] Also, as a young country—65 percent of its population is under thirty-five—India can't afford to have stagnant job growth.

"In India and Africa there is a surplus of drivers," says Venkat Sumantran. "While I accept that in rural Idaho, an AV might be an improvement for an eighty-five-year-old farmer who has had his license
taken away, or for people who want to strap their twelve-year-old into
an AV to visit Grandma, I can't make the same argument in places like
Lagos, Nigeria, where you can hire a driver for ten cents a mile to take
you where you need to go."[45]

Not So Easy Riders

Driverless vehicles could be a death knell for motorcycles, especially in
the United States. A report from industry insiders finds that the motorcycle industry is in deep trouble, and autonomous technology will
only make things worse.[46] "There is a very real risk of motorcycling being
completely cut out of the conversation for future vehicle infrastructure
systems," concludes the report. Moreover, the report points out, as autonomous technology grows, traffic and city planners, insurance companies, and AV manufacturers may see motorcycles as increasingly risky. In
2017, an AV hit a motorcycle in San Francisco, but the motorcycle rider,
who was injured, was, according to police reports, to blame.[47]

Sales of motorcycles are declining for several reasons.[48] As baby
boomers age, they are giving up motorcycling, and millennials don't
seem interested in picking up the slack. Manufacturers have never ag-
gressively marketed to women and minorities, so there are few customers in these demographic groups for the machines. About 65 percent
of American motorcycle riders are middle-aged white men who make
more than $50,000 a year and ride for fun.[49] In contrast, 70 percent
of European motorcycle riders and the majority of people in the Asia
Pacific countries see motorcycles as basic transportation.[50] I cannot
imagine cities like Rome or Barcelona without motorbikes. In Australia, a report on AV testing from the Austroads and National Transport
Commission makes no mention of motorcycles, but it does discuss both
cars and bicycles.

The LiDAR systems of cars and AVs will need to improve so that they better recognize and respond to smaller vehicles, like motorcycles, if they are to share the roadways safely. Designing autonomous motorcycles may not be cost-effective—and the concept somehow flies in the face of what people who own motorcycles want them for in the first place. In 2016, however, Eric Unnervik, a microengineering student at the École Polytechnique Fédérale de Lausanne, designed a miniature prototype of an autonomous motorcycle that he hopes will be developed as a full-size model that could outperform human riders. The motorcycle can go 37 miles an hour without falling over.[51]

AVs may present all-terrain vehicle (ATV) manufacturers with opportunities to make more vehicles. While most ATVs are used for off-roading leisure riding or sport, which may continue even as AVs take over roadways, they can also be used for industry. For instance, Honda is developing an ATV that can carry just about anything *except* a driver.[52] These machines could be used in various settings, from farming and construction to search-and-rescue teams to the movement of goods in large warehouses or other places.

Insurance

Since most crashes are caused by human error, AVs will certainly reduce their numbers. Some estimates expect a reduction in crashes of 90 percent.[53] If this happens, there will be a major shift in the insurance model. As the risk of crashes drops, demand for the kind of car insurance sold now will most certainly take a dive. In anticipation of this change, some insurers are rolling out usage-based insurance policies (UBIs), which charge consumers based on how many miles they drive and the safety of their driving habits.

Donald Light, head of the North America property and casualty practice for the research firm Celent, says that as driverless cars hit the roads, premiums could drop as much as 60 percent. He warns insurers to "be prepared to see that part of your business shrink, probably considerably."[54] Because of safety features, particularly brake sensors, insurers have already noted a decline in claims. The Insurance Institute for

Highway Safety has found a 7 percent reduction in crashes for vehicles with a basic forward-collision warning system and a 14 to 15 percent reduction for those with automatic braking.[55] The Highway Loss Data Institute's 2014 study of insurance claims found that bodily injury liability losses dropped by 40 percent that year and medical payments saw a 27 percent drop.[56]

Some insurance companies are writing new policies for AV owners, perhaps in an attempt to preempt what some see as an AV threat to the insurance industry.[57] The British insurance company Adrian Flux offers a policy specifically for semi- or fully autonomous vehicles. The firm says that it expects fewer crashes and fewer liability claims from such vehicles. "We expect premiums for fully autonomous cars to be considerably cheaper than regular cars, purely because of the expected reduction in accidents and claims." The company says that it will reduce its revenue, but as the *Washington Post* reports, "the lower rate of accidents means the insurance company will get to save money overall because it won't be forced to issue as many payouts."[58]

Eventually, as AVs become more widespread, the insurance market will evolve to a point where it becomes extremely expensive for individual motorists to buy insurance to cover driven cars. If the business of selling insurance to individual drivers shrinks, selling insurance to carmakers may open up. Liability insurance for failing systems could become one way in which insurers recover lost revenue.

With fewer crashes and claims comes a reduced need for personal injury lawyers specializing in car crashes. Vehicle collisions, which accounted for 35 percent of all civil trials in 2005, could be eliminated with AVs.[59] About 76,000 attorneys in the United States specialize in personal injury and make up approximately 6 percent of the country's population of lawyers.

The Hospitality Industry

AVs will also have an impact on the food and drink and lodging industries. As cars are redesigned and reimagined, there may be significantly less demand for hotels and motels and more demand for areas where cars can hook up to energy sources and people can sleep overnight in vehicles (which could very well have first-class convertible chair-beds). The luxury business may not be as heavily affected as midrange and budget hotels, but surely there will be a shift in how these businesses operate and who they serve. Audi's vice president of brand strategy and digital business, Sven Schuwirth, has predicted that car interiors will morph between driving mode and sleeping mode. This adaptability will present a major challenge to the hotel industry by eliminating the need for business travelers to take short-distance domestic flights or check into city-center hotels.[60] "We can disrupt the entire business of domestic flights," he says, noting that cars will increasingly resemble mobile apartments, and service stations along highways will evolve to support them, offering drivers facilities for washing, dining, and shopping.

The liquor industry could win big—since driving and drinking will probably no longer be an issue. With a high-level AV, you wouldn't have to worry about finding a designated driver or car service to get yourself home after a night of partying. (Some semi-autonomous driven cars may not even start if they sense that the person at the wheel is intoxicated.) Eliminating the danger of drinking and driving may have other serious health consequences; nevertheless, I'm sure that the industry will capitalize on AV technology. Bars may no longer have to worry about getting sued if they serve one too many to a customer.[61] The food and food delivery business will see huge gains from AVs, which will be able to deliver more food to more people, more cheaply, than human drivers could—and at all hours.

Media and Entertainment

As cars become pods for relaxation and work, people will spend more time in them consuming media, watching movies, reading books, surfing the internet, and so on. A McKinsey and Company report says that future owners of self-driving cars could save up to fifty minutes a day previously spent concentrating on driving and spend some of that time on other activities, like going online. The consulting firm estimates that the additional free time spent in cars could generate about $5.6 billion a year in digital revenue for each additional minute that vehicle occupants spend on the internet—which adds up to as much as $140 billion if they devote half of their free time in the car, or roughly twenty-five minutes, to daily web surfing and shopping.[62] That means retailers could win too if online shopping accelerates during car trips.

Israel's Mobileye, Germany's Continental AG and Robert Bosch GmbH, Delphi and Nvidia Corporation in the United States, and other software component makers could also win big. Silicon Valley's Nvidia, which began by making graphics for video games, now counts automotive as its fastest-growing business segment, with revenue nearly doubling every year.[63] Its automotive division creates artificial intelligence platforms for cloud-to-car communications, among other communication technologies.

Auto Repair and Manufacturing

"More than [$2 trillion] is spent each year in the US on car-related spending, encompassing suppliers, carmakers, dealers, financing, service, repairs, insurance, energy, rentals, taxes, etc.," writes Chunka Mui for *Forbes*.[64] "Car dealers in the US handle more than $650 billion in new and used car sales," and "profits would be squeezed if robotaxis cut into the sales of large expensive models that provide most of today's margin."

US car sales could plunge 40 percent in the next twenty-five years, Barclays analyst Brian Johnson wrote in a 2015 report. General Motors and Ford Motor Company, he noted, would have to cut the combined number of their assembly plants in the United States and Canada to seventeen from the current thirty, and some 25,000 autoworkers would lose their jobs. That's why many automakers are moving to offset any loss of sales with revenue from providing transportation as a service. Mike Ableson, GM's vice president of strategy and global portfolio planning, told the *Insurance Journal*, says "Some scenarios show a decline in volume, but we have some scenarios that show it going up."[65]

Most car trips today involve only one or two people. If robo-taxis allow riders to call for the type of car needed, when they need it, customers might opt for smaller, less expensive cars most of the time. A larger car may only be needed to shuttle a bunch of kids to a lacrosse game or three or four adults to a dinner party. For the same reasons, the tendency to purchase second or third cars for occasional use might be diminished.

Law

It's a toss-up in terms of how AVs will affect personal injury and property damage cases. There is a possibility that personal injury lawyers could find new ways to benefit from AVs. There are already law firms advertising a specialty in ride-sharing complaints. LegalRideshare, a two-person Chicago firm, only handles cases linked to the ride-sharing business, primarily personal injury or property damage claims.[66] Firms that specialize in understanding AV laws and AV-related injuries could start to spring up once driverless cars become more common. We already know that AVs don't guarantee safety—one killed pedestrian Elaine Herzberg, a forty-nine-year-old Arizona woman, when she was walking her bike across the street in Tempe, Arizona, in March 2018. In California the same month, a Tesla owner was killed in his car, which featured autopilot, and as of this writing, evidence suggests that the car was in autopilot and the driver's hands were not on the wheel for about six seconds before it collided with a highway median.[67] Autopilot in this case does not mean a fully autonomous feature. Firms that can sort out such cases stand to benefit.

However, some lawyers see driverless cars as damaging the personal injury business, since experts predict that accidents (and claims) overall will be reduced. Jim Herrick, a civil litigator in Wisconsin, says that AVs will bring unprecedented change to small litigation firms. He claims that with the cumulative safety effects of seat belts, airbags, self-braking systems, and, eventually, self-driving vehicles designed to follow the rules of the road, there will be an 80 percent decline in both the frequency and severity of crash injuries—and a parallel reduction in claims. "I see the survival of smaller litigation firms as dependent upon their ability to cultivate alternative sources of revenue. My recommendation, particularly for the younger litigators, would be to begin that process as soon as possible," he says. This concern is echoed by other litigators across the United States.[68]

Technology

Data crunchers at Intel and the research company Strategy Analytics, who have stakes in autonomous technology, claim that the robo-car sector could add as much as $2 trillion to the US economy by 2050. Although much of that money will go to the carmakers and mobility companies like GM, Uber, and Google, technology companies and developers will also be winners.

Grayson Brulte foresees how "autonomous logistics officers will manage fleets of vehicles from a remote command center in multiple daily shifts. When these roles merge, drivers' quality of life will improve immensely. This new job category will create thousands of jobs for individuals with a new, unique skill set. Individuals with this new skill are already in demand." Brulte sees automated vehicles as part of the emerging digital "platform economy," from which myriad other business possibilities are likely to evolve.[69] Smart Car, RideCell, and Otonomo are all developing software platforms to enable entrepreneurs and established companies to build applications and other services that will be used by and in AVs. This technology sector could create jobs for many more people with the right training and skills.

Additional economic gains will include "savings of a minimum of $5,600 per year per average American household," which "will add $1 trillion to the annual disposable income of US households, the single largest economic boost in US history," say Tony Seba and James Arbib of RethinkX, an independent think tank that analyzes and forecasts the speed and scale of technology-driven disruption and its implications across society. They add: "We foresee another $1 trillion in productivity gains as people work, study or shop instead of wasting time behind the wheel."[70] This sort of hype sounds good, but how realistic is it to imagine that people will automatically stop wasting time because of autonomy? Given the amount of time people spend on social media and online game playing, it's hard to imagine AVs will make most of them use their time more wisely.

AVs could also become a highly efficient and profitable source for data collection. According to Barry Devlin, "Whether urban or intercity, providing entertainment, information, or education to a captive and otherwise unoccupied audience will be big business and, indeed, big data business. Cellular and other networks will need to be upgraded to cope with vast data volumes."[71] Karl Brauer, auto analyst for Kelley Blue Book, concurs: "They will know when he's going, where he's going, what he's doing. Talk about opportunities for targeted advertising."[72] This may be true, and the advertising industry may be safe—but will the need for big data collection really result in hiring more people?

"All those cars will generate loads and loads of data about, well, just about everything," says Aarian Marshall. "Who you are. Where you go. What you do. How often you do it. Coupled with data gleaned from your smartphone, credit cards, and, in a particularly creepy twist, maybe even biometrics, and anyone who wants to can get a highly detailed picture of you. That kind of data is worth a lot, and the consulting company McKinsey predicts the car data industry could be worth as much as $750 million by 2030. Storing, organizing, and analyzing that data will be a big job."[73]

Barry Devlin, among others, thinks that this Orwellian, though potentially highly profitable, aspect of the AV revolution is inevitable. "Autonomous vehicles may become the most prolific creators and consumers of data imaginable. They will collect every detail of their internal activities. They will store a complete, continuous record of their location. They will gather details of every passenger. Such information will amount to a continuous and permanent record of every journey taken by every traveler. The automobile that used to be the most private spot for your first hot date becomes the ultimate surveillance device."[74]

CHINA

The United States was the dominant force in automobile manufacturing and road planning from the 1930s to about 1980, when Asian and European firms and governments competed for the industry vanguard. The most likely country to "set the stage" for AV technology, manufacturing, road design, and government policy from now until midcentury is China. While the United States, Europe, Japan, Korea, and others will certainly make money from AV technology, manufacturing, and sales, China's reputation for high adoption rates of new technologies and the ways in which the government sets national policy make it poised to become a substantial market for AV manufacturing and consumption.[75] A World Economic Forum survey found that "75 percent of Chinese say they are willing to ride in a self-driving car."[76] This view was echoed in a separate survey undertaken by the Roland Berger consulting firm, which found that an even higher number of Chinese, 96 percent, say they would consider an autonomous vehicle for everyday driving, compared with 58 percent of Americans and Germans.[77]

Road-testing for AVs has already begun in China and the scale of it is likely to increase. On December 15, 2017, three Beijing government agencies—the Beijing Municipal Commission of Transport, the Beijing Traffic Management Bureau, and the Beijing Municipal Commission of Economy and Information Technology—jointly released a document called "The Guiding Opinions of the Beijing Municipality on Accelerating the Work of Road Tests for Autonomous Vehicles (for Trial Implementation)" (the "Guiding Opinions") and "The Detailed Implementation Rules of the Beijing Municipality for the Administration of the Road Tests of Autonomous Vehicles (for Trial Implementation)" (the "Implementation Rules"). Although the "Guiding Opinions" and the "Implementation Rules" cover only Beijing, they represent the first guidelines dealing with road tests of autonomous vehicles in China.

On January 4, 2018, a report said a testing zone would be established in Yizhuang, a suburb of Beijing, making it the first designated area for road tests of AVs in Beijing. Then, in April 2018, China's, ministry of Transport gave all provincial and city governments permission to test AVs on roads.[78] The country's top-down approach to setting national policies helps simplify the sort of regulatory procedures that characterize federal systems, like the United States.

China has also identified autonomous cars as a key sector for development in its "Made in China 2025" program, meant to transform the country into a world leader in innovation. In December 2017, Beijing became the first Chinese city to allow autonomous vehicle road tests. The city's autonomous driving guidelines allow organizations registered in China to test up to five vehicles simultaneously after successfully completing tests in designated restricted areas. In late January 2018, China completed a draft of national rules for driverless vehicle road testing. They detail requirements for drivers, cars, and companies, and road conditions.[79]

"Chinese carmakers started making cars 100 years after others and a lot of the core technology aren't [sic] in Chinese hands, such as engines," said Jin Wang, senior vice president at Baidu, China's largest search engine (China's version of Google), and general manager of its Autonomous Driving Unit. "With electric cars, with intelligent cars, the core technology shifts from the engine and gearbox to artificial intelligence and that's an area where China is very close to the US, giving China the chance to catch up and seize leadership."[80] This could mean that the cell-phone analogy, which may not work for Africa, *could* work for China in that people who don't own cars now may opt to buy one, especially if China's manufacturing and computing make them small, efficient, and inexpensive—that is, highly accessible.

Some estimates say that by 2035 there will be around 21 million autonomous vehicles on roads worldwide. According to *Bloomberg*, Chinese officials believe that "the Chinese market for car sales, buses, taxis and related is potentially worth more than $1.5 trillion in revenue."[81] Work is also being done on other kinds of mobility solutions in this country of 1.4 billion people, from low-tech bicycle-sharing to high-tech speed rail systems. However, its artificial intelligence technology and large-scale manufacturing capabilities could make China an AV business powerhouse.

China has already pulled ahead of the United States with its super-computing technology, which will certainly play a part in AI and AV technology.[82] In July 2017, the State Council of China published a road-map to make China the global center for artificial intelligence by 2030.[83] A timeline established by the National Reform and Development Commission (NRDC) called for China to have a framework in place for safe and timely development of AI technologies by 2018. China is known for setting target dates it knows it can hit before or on deadline.

In April 2017, Chinese authorities issued a draft of potential AV regulations. According to media reports, this document, titled "Auto Industry Mid- and Long-Term Planning," includes technical standards for driverless cars in China and tries to centralize rule-making jurisdiction on autonomous vehicles. China aims to have half of its cars sold to incorporate some forms of autonomy by 2020 and 10 percent of cars sold by 2030 to be fully autonomous.[84] Policymakers are also considering rules that would shift legal liability away from drivers. Li Shufu, chair of the automaker Geely, said that "China must revise its laws so the manufacturer, not the driver, is held responsible for crashes when a car is in self-drive mode."[85]

Another complicating feature of Chinese lawmaking is that multiple ministries are responsible for supervising laws and jurisdictions often overlap. Lawmakers may have to clarify who regulates what, and how regulations are developed and approved. For AV advancement, the government would need to eliminate the current national prohibition on road-testing and reduce restrictions on roadmap development so that carmakers and software designers could devise accurate navigational guides.[86]

Culture will make a difference in how AV ownership models play out in China. Optimistically, China will embrace ride-sharing over private ownership, a completely plausible scenario since the Chinese don't have the same positive emotional relationship with driving and car ownership as Americans do and may be more amenable to shared self-driving cars.[87] The Chinese, especially young people, actually seem to have a preference for sharing over owning.

A Roland Berger survey showed that "51 percent of Chinese car owners said they would prefer to use robot taxis rather than buy a new vehicle themselves, compared with 26 percent of Americans."[88] The cellphone analogy of individual ownership may only work if the culture changes along with the other factors mentioned here. Didi Chuxing, the largest ride-sharing service in the world (based on number of rides), has a valuation of $35 billion and makes 14 million trips each day in 400 Chinese cities. By comparison, Uber makes more than 10 million trips daily worldwide.[89]

There is some skepticism about Chinese adoption of AVs. Didi Chuxing says that AVs may not be on Chinese roads by 2030, the time by which they are predicted to be ubiquitous on US and European roads. The first hurdle they would have to jump is infrastructure—China's dangerous and congested roads. "If you take one of Google's self-driving cars and put that into one of the main streets in Beijing, the car will show you a crash alert all the time. It will stay there forever, not moving an inch," said Stephen Zhu, Didi's vice president of strategy, during an investor conference sponsored by Credit Suisse in 2016.[90]

Despite the challenges, manufacturers are betting on AVs in China. Volvo, the Swedish carmaker now owned by China's Geely Automobile, announced in April 2016 that it would test 100 driverless cars in China, but didn't offer a specific time frame for the experiment. Baidu has partnered with BMW to mass-produce driverless cars by 2018.[91] In April 2018, China held its second "Autonomous Vehicle Summit," which focused on the "roboconomy." Executives from Nissan, Tesla, Toyota, General Motors, Ford, Cisco, Bosch, the Eno Center for Transportation, and others from technology, automotive, and research organizations attended.[92] China, as a maker and exporter, is clearly positioning itself to win in the AV market.

PEAK OIL?

Oil demand could collapse in the future, along with the need for high-cost oil fields, maintenance, and infrastructure, though big oil-producing companies don't seem to be taking this threat very seriously at present. This is despite the reality that oil companies are feeling the effects of the spread of fuel-efficient vehicles that don't burn as much oil or gas as older cars do. About one-quarter of all the energy used in the United States each day goes to propelling vehicles, according to the US Energy Information Administration. In 2016, US motorists consumed less than 390 million gallons of gasoline a day, a 1.5 percent reduction from peak consumption in 2007.[93] Fuel and energy companies may soon have to reinvent themselves, becoming leaner and meaner and expanding into other areas, just as other businesses have had to do over the years.

Electric vehicles are likely to get a big boost if AVs become mostly fleet-owned, as many predict. With their own charging stations, fleets can manage charging times based on algorithms to put the proper number of vehicles on the road at any one time. Fleets of EVs that run at consistent speeds and can partially charge themselves will most certainly reduce the need for more fossil fuels. There will be less braking, stopping, and accelerating, all of which use the most energy (fuel) in the operation of a car.

A 2014 study by the National Renewable Energy Laboratory found that cars and trucks could achieve 15 percent reductions in fuel consumption by maintaining an optimal speed and avoiding stop-and-go traffic—a way of driving that AVs will be programmed to do.[94] When the national speed limit was changed to 55 miles per hour during the energy crisis of the 1970s, both fuel and lives were saved. If every AV could be regulated to go no more than 45 or 55 miles per hour, we could save billions of gallons of gas or fuel.

As cars become more autonomous, energy demand per vehicle could decrease (although the power to run the electronic features in AVs, from sensors to entertainment equipment, may make power usage go up or stay the same). If ride-sharing goes up and individual ownership goes down, demand will drop significantly. If individual vehicle ownership expands, overall demand will go up. Still, increased efficiencies may balance out demand even if everyone who could have an AV decides to buy one. Studies show that advanced forms of eco-cruise control can reduce a vehicle's fuel use 5 to 15 percent.[95]

The potential energy savings are so great that in 2016 Advanced Research Projects Agency-Energy (ARPA-E), the advanced research division of the US Department of Energy, gave out $30 million in grant money for engineers to find ways for AVs to help cars use less fuel.[96] (Grant giving was suspended temporarily in 2017 by the Trump administration.[97]) The Southwest Research Institute in San Antonio, where engineers work on developing (not manufacturing) autonomous vehicles for everyone from the US military to farmers to major car manufacturers, is also working on fuel-efficient strategies. Ryan Lamm, director of research and development at the institute's Automation and Data Systems Division, told the *Houston Chronicle*, "There's a lot of venture capital funding flowing into this right now. It's almost like an arms race."[98]

Increasing fuel efficiency could have an impact on the environment as well, even as it reduces the fuel industry. "The environmental impact of autonomous cars has the potential to reverse the trend of global warming and drastically reduce our dependence on fossil fuels," writes Zack Kanter.[99] "Passenger cars, SUVs, pickup trucks, and minivans account for 17.6% of greenhouse gas emissions—a 90% reduction of vehicles in operation would reduce our overall emissions by 15.9%. As most autonomous cars are likely to be electric, we would virtually eliminate the 134 billion gallons of gasoline used each year in the US alone. And while recycling 242 million vehicles will certainly require substantial resources, the surplus of raw materials will decrease the need for mining," he says. Even if we don't go the electric route, we will save energy through better driving and ride-sharing.

COMMUNITIES COULD LOSE CASH—AND REPLACE IT IF THEY'RE SMART

If vehicles become more fuel-efficient, they will deliver less gas tax revenue. How will state governments replace that revenue, as well as the revenue from parking fines and moving violations? Governments may naturally end up paying for infrastructure and public transit (which today benefit from gas taxes and, to an extent, fine revenue) by instead instituting fees based on use of roads by distance and/or time, congestion pricing, and more substantial fuel taxes. To assess how vulnerable cities' budgets could be, *Governing* magazine conducted the first national analysis of the impact of AVs on city revenues. For the twenty-five largest US cities, this analysis looked at parking collections and fines, traffic citations, traffic camera fines, gas taxes, and vehicle registration, licensing, and other fees. These twenty-five cities collectively netted nearly $5 billion in auto-related revenues in fiscal 2016, or about $129 per capita. While some cities will see hardly any effect on their budgets, the fiscal consequences of AVs for others could be big.[100] Cities and towns could face unprecedented losses in revenue from parking tickets alone.

New York City collected a record $1.9 billion in fees and fines during its 2015 fiscal year, many from parking and driving violations, but also from littering and noise pollution (which is often triggered by blasting car and truck horns).[101] The 2015 total was an increase of 5.5 percent over the $1.8 billion collected in 2014, and a 13 percent increase from 2012, when the city collected $1.7 billion. The largest jump in fines and fees came from violations of red light, bus lane, and speed cameras near schools. Vehicles programmed to obey traffic laws won't need nearly as much policing, which also means fewer traffic police will be needed, fewer traffic tickets will be issued, and less revenue will flow into municipalities.

The analysis found that the cities most likely to suffer the steepest revenue losses per capita include San Francisco ($512), Washington, DC ($502), and Chicago ($248). "Totals were much larger in cities assessing special taxes on parking operators, deploying traffic cameras or those receiving substantial shared revenues from states in the form of gas taxes or vehicle registration fees," the report says.[102]

Other countries around the world also depend on ticket revenue. Florence, Italy, for example, takes in more than €50 million each year from traffic tickets, a good percentage of them issued to visitors in European rental cars, according to Gemut, a European travel agency.[103] Technology has allowed municipalities to catch more violators, and most tickets in Europe are issued electronically. Cameras, not cops, catch drivers speeding, talking on a cell phone, not wearing a seat belt, driving in a restricted zone, or following too closely.

Autonomous technology would make VMT fees much easier to administer, says Paul Lewis of the Eno Center for Transportation, a foundation dedicated to improving transportation. Eno proposes a national baseline per-mile fee on autonomous vehicles that would vary rates depending on the type of vehicle, the number of passengers, and other factors.[104] Oregon operates a voluntary VMT program that charges participants 1.5 cents per mile and gives them a tax credit for fuel taxes paid. The state's Department of Transportation is considering testing new technology that would enable localities to assess their own fees on top of the state rate. That would probably require federal approval. I have long advocated for congestion pricing in dense cities that includes not only a vehicle-miles-traveled charge but a vehicle-hours-traveled (VHT) charge. This is an important distinction, since slower speeds in cities make the number of miles traveled relatively low.

Large cities like New York could recoup lost ticketing revenue by taxing or licensing autonomous vehicle services. Seattle collected $2.4 million in the 2016 fiscal year through fees paid by car-sharing services. New York State is estimating over $400 million to be collected in 2019 when a law charging Uber, Lyft, taxis, and other car services up to $2.75 per trip in the business district goes into effect. But this kind of revenue source can't overcome sizable revenue reductions elsewhere.[105]

Smaller cities and towns, as well as suburban towns and rural villages that raise funds via ticketing, could experience a renaissance. If individual vehicle ownership is reduced and parking spaces and garages are repurposed as more aesthetically pleasing mixed-use spaces, downtowns could become more active. Lost ticketing monies could thus be recouped through the reuse of parking and driving land for ongoing public events like farmers' markets, art exhibitions, concerts, and other old-fashioned events like those that used to bring people into the town square.

By allowing a greater variety of development, mixing in affordable residential ownership with retail, hospitality, and professional businesses, communities of every size can draw people into downtowns, where they'll spend more money the longer they stay in the area. Real estate tax revenue is likely to rise too. Machines can't run all of these businesses, and as many futurists predict, a rejection of technology among current and future generations may increase the demand for vibrant places that promote human-to-human contact. In this regard, smaller towns and cities that engage their populations could win economically without writing a single speeding or parking ticket.

WORK JUSTICE AND EQUITY

Forward-looking entrepreneurs who can successfully identify changing market dynamics and create new businesses may create new jobs. But what about economic justice? What about those who suffer from employment inequity already? Will AVs save them or hurt them further? The new technology could provide some advantages to the most vulnerable and disadvantaged by supporting cheaper and more convenient ways to get around if public and private transit work together to serve communities that are ill served by current transit options. Robo-buses and shared robo-taxis could increase the mobility of disadvantaged, disabled, and elderly people. A US Bureau of Transportation Statistics survey found that almost 15 million people, six million of whom are disabled, have difficulty getting the transportation they need.[106] Moreover, the infrequency and inefficiency of public transit is often cited as a barrier to people looking for work and who do not have access to a personal vehicle.

In 2017, CBS reported on a young man, Justin Korva, who walked three miles to and from his job at a restaurant in Rockwall, Texas.[107] He was picked up by a friendly stranger, who posted about the encounter on social media, and in short order those who saw the post raised enough money for Korva to buy a used car—which he of course would have to insure, fill with gas, and maintain to keep in working order. The kind stranger, Andy Mitchell, also bought him a $500 car card and one year's worth of insurance. It can certainly get punishingly hot in Texas, and walking to a job where you stand all day, and then walking home, even three miles, is not easy. However, just imagine if Korva had access to autonomous transit—a public or private bus or van that could take him where he needed to go for work at far less cost per year than a car. Why is the car our default solution to transit issues? The feel-good story did not delve into this, but according to autotrader.com, it costs at least a few thousand dollars a year to keep a used car running and insured at minimum standards.[108]

In order for cities and downtowns of any shape or size to increase commerce, they have to be friendly not just toward commuters but toward visitors and residents. Barbara Gray, the general manager of transportation services for Toronto (and formerly of the Seattle Department of Transportation), says that businesses are always prickly about modifying curb space for anything other than parking. "However, we have seen clearly in Seattle and in Montreal that people prefer to travel to get all of their basic needs filled via walking, biking, and public transit if it is safe, reliable, and convenient and if driving is not convenient or reliable."[109]

This preference for travel is why it is so important for planning and public policy to be pro pedestrian and cyclist and less congenial toward AVs. Although Gray says that businesses can be reluctant to make curb changes that do not address parking, they shouldn't be. People on foot and on bikes can actually spend more than people in cars in downtown areas. The conventional wisdom is that "kids on bikes" have no money but "people in cars" do. According to a study done by the Oregon Transportation Research and Education Consortium, drivers still make up a plurality of customers at businesses.[110] It's not surprising that drivers, having greater trunk capacity, would far outspend people who travel to grocery stores by foot, bike, or transit. But for all of the other business types, the study found, including restaurants, bakeries, boutiques, specialty shops, and wine stores, cyclists and pedestrians actually *outconsumed* drivers over the course of a month. Although cyclists and pedestrians spent less per visit, both made more frequent trips, and that added up to more engagement and more spending. Engagement also links to customer loyalty. "Such frequent visits are part of the walkable culture. Compare European communities—where it's common to hit the bakery, butcher and fish market on the way home from work—to US communities where the weekly drive to Walmart's supermarket requires an hour of dedicated planning," said CityLab in its report on the findings.[111]

LIVES SAVED

One major economic advantage of AVs may be the side effect of reductions in traffic crashes and related health care costs. Indeed, the insurance industry may have to reinvent itself: according to a study from the nonprofit Eno Center for Transportation, if just 10 percent of cars and trucks in the United States were self-driving, the number of traffic deaths could be cut by 1,000 per year. There could also be a savings of just under $38 billion a year. If 90 percent of vehicles in the United States were self-driving, the study predicts, 4.2 million crashes could be avoided, with 21,700 lives saved along with about $450 billion in related costs annually. Worldwide over a million lives could be saved.[112] With these stats, no wonder there is such a strong push for AVs. As we'll see in the next chapter, however, we need to look carefully at safety and other health-related claims before turning over our streets to AVs en masse.

FIVE

Saving Lives: Are AVs Good for Our Health and Safety?

Because if, in writing some article that's negative, you effectively dissuade people from using an autonomous vehicle, you're killing people.

—ELON MUSK, AMERICAN INVENTOR[1]

O NE SPRING DAY IN 1968, THREE OF MY BROOKLYN COLLEGE buddies and I had decided to play hooky from school and drive out to Stony Brook on Long Island, about sixty miles away. We were cruising in my friend Gerard's 1957 Chevy, built like a tank, with rockets for headlights. And no seat belts, of course. I was in the backseat. We were on the Southern State Parkway on our return home, approaching the toll booths (now long gone), when Gerard said his brakes weren't working. "The brake pedal was completely to the floor," he recalled later, "but the car just kept going." Since it was rush hour, there was a long queue of cars waiting to pay the toll.

Gerard drove between the lines of cars, and naturally the people in the other cars thought we were cheating and trying to cut the line. "Of course, I was really just trying not to cause a chain-reaction collision," he said. Eventually, we crashed into a concrete barrier in front of the toll booth, which protected the operator and kept him from being injured. The car was totaled, and Gerard was stuck in the driver's seat with the steering wheel jammed against his chest. We were slightly bloodied, but no ambulance was called. Why would they bother for a few college kids? The car was towed to a service station, and we made it back to school.

A smart car would have prevented this crash because it would have known the brakes weren't working properly long before it got to the point of impact. My 2017 Volvo would have just stopped—it wouldn't have let us get very far. We don't need AVs to keep us safe from these or many other kinds of crashes.

Still, AVs bring up myriad health issues, from traffic safety to personal fitness. For instance, one of the best-case scenarios envisioned by developers, academics, and futurists who hype AV technology is far fewer deaths and injuries from car crashes. I have little doubt that AVs will be far safer mile for mile than conventional driven cars are today. The track record of the car industry in reducing casualties over the years has been impressive, owing in large part to mandated safety features such as seat belts, antilock brakes, puncture-resistant tires, airbags, crushable steering columns, crumple zones, and more ergonomically friendly interior design—all now standard features on most new vehicles. Current car models at every price point are now significantly safer than those produced when Ralph Nader published his 1967 classic *Unsafe at Any Speed*, which showed that bad car designs contributed to 47,000 annual deaths at the time. In the ensuing fifty years, the traffic death rate by miles traveled in the United States dropped by 77.75 percent (the 2017 estimate is 1.25 percent).

Still, far too many people die in car crashes. There were 37,461 people killed in crashes on US roadways in 2016, an increase from 35,485 in 2015, which itself was a 8.4 percent increase from 2014, according to the National Highway Traffic Safety Administration (NHTSA). That agency reports that the largest percentage increase prior to the 8.4 percent increase from 2014 to 2015 was the 9.4 percent increase from 1963 to 1964—over a half-century ago! The back-to-back total motor vehicle fatality increases from 2014 to 2015 (8.4 percent) and from 2015 to 2016 (5.6 percent) exceeded the highest two-year increase in sixty years, beating the previous record increases in 1963 and 1964 of 9.4 and 3.2 percent, respectively.[2] Ironically, one of the explanations for this unusual jump may be technology: we are getting distracted by our dashboards, phones, and navigation tools.

Nonetheless, the fact is that "cars today are substantially safer than vehicles were even five or even ten years go," says Richard Retting, the renowned traffic safety expert. "There is no question that cars will become even safer over the next twenty years, due especially to improvements in crash avoidance technology, which will be dramatically more advanced than it is today."[3]

Even though cars are becoming exponentially safer, drivers don't always keep up with technology. Moreover, even high-level standard safety features don't save everyone—not even, perhaps, when AVs reach their highest technological levels. "We don't know if safety features make people drive more safely; there is no empirical data on that," Retting says. "Admittedly, the human condition has not changed much over time, therefore our ability to be good or bad drivers hasn't either. Some AV technology can compensate for the shortcomings of human beings, but at the same time, there is a dramatic increase in distractions available to us in a car, and human beings are susceptible to distraction." More than 40 percent of fatal traffic crashes involve alcohol, distraction, drugs, or fatigue.[4]

Crashes are also often due to aggressive driving, overcompensation, inexperience, slow reaction times, inattention, and many other human variables. AVs won't fall prey to these human failings, and their computers will reduce human error, but they probably won't entirely eliminate it. Consider the March 2018 crash that killed pedestrian Elaine Herzberg as she crossed a street with her bicycle in Tempe, Arizona. The autonomous car, operated by Uber, did have an emergency backup driver behind the wheel, who may or may not have been paying attention to the road (the investigation is ongoing as of this writing). It is believed to be the first pedestrian death associated with self-driving technology. Uber subsequently suspended testing in Tempe, Pittsburgh, San Francisco, and Toronto.[5] Arizona governor Doug Ducey banned Uber from testing driverless vehicles in the state; he did not, however, ban other companies from testing AVs. And Ducey has been a strong proponent of AV testing and development.[6]

Still, I believe that, on a per mile basis, AVs could be 70 percent safer than driven cars—or even more—in terms of property damage, personal injuries, and fatalities. But if VMT rises signficantly, as predicted by many, the absolute decrease in number of crashes could be far less than 70 percent. I worry, however, that greater AV-related inactivity, by making people less healthy, could wipe out these gains. But I also worry that increases in VMT could wipe out some gains.

Speeding is also an issue, which could ostensibly be mitigated by programming AVs to default to safer or slower speeds depending on road conditions and other factors. But will Americans give up their impulse to speed? In 2015, speeding was a factor in 27 percent of motor vehicle crash deaths. The Insurance Institute for Highway Safety's Highway Loss Data Institute says that speeding has been a factor in more than one-quarter of crash deaths since 2005.[7] The IIHS defined going too fast to include crashes in which the driver was issued a traffic citation for speeding or driver-related factors included driving too fast for the conditions, racing, or exceeding the posted speed limit.

In 2015, the percentage of crash deaths involving speeding was higher on minor roads (32 percent) than on interstates and freeways (30 percent) or other major roads (24 percent). Of the 9,557 speeding-related fatalities that occurred in 2015, about half (52 percent) occurred on roads with speed limits lower than 55 miles per hour.[8] The National Transportation Safety Board (NTSB) released a study in August 2017, "Safety Study: Reducing Speeding-Related Crashes Involving Passenger Vehicles," aimed at reducing speeding-related injuries and fatalities. That study reports that between 2005 and 2014, 112,580 fatalities, representing 31 percent of all traffic fatalities, resulted from crashes in which a law enforcement officer indicated that a vehicle's speed was a factor. In 2014, it states, passenger vehicles constituted 77 percent of speeding vehicles involved in fatal crashes.[9] A driverless car that has preset speeds or is programmed to reduce speed or stop acceleration after a certain speed is reached would go a long way toward preventing crash fatalities. But the technology is available today to control speeding even with driven cars.

The Eno Center for Transportation says that, with AVs, 50 to 60 percent fewer crash-related deaths are expected each year. Its report contends that if only 10 percent of cars and trucks on the road were self-driving, traffic deaths could be reduced by 1,000 per year, producing nearly $38 billion in economic and other savings. If and when self-driving vehicles reach critical mass, as many as 21,700 lives per year could be saved.[10] The consulting firm McKinsey also reports reductions in crash-related deaths, saying that 90 percent of crashes could be avoided with AVs.[11] Today, for every person killed in a motor vehicle crash, according to the McKinsey study, eight people are hospitalized and one hundred are treated and released from emergency rooms.

I'm not convinced by the 90 percent reduction in deaths being hyped, because the fact is that more than one-quarter of traffic fatalities in the United States (and more worldwide) occur among motorcyclists, pedestrians, and cyclists. For instance, according to Emilia Crotty, executive director of the pedestrian advocacy group Los Angeles Walks, in the United States, African Americans and Latino Americans are 60 percent and 43 percent more likely, respectively, to be killed in traffic crashes while walking than are white Americans. "The traffic deaths and injuries that are so common in these neighborhoods are a result of historical neglect and disinvestment in the streets, crosswalks, sidewalks, traffic signals, medians, and curb extensions that other communities have enjoyed for years," she notes.[12] I'm not convinced that AVs will have as much success reducing these fatalities and other person-to-vehicle fatalities as they will with vehicle-to-vehicle deaths.

The overall annual cost of crashes for Americans is approximately $871 billion in economic loss and societal harm. About $277 billion represents economic costs—that's close to $900 for each person living in the United States based on calendar year 2010 data—and another $594 billion represents harm from the loss of life and the pain and diminished quality of life due to injuries.[13] Using that number as an example, the reduction in car crashes from AVs could save $105 billion to $190 billion a year (depending on whose estimate of crash reductions is used) in the United States. Moreover, when AVs are ubiquitous (by the middle of the twenty-first century), vehicle crashes in this country could move from second place to ninth place in rankings of types of human activities that lead to death.

Alain Kornhauser, professor of operations research and financial engineering at Princeton University, stresses the distinction between *safe cars* and *self-driving cars*. He maintains that much of the 50 to 90 percent estimated reduction in traffic fatalities could be achieved if carmakers simply continue to make cars themselves safer. And instead of waiting for fully autonomous vehicles—which may be decades away, he notes—this could happen in the next five to ten years. Safe cars are feasible now.

Several studies support Kornhauser's distinction between safe cars and self-driving cars. A 2016 study from Carnegie Mellon found that three recently introduced safety features in particular could prevent crashes caused by human error and distracted driving: blind spot monitoring (BSM), lane departure warning (LDW), and forward collision warning (FCW) crash avoidance systems.[14]

By alerting drivers when a vehicle is encroaching into their blind spot—via cameras or sensors that monitor areas to the side of the vehicle—BSM is useful in preventing or reducing the severity of lane change crashes. A lane departure crash happens when one vehicle inadvertently departs a travel lane and hits another vehicle in the process. An LDW system issues warnings (such as "Vehicle traveling over left of lane" and "Vehicle traveling over the right lane line") that help drivers get back into their own lane. FCW systems prevent or reduce the severity of rear-end collisions by using a camera or radar to detect whether a vehicle is approaching another vehicle or an object like a bicycle, pedestrian, or large animal, especially during inclement weather. My 2017 Volvo lets me know with a slight tug on the steering wheel if I'm veering too close to the lane line; it flashes an amber light in my mirror if I try to change lanes when another vehicle is too close; and it beeps and depicts on a screen when and where another vehicle, person, or object is too close.

According to the Carnegie Mellon study, if these features were standard across all vehicles, they could collectively prevent or reduce the severity of as many as 1.3 million crashes a year, including 133,000 injury crashes and 10,100 fatal crashes, or about one-quarter of annual fatal crashes in the United States. At that rate, the technology could save $18 billion a year (*note:* if a 25 percent reduction in crashes is achieved, I believe the savings would be far higher), but making these features standard in every vehicle may be wishful thinking. According to the Insurance Institute for Highway Safety, "only 6 percent of new cars in model year 2017 have lane departure warning as a standard feature."[15] Right now, the costs involved may be discouraging carmakers from adopting standardization. Using 2015 as a pricing guide to add these options to the 4.25 million cars (and 7.4 million commercial vehicles) manufactured in the United States each year, the Carnegie Mellon study says that the total cost would be about $13 billion, or $20 per vehicle. So for now, better safety can be bought only by those who can afford it. The industry that touts safety as the paramount reason we should buy into AVs could eliminate one-quarter of crashes right now, with the mandated safety features in existing models, without waiting for widespread adoption of AVs. This adds a hollow ring to safety being the impetus for AVs.

Pedestrians and cyclists could also be safer alongside vehicles with BSM, LDW, FCW, and other safety systems built into them. In 2015, 5,376 pedestrians were killed in traffic crashes in the United States. This averages to one crash-related pedestrian death every 1.6 hours. Additionally, almost 129,000 pedestrians were treated in emergency departments for nonfatal crash-related injuries in 2015.[16] Vehicles programmed to brake for pedestrians in their path could prevent a large percentage of these kinds of crashes. Even without more advanced autonomous technology, we could save lives with these systems. In 2016, twenty carmakers committed to making automatic emergency braking systems a standard feature on virtually all new cars sold in the United States by 2022.[17] Forward collision warning systems went from being standard in 4 percent of new cars in 2016 to 14 percent in 2017.[18]

However, as humans become more comfortable with AVs and expectations rise that these vehicles will stop when confronted with foot traffic, people may take more chances around them, with unpredictable results. People may cross streets wherever and whenever they like (as they did in pre-automobile days), and the outcome may not always be in the pedestrian's favor. One of the most critical safety factors in vehicle-related fatalities is speed. In a 2016 position paper, the National Association of City Transportation Officials—a US group representing more than fifty-seven cities, including Baltimore, Atlanta, Seattle, Charleston, Montreal, Toronto, and Vancouver—called for AV speeds to be restricted in densely populated areas.[19] The group recommended a limit of 40 kilometers (25 miles) per hour in cities. Being hit at that speed, the majority of pedestrians would survive, although almost all would certainly sustain some type of injury.

Michael Clamann, a senior research scientist in the Humans and Autonomy Lab at Duke University, conducted an experiment to explore ways in which an AV could communicate with pedestrians.[20] He fitted a van with a display board that showed the vehicle's velocity using either a number or an icon (such as a "walk" or "don't walk" image). Pedestrians were told that the van was an AV (it actually had a human driver) and were asked to assess the displays to determine when it was safe to cross. A majority, 76 percent, saw the displays, but only 12 percent said that they used them to inform their decisions on whether to cross.

Figuring out how people will communicate with AVs is imperative because much of the communication between drivers and pedestrians today occurs through eye contact, gestures, honking, and shouting. The Swedish company Semcon has suggested displaying an LED smile or grimace on a vehicle's grill that would tell pedestrians to stay away or keep coming. A 2015 study prepared for Toronto's Transportation Services Department raises the prospect that all road users will have to embrace this kind of technology as a replacement for subtle human signals: "As a safety measure, pedestrians and cyclists may one day passively announce their presence to connected vehicles via mobile apps or wearable technology."[21]

In September 2016, the US Department of Transportation (DOT) released a 116-page policy paper on autonomous vehicles and behavioral issues.[22] The paper identifies the ability to "yield to pedestrians and bicyclists at intersections and crosswalks" as one of the "behavioral competencies" that AVs must have. This is a key point, and one that Adam Millard-Ball believes could lead to a profound change in how roads are used. For a paper first published in 2016, the assistant professor of environmental studies at the University of California–Santa Cruz applied game theory "to develop a new model of road-user interactions" between pedestrians and drivers.[23] Millard-Ball argues that pedestrians often don't assert their right to cross because they fear the oncoming vehicle won't stop. However, a pedestrian who *is* certain that the vehicle will yield will take the initiative and cross. Even before AVs become ubiquitous, he argues, human drivers who encounter newly assertive pedestrians will learn to be more careful. AVs could learn this too. This new caution on the part of drivers and/or vehicles could be self-perpetuating, making walking safer and prompting other pedestrians to assert their rights as well. This is a best-case scenario for pedestrians, but it clearly would have a cost for vehicle owners.

"At a crosswalk . . . driverless cars potentially might be stuck for hours," MIT professor emeritus of robotics Rodney Brooks says in one of his blog posts.[24] "Will people take pity on [AVs] as they do on human drivers? To take advantage of this, the cars would need to understand human social signals of giving them a turn, but without a reciprocal signal [from the vehicle] it is going to be confusing to the generous pedestrians and they may soon decide to not bother being nice to driverless cars at all." This sort of pedestrian assertiveness requires technology that is wholly reliable and pedestrian-friendly—a level of predictability that has yet to be reached. "So much of our current driving is based on nonverbal cues. While technology is capable of doing many things, and I don't put it beyond possibility that a computer could understand the nuances of human communication, the challenge seems extraordinary," says Jason Levine, executive director of the Washington, DC–based consumer advocacy group Center for Auto Safety.[25]

Whether an AV can be designed to avoid pedestrians at night depends on whether its sensors can be highly developed enough to detect a person on the road dressed entirely in black and in all weather conditions.

The warnings from Toyota's 2017 handbook about situations where sensors may not recognize pedestrians highlights their current limitations. The handbook says the system may not detect pedestrians if they are:

- Shorter than 3.2 feet or taller than 6.5 feet
- Wearing oversized clothing
- Carrying luggage or holding an umbrella
- Bending forward or squatting
- Pushing a stroller, wheelchair, or bicycle
- In a group of pedestrians close together
- Wearing white
- In the dark, as at night or in a tunnel
- Wearing clothing of a similar color to the environment
- Walking near fences or walls
- Standing on a metal object like a manhole cover
- Walking fast, or changing speed abruptly
- Running out from behind a vehicle
- Extremely close to the sidewalk

"It's hard to assign distraction—statistically speaking, crashes are rare events where typically more than one thing goes wrong, particularly in serious crashes," Richard Retting says. As the collection of data from wired cars communicating with each other and with cell towers or other data collection technology becomes the norm, more information may lead to better and more advanced ways to prevent more crashes.[26] "If you look at seat belt use in the 1960s," he observes, "it was maybe at 10 or 15 percent, and today it is close to 90 percent compliance." Of course, there is pushback against laws that curb pedestrian behavior, but over time such laws, in some settings, have changed the way pedestrians act on the street, though they haven't necessarily increased pedestrian safety. In New York City, which has virtually no jaywalking enforcement, pedestrian fatality rates are lower than in Los Angeles, where enforcement is quite strict and compliance is very high. Since I feel that we went overboard a hundred years ago when we started criminalizing jaywalking, I lean heavily toward not adding more, if any, regulations regarding pedestrians.

Some feel that pedestrians will learn, over time, how to live with AVs. "If you want to act like a jerk and walk in front of an AV to make it stop, you can do that," says Alain Kornhauser. "Maybe AVs have to kill a few pedestrians so that people start behaving. Pedestrians have responsibilities too."[27] Richard Retting agrees. "Without a law, people are doing something dumb [when they walk into the road with their head buried in a cell phone]. Now they can do something dumb and illegal. There is more pressure to stop a stupid behavior," he says.[28]

According to MobilityLab, emerging yet still limited experience between bikes and AVs has shown that cyclists may be more comfortable sharing the road with an AV than with human-driven vehicles—probably because AVs are thought to be more predictable than human-driven cars.[29] Even this comfort or trust may cause issues. Carlos Ghosn, CEO of Renault and former CEO of Nissan, told CNBC that cyclists are "one of the biggest problems for driverless cars."[30] Ghosn says that bikes can confuse AVs because they sometimes act like pedestrians and sometimes act like vehicles, and also because cyclists "don't respect any rules." It's not just bikes that can confuse AVs: motorcycles, animals, tumbleweeds, and severe weather conditions have confounded their systems.

Tesla's Autopilot system was cleared in the deadly crash involving the Model S sedan in May 2016 that collided with a semitrailer truck on a Florida highway, killing the sedan's owner, Joshua Brown (giving him the distinction of being the first known fatality in a self-driving car).[31] The case demonstrated AV technology's current limits. "Not all systems can do all things," said Bryan Thomas, a spokesman for the National Highway Traffic Safety Administration, which investigated the Tesla crash. "There are driving scenarios that automatic emergency braking systems are not designed to address."[32]

As consumers, we have a lot to learn about self-driving technology if we are to optimize AV safety levels when a person is in the vehicle but not controlling a steering wheel. Tesla's owner manuals make it clear that drivers must be prepared to take charge of the steering wheel if its Autopilot system acts unpredictably or is unable to correctly process a specific traffic condition.[33] When was the last time, however, you sat down and read the owner's manual for your car? Humans don't much like reading instructions. Did Joshua Brown take the time to read his Tesla's manual before getting in the vehicle? Frank Baressi, the owner-driver of the truck that slammed into Brown, said that the forty-year old tech enthusiast was speeding and "went so fast through my trailer I didn't see him."[34] That testimony indicates that Brown felt completely comfortable handing over all responsibility to the car.

We can't forget that while high-level autonomy could be nearly fool-proof in preventing crashes (although so far no evidence supports this), during the transitionary period, when AVs share roads with driven cars, crashes will happen. It will take time for older cars, which are durable, to be completely replaced.

So are we really on track to eliminate as much as 70 to 90 percent of driving fatalities? Maybe, if AV makers can standardize advanced safety features. However, if we allow the AV industry to decimate transit systems, as cars did from the 1930s to the 1950s, the answer could be no. Transit is already about 95 percent safer than cars per mile traveled and may already be twice as safe as AVs at the highest levels of safety they may ever achieve. If we repeat the past, some people who would otherwise have been safe on transit will die because frustration combined with the affordability of individual vehicles persuaded them to abandon public transport.[35]

Public transit is especially effective at reducing crashes among high-risk drivers, such as impaired drivers, seniors, and teens. A study by the American Public Transportation Association analyzed DUI rates around DC Metro stations and found that crashes involving drunk drivers declined 70 percent after an increase in late-night transit service.[36]

Another benefit is that cities with good transit have lower rates of unlicensed drivers, according to the NHTSA. Unlicensed drivers are almost three times more likely to cause a fatal car crash than licensed drivers, according to a report by the California Department of Motor Vehicles.[37]

We could also miss out on the lifesaving potential of AVs if we don't pass legislation that puts limits on how AVs operate and on who operates them, or if we yield lawmaking to the AV industry. Regulators first need to define what "safe" actually means when it comes to AVs. Should autonomous vehicles drive flawlessly? Is the bar of perfection even possible to reach considering that, for instance, even the most advanced navigation systems can still send people onto nonexistent roads?[38] Or do AVs simply need to be noticeably better than human drivers? As of this writing, there isn't a specific test that can determine the safety of self-driving cars, according to Steven Shladover, a research engineer and manager of the Partners for Advanced Transportation Technology program at the University of California–Berkeley. "There is a need for fundamental research to support the development of dependable and affordable methods for assessing the safety of an automated driving system when it is confronted with the full range of traffic hazards," he told *Scientific American*.[39]

The right kind of legislation, based on science, is crucial to ensure the safety of people both inside and outside of cars (not just drivers but pedestrians, cyclists, and others) in a world of AVs. Good legislation can go a long way toward preventing the problems that will arise if AV technology is less predictable and more malleable than humans would like to believe, or if AV makers control the rules of the road and marginalize people on foot or bikes through legal means.

There are several safety issues we should be concerned about. The 114-page Federal Automated Vehicles Policy (FAVP), released in 2016 during the Obama administration, signaled the first time that federal guidance was offered to unify AV safety rules and make them consistent across the states.[40] However, critics took a dim view of the guidance. CityLab's Laura Bliss wrote that the FAVP amounted to "a federal endorsement of full autonomy" that was engineered to speed the industry's rapid development.[41]

The Trump administration also took a shot at writing AV safety guidelines, in September 2017. Transportation secretary Elaine Chao released "Automated Driving Systems 2.0: A Vision for Safety," a 36-page report focused on making "department regulatory process more nimble," encouraging "new entrants and ideas," and removing "barriers to innovation" by trimming what Chao considered to be the most restrictive parameters outlined in the 2016 report.[42] Bliss is skeptical about this plan. She writes that the "Trump administration has yet to produce any concrete proposals that outline the president's infrastructure priorities, ambitions, and policies. What is known about the $1 trillion plan, insofar as one exists, is that it leans heavily on partnerships between public and private actors."[43]

The document offers a nonregulatory approach to automated vehicle technology safety. In its section on "Voluntary Guidance for Automated Driving Systems (Voluntary Guidance)," the paper supports the automotive industry "and other key stakeholders as they consider and design best practices for the testing and safe deployment of Automated Driving Systems." The bulk of the document encourages companies to submit documents to the DOT that address twelve aspects of vehicle safety and accountability. It recommends (but doesn't require) that manufacturers disclose vehicle designs and the technologies that make them work (all of which should adhere to federal, state, and local laws), and it lays out a plan for consumer education and training. Cybersecurity should be incorruptible, and data recording should be comprehensive.

"The purpose of this Voluntary Guidance is to help designers of AVs analyze, identify, and resolve safety considerations prior to deployment using their own, industry, and other best practices," the report states. It's important to point out that while this guidance encourages carmakers to publicly disclose their "Voluntary Safety Self-Assessments," there is neither a requirement that they do so nor enforcement methods to encourage such disclosure. In fact, the word "voluntary" is used fifty-seven times in the report, which also encourages states not to interfere with DOT's regulations.

To be clear, the 2016 FAVP wasn't mandatory either, but manufacturers and automakers tended to interpret that relatively lenient document more strictly, according to Greg Rogers, a political analyst at the Eno Center for Transportation. It too listed safety areas (fifteen to the twelve in the Trump administration report), and it recommended that states require that safety assessments be submitted before allowing more AV testing.

It's not surprising that auto industry groups like the 2017 guidelines. In a statement, a General Motors spokesperson called them "clear, streamlined, and flexible" and applauded the specificity around state and federal roles.[44] "In issuing the new guidance and policy framework, NHTSA and DOT have been very responsive to the concerns and suggestions of stakeholders, while appropriately maintaining safety as the paramount goal," the spokesperson said. "In particular, General Motors appreciates DOT's clarification of the separate roles of federal and state governments in regulating self-driving vehicles and its guidance for state policymakers."

Whenever I see a reference to auto industry "stakeholders," I recall the public committees formed a hundred years ago to address the conflicts occurring between motor vehicles and pedestrians across the United States. Those panels heavily favored cars over people, and we know who won. Moreover, car-sponsored groups of that era freely used the word "safety" to advance their agenda, but in the ensuing 100 years, 70 million people died in car crashes worldwide and 4 billion were maimed. So you can understand my suspicion when I once again hear the car industry use the word "safety" to advance its cause. "With more than 35,000 motor vehicle deaths in 2015," says David Strickland, general counsel for the Self-Driving Coalition for Safer Streets, which represents Google, Uber, Lyft, Volvo, and Ford, "the potential safety benefits of fully self-driving technology are too important to delay." The former NHTSA administrator adds, "We look forward to continue working with Secretary Chao, NHTSA and Congress in pursuit of the right policy solutions to make self-driving technology's safety and mobility efforts a reality."[45]

Automotive safety advocates are also concerned about other bills surrounding state-specific AV regulation in Congress. In September 2017, the US House of Representatives passed the SELF-DRIVE Act with enthusiastic bipartisan support. It gives NHTSA jurisdiction over states in regulating AV design, performance, and safety requirements. The House measure applies only to vehicles under 10,000 pounds (4,536 kilograms). Under the bill, automated semitrucks and other commercial vehicles without drivers can't be deployed in the same way passenger vehicles would be.[46] It would allow automakers to obtain exemptions to deploy up to 25,000 vehicles without meeting existing auto safety standards in the first year. The cap would rise over three years to 100,000 vehicles annually. While 99 percent of the vehicles on the road today can withstand a front-end crash at 25 miles per hour, next year you could be riding in a lightweight, eggshell-like AV that might only withstand a 5 mile per hour crash.

The US Senate developed its own version of the federal legislation, called the American Vision for Safer Transportation through Advancement of Revolutionary Technologies (AV START) Act, which was passed in October 2017.[47] The Senate bill is similar to the House proposal (as of this writing). It stipulates that states would continue to license cars, regulate insurance, and enforce traffic laws, but that the National Highway Traffic Safety Administration would oversee the design and manufacture of the vehicles. Like the House bill, the Senate legislation would allow the transportation secretary to exempt automakers from existing safety standards, eventually permitting the sale of 100,000 cars a year as the self-driving technology develops. It also requires manufacturers to develop plans to protect autonomous cars from cyberattacks. Both the House and Senate bills pertain only to the development of driverless cars, not to the driverless trucks that may become a presence on the highways in ten or twenty years.

Legislation is likely to be in need of modification across Europe as well. For instance, European roads fall under the United Nations' 1968 Vienna Convention on Road Traffic, which originally limited self-driving cars to speeds of no more than 10 kilometers per hour.[48]

Seventy-two countries are party to the convention, which covers the European countries, Mexico, Chile, Brazil, and Russia, but not the United States, Japan, or China.[49] In 2014, the convention was amended to allow driverless vehicles on the road and to allow drivers to take their hands off the wheels of self-driving cars and to transfer driving tasks to their vehicles, provided that they conform to UN vehicle regulations.[50]

In 2012, the European Commission said that all commercial vehicles would have to be fitted with autonomous emergency braking (AEB).[51] As of 2014, the European New Car Assessment Program (Euro NCAP) included AEB in its assessment of new cars, which made it impossible for any model without this technology to achieve a five-star safety rating from the group.[52]

In 2016, the German transport minister Alexander Dobrindt put forth a proposal mandating that drivers be able to intervene in an emergency, a requirement that would necessitate steering wheels in AVs. German legislation could also require vehicles with an autopilot function to have a black box to help determine responsibility in the event of a crash.[53]

While European countries and the EU continue to look at laws governing self-driving, the most challenging issue for lawmakers and AV developers may be Europe's strict privacy laws regarding data collection, as well as its laws around liability and insurance. Both EU and national privacy laws might have to be revised or at least reinterpreted. Both collectively and individually, Europe must find ways to balance the need to protect driver data with the need to collect that data, which is so vital to high-definition mapping for autonomous vehicles.[54] "Privacy is one issue that will affect the way in which AV and AI technology are developed in Europe. I don't think it will prevent these technologies from developing in Europe, but it will shape the way in which the technologies are deployed and relied upon," says Oliver Yaros, a London partner in the international law firm Mayer Brown's Intellectual Property and IT Group and an expert in privacy laws and data protection.[55]

The EU's restrictive stance on data collection and analysis limits the ability of tech companies to collect data on road conditions and map street views. European data protection law imposes use limitation and data minimization requirements that may restrict the manner in which "big data" are typically collected and used. Specifically, the EU's new General Data Protection Regulation (GDPR, in effect as of May 2018) prohibits the use of personal data for purposes other than the original reason collected. The GDPR also requires that the processing of personal data be kept to a minimum and that no data are held for longer than necessary.[56]

Anger over tech companies' aggressive data collection practices (especially Google's) has been brewing for some time. In 2010, European privacy regulators and advocates were frustrated when Google revealed that it had been systematically collecting private data since 2006 while compiling its Street View photo archive.[57] In 2013, a German privacy regulator imposed what is a pretty nominal fee for an organization like Google, €145,000 (about $171,000), for "the systematic, illegal collection of personal data while it was creating the Street View mapping service."[58] It also called on European lawmakers to significantly raise fines for violations of data protection laws. In Germany, for instance, Google is obligated to notify the public before it collects Street View data on public roads.[59] Germany also limits the length of time the company can keep imaging data about the streets and highways surrounding private homes. Germans can opt out of data collection. So far, 3 percent of its population have done so.[60] These requirements and others limit the accuracy of navigational maps and the ability to keep them up to date.

The GDPR, adopted in April 2016 to replace the EU's Data Protection Directive, stems in part from many European countries' concern that people's personal information in unencrypted Wi-Fi networks could become part of overall data collection used for unknown—and potentially unsafe—purposes.[61] The EU has fined Google, Facebook, and Twitter on several occasions for data collection infractions.[62] As recently as June 2017, Google received a substantial $2.7 billion fine from the EU, and another EU regulation forced Google and other companies to purge inaccurate or outdated personal information from their search results.[63] These kinds of restrictions, if unchanged, could make it difficult for tech firms to develop the high-definition maps that AVs need to navigate roadways safely.

The GDPR also places strict constraints on the use of artificial intelligence (AI) and machine learning. According to the guidelines, "regulations prohibit any automated decision that 'significantly affects' EU citizens. This includes techniques that evaluate a person's 'performance at work, economic situation, health, personal preferences, interests, reliability, behavior, location, or movements.'"[64] The rules also give citizens the right to review how digital services make specific algorithmic choices that affect them.

Regulations this stringent could make it hard for developers to incorporate artificial intelligence that provides safety features and high-definition mapping in autonomous vehicles, but it would not be impossible. "Privacy laws may require organizations to think about how they get the data. If countries see that the benefits are so great and outweigh some privacy concerns, mapping will happen. In short, it may take longer than in places with more relaxed privacy laws [like the United States and China]," says Oliver Yaros.[65]

Tracking locations and movement is central to AV navigational powers. Those who champion the manufacture of AVs, including Darrell West at the Center for Technology Innovation at the Brookings Institution, say that European manufacturing will stagnate without loosened standards around data collection for mapping purposes.[66]

Of course, countries within Europe have different approaches to policy, legal, and regulatory questions. "Differences in laws sometimes depend on cultural differences," says Yaros. "National laws vary from country to country [much as laws vary from state to state in the United States]. Privacy is seen as a fundamental right in Europe. It cannot be commoditized in terms of being given away as part of a bargain when someone enters into a contract. The UK is less protective of privacy compared to France, for instance, where they are very protective of privacy."[67] At the same time that the very restrictive privacy laws in countries like France hamper the ability of AVs to talk to each other or to infrastructure, the lack of uniformity in privacy laws also creates headaches for systems designers. Countries generally prefer maintaining their sovereignty, as recent moves toward independence by many EU members make apparent, but with the spread of autonomous technology, there may be resistance by citizens to force standardization of privacy laws across the continent.[68]

Will consumers want to get into a car that has been exempted from safety standards or that reveals passenger information to governments and private companies? Will they want to put their elderly mother or their blind uncle into one of these vehicles? Some polling says no. A majority of respondents to an AAA survey, 78 percent, said that they would not want to ride in a self-driving car.[69] Just 13 percent of people surveyed by MIT said that they would feel comfortable with autonomous car technology that relieved them of any responsibility.[70] Regardless of what laws are passed, people won't adopt the technology if they don't feel safe using it, according to Alain Kornhauser: "AV technology has to be safer for vehicle occupants or the technology won't get off the ground. AV cars are at absolute zero right now regardless of what you read in the newspaper. And AVs won't be in demand by consumers unless they are much safer than driven cars. They won't exist if they aren't safer."[71]

The National Association of Transportation Officials and Transportation for America reacted negatively to the US Senate's draft of the American Vision for Safer Transportation Through Advancement of Revolutionary Technology (AVSTART) Act, issuing a statement that said, "The bill's requirement of a safety report is just an exercise. . . . The bill strips states and local governments of the authority to manage the vehicles on their roadways and leaves them without the tools to deal with problems already arising during the testing and deployment of automated vehicles."[72] Critics may be frustrated, however, since industry lobbying and political pressure will continue to grow and lawmakers will be seduced by the money, power, and promise of being on the cutting edge of innovation. Such lobbying has now started in earnest.

Some US states have presciently noted the potentially hand-tying effect of federal regulations and crafted their own legislation regarding AV safety. In 2017, thirty-three states introduced AV-related legislation, up from twenty in 2016. Twenty-nine have passed some kind of AV legislation as of this writing.[73]

Michigan was the first state to pass comprehensive self-driving legislation.[74] In that state, AVs can take to the roads only if their high-tech manufacturers have collaborated on some level with the traditional automotive industry—Detroit carmakers obviously had some say in that rule. California requires that self-driving vehicle crashes be publicly reported, and that the reports state how often humans had to take control in order to avert or minimize the impact of a crash.[75] In April 2018, a California regulation allowing the testing and public use of fully driverless cars (those with no human backup driver present) took effect. Governor Jerry Brown signed the legislation at Google headquarters in Mountain View, boasting that "California's technological leadership is turning today's science fiction into tomorrow's reality."[76] Arizona so far requires only standard vehicle registration, as for any conventional driven car, to operate an AV.[77]

There are those who believe that no laws should be written until we have more data about how AVs operate. The RAND Corporation think tank says, "A fleet of 100 cars would have to drive 275 million miles without failure to meet the safety standards of today's vehicles in terms of deaths."[78] Kornhauser told *Scientific American*'s Jeremy Hsu in early 2017 that, without federal laws, "the US government could simply step aside and allow companies to put more self-driving cars on public roads to collect the necessary safety data." He added that "it would be worth the risk to let autonomous cars roam more freely and 'learn' faster."[79]

Such learning could be as straightforward as data-sharing between tech companies and carmakers. Sebastian Thrun, CEO and cofounder of the online education provider Udacity and a self-driving technology pioneer who formerly worked at Google, agrees: "There is no doubt in my mind that if companies openly shared data, the development would go faster and the cars would take off"—and presumably safety would increase. Barring regulations that force them to do so, however, companies are reluctant to share this information with each other or across industries.[80]

All of Europe wants to be ready for the potential economic and social benefits of the technology. Greece knows AVs are coming and is trying to prepare for them. In 2013, the Greek Ministry of Infrastructure,
Transport, and Networks began discussions about allowing driverless
vehicles within the Greek transit system.[81] The ministry convened
a meeting in Athens in May 2014 to discuss different approaches to
AV transit with representatives of other foreign ministries, including
France, Italy, Finland, Spain, Sweden, Germany, the United Kingdom,
Poland, Malta, and Cyprus. As a result, a legislative act was proposed to
the Greek parliament that allowed AV testing on roadways. Greece has
tested autonomous buses since 2015.[82] A 2017 study found that Greeks
are willing to accept AVs if they are affordable and safe—findings that
echo the sentiments of many other people around the world.[83]

In 2013, the United Kingdom authorized the testing of autonomous cars on public roads, and in 2015 it published a code of practice—a nonstatutory guidance to promote responsible AV testing.[84]
In July 2016, the UK government also began looking at changing
regulations on driver insurance and road regulations for self-driving
cars. In 2014, France announced that testing of autonomous cars on
public roads would be allowed by 2015. Approximately 1,243 miles
(2,000 kilometers) of road would be opened for testing, particularly
in Bordeaux, Isère, Île-de-France, and Strasbourg.

Self-driving tests are also legal in the Netherlands. In the spring of
2015, Switzerland allowed Swisscom to test a driverless Volkswagen
Passat on the streets of Zurich.[85] In 2017, Sweden also allowed Volvo
to test driverless vehicles on public roadways, and it continues to look at
ways to modify existing legislation to enable acceptance of AVs.[86]

In mid-2016, European Union policymakers and European vehicle
manufacturers reached an agreement on the future of AVs.[87] The "Declaration of Amsterdam" lays out an agreement on the steps necessary
for the development of connected, autonomous driving technology in
the EU. The signatories pledged to draw up rules and regulations that
will allow autonomous vehicles to be tested and used on the roads of
Europe.[88] The Declaration also defines the following objectives:

- To work towards a coherent European framework for the deployment of interoperable connected and automated driving, which should be available, if possible, by 2019;
- to bring together developments of connected and automated driving in order to reach their full potential to improve road safety, human health [i.e., safety], traffic flows, and to reduce the environmental impact of road transport;
- to adopt a "learning by experience" approach, including, where possible, cross-border cooperation, sharing and expanding knowledge on connected and automated driving and to develop practical guidelines to ensure interoperability of systems and services;
- to support further innovation in connected and automated vehicle technologies to strengthen the global market position of European industry; and
- to ensure data protection and privacy.[89]

Dutch official Melanie Schultz van Haegen said, "We want to pick up the pace because there are many gains to be made for mobility. Connected automated vehicles will make our roads safer, more sustainable and more efficient."[90] The two parties acknowledged that the agreement is only the first step, but it represents a collective effort to address some of the issues that AVs bring to the EU, and it seems oriented toward getting AVs on the road "the sooner the better."

Liability laws will also have to be reviewed, as is already happening in the United Kingdom. Its 2017 Vehicle Technology and Aviation Bill lays out rules for liability in crashes involving automated vehicles, factoring in whether the vehicle owners are insured and whether they have made "unauthorized alterations" to the vehicle or failed to update its software.[91] According to the UK government, the bill is designed to "help the UK to become a world leader in these technologies by breaking down some of the barriers that could limit companies from testing them here." The Association of British Insurers (ABI) has backed the UK government's plans, under which the government would keep a list of all AVs in the country. Those vehicles would be defined as ones "designed or adapted to be capable, in at least some circumstances or situations, of safely driving themselves without having to be monitored by an individual."[92] Vehicles on the list would be subject to the new insurance and liability provisions.

Ultimately, for AV safety legislation to be the best it can be, it must include the interests of an entire network that includes automakers, tech firms, research institutes, and local, state, and federal government—and the public. "Our preference is to fund the NHTSA appropriately," says the Center for Auto Safety's Jason Levine, "and let them work with the industry to develop the right regulatory framework over time. There are many people working in the AV industry who don't come from the world of car-making. For all its faults, the auto industry has traditionally put out safety features in an integrative way—and that's not something the tech industry is accustomed to doing. They just want to get the product out and issue updates later." Moreover, every car safety feature has been added only after much kicking and screaming from carmakers. "The airbag is the perfect example—carmakers didn't want them to be mandatory and even after they put them in, many manufacturers took the cheap way out, and defective airbags cause more injuries than no airbags at all," Levine says.[93] Safety laws are only as good as the products made for carrying them out.

AI AND AVs—WEAPONS OF MASS DESTRUCTION?

Do we need to worry about AVs being hacked? If you talk to computer experts, most admit that anything that can be hacked will be hacked. The closer cars come to being giant smartphones-with-seating, the more vulnerable they will be to high-tech attacks. In July 2017, Elon Musk, chief of Tesla and SpaceX, told a meeting of governors that they should enact AI legislation before robots start "going down the street killing people." In August 2017, he tweeted that AI going rogue represents "vastly more risk than North Korea." Following that, in September 2017, he tweeted out a Gizmodo story that was headlined "Hackers Have Already Started to Weaponize Artificial Intelligence" and reported that researchers had proven that AI hackers are better than humans at getting Twitter users to click on malicious links.

Patrick Lin, director of the Ethics + Emerging Sciences Group at California Polytechnic State University–San Luis Obispo, sees hacking as a genuine threat. "So far, just about every computing device we've created has been hacked. If authorities and owners (e.g., rental car companies) can take control of a car remotely, this offers an easy path for cyber-carjackers. If under attack, whether a hijacking or ordinary braking-in, what should the car do: speed away, alert the police, remain at the crime scene to preserve evidence, or maybe defend itself? For a future suite of in-car apps, as well as sensors and persistent GPS/tracking, can we safeguard personal information, or do we resign ourselves to a world with disappearing privacy rights?"[94] Data collected from cars by rogue nations or malicious people or groups could be used in various destructive ways, from identity theft to cyber and other kinds of warfare.

AVs could be the target of other forms of abuse as well, says Lin. "If the cars [AVs] drive too conservatively, they may become a road hazard or trigger road-rage in human drivers with less patience. If the crash-avoidance system of a robot car is known, then other drivers may be tempted to 'game' it, e.g., by cutting in front of it, knowing that the automated car will slow down or swerve to avoid a collision. If those cars can safely drive us home in a fully-auto mode, that may encourage a culture of more alcohol consumption, since we won't need to worry so much about drunk driving."

Lin further notes that "our laws are ill equipped to deal with the rise of these vehicles. For example, is it enough for a robot car to pass a human driving test? In licensing automated cars as street-legal, some commentators believe that it would be unfair to hold manufacturers to a higher standard than humans, that is, to make an automated car undergo a much more rigorous test than a new teenage driver.

"But there are important differences between humans and machines that could warrant a stricter test. For one thing, we're reasonably confident that human drivers can exercise judgment in a wide range of dynamic situations that don't appear in a standard forty-minute driving test; we presume they can act ethically and wisely. Autonomous cars are new technologies and won't have that track record for quite some time."

Not everyone believes that AI presents the threat that Musk fears; other AI experts, like the lawyer and entrepreneur Martine Rothblatt, say that AI represents neither a utopia nor a dystopia, but is just another technological breakthrough that we will incorporate into our daily lives. Alain Kornhauser thinks that people with fears such as those voiced by Musk need to "get a life." He says, "Are you kidding? If you want to be a bad actor, you don't need to hack into a car. On the list of things to do to be a bad actor, hacking into a car is number 6,482. You have nothing to worry about. We saw someone kill 59 people from the upper floor of a hotel room in Las Vegas. Worry about someone hacking into the Minute Man silo in Nebraska. Hacking into a Cadillac going down I-95 could not kill 59 people, even in heavy traffic. The probability for a serious level of destruction from a hacked car is very low."

Yet, on July 11, 2016, Bastille Day in Nice, France, a 19-ton refrigeration vehicle rented by thirty-one-year-old Mohamed Lahouaiej Bouhlel sped down a crowded promenade for about one mile. The assailant exchanged gunfire with three police officers before he was shot to death. More than eighty people were mowed down and killed—including ten children and teenagers—and more than two hundred were wounded in the attack.[95] According to reports, the attackers deliberately chose a target with many exit and entry points and with a crowd large enough that law enforcement response times would be slowed. The truck was able to drive just over a mile before the driver was shot and killed by police. It took ambulances nearly twenty-five minutes to get to the scene.[96]

Then, on October 31, 2017, in New York City, took eight lives and is another stark reminder that the use of vehicles as weapons is on the rise.[97] The Global Terrorism Database at the University of Maryland has documented more than 350 vehicle-as-weapon deaths since 2006, and many more injuries.[98] According to the Counter Extremism Project, a nonpartisan international policy group, such attacks have increased each year over the past decade. In 2017, at least 32 people died and more than 240 were wounded from vehicles used as weapons.[99] The numbers are particularly chilling because victims are ordinary people engaged in the most innocent of activities—biking and walking in the case of the attack in Lower Manhattan. With the advances in autonomous driving technology and artificial intelligence, such attacks theoretically could accelerate, with faceless perpetrators operating several vehicles at once in different locations.

Since writing this, several more vehicle attacks have taken place, and they will continue. So the fears of Elon Musk and so many other people may be justified. If a conventional truck can cause devastation, "smart" autonomous cars, deployed from afar with no driver to shoot and kill, could cause even worse chaos and destruction. And smart cars have already been hacked. Researchers at the University of California–San Diego and the University of Washington conducted a field experiment where they successfully infected driverless vehicles with computer viruses that shut off their lights, killed their engines, and slammed on their brakes, causing them to crash in each case.[100]

In September 2016 and again in March 2017, Chinese researchers discovered "security vulnerabilities" in the Tesla Model S and a Model X and remotely hacked into the cars to send malicious software through the cars' web browsers by way of a series of circuitous computer programs. Once they'd gained entry into the Tesla systems, the hackers were able to remotely control the cars via their Wi-Fi and cellular connections.[101] In both cases, Tesla was informed of the vulnerabilities, and the company was able to correct them. Charlie Miller and Chris Valasek were also able to hack into a Jeep, making its systems go haywire, despite the efforts of the driver to regain control.

Researchers from the University of Washington, the University of Michigan, Stony Brook University, and UC Berkeley were able to disrupt the way machines read and classify street signs by using everyday items: a color printer and a camera.[102] Their paper "Robust Physical-World Attacks on Deep Learning Models" explained how they camouflaged signs in ways that didn't disrupt human understanding but did disrupt AV technology's ability to read the signs correctly.[103] The signs were manipulated with graffiti, art, or images incorporated into the existing sign— all changes that humans can "edit out" when they see the basic iconic shape of a stop sign or another common street sign. Some manipulations involved placing strategically placed stickers on a stop sign. In another example, researchers printed out a true-size image similar to a sign for a right turn and overlaid it on the existing sign, completely confounding a car computer, which read it as a Speed Limit 45 sign.

To ensure the effectiveness of these "sign attacks," a hacker would have to know how a car's vision system classifies the road signs it sees. Once that is understood, the rest is easy: the hacker works with a photo of the target sign, a color printer, and some sticky paper and then sits back and watches the consequences when someone's AV blows through a stop sign at 45 miles per hour.

Tarek El-Gaaly, a senior research scientist at the autonomous driving startup Voyage, told *Car and Driver* that there are solutions for these kinds of attacks that could be incorporated into AV computer systems.[104] One would be the Context Driving Speed Limit Alert (CDSLA) system, which collects data about road signs, location, and mapping, among other things.[105] Such a system would know that a sign was being misidentified because it would also know that you need to stop at an intersection or that 45 miles per hour is too fast in an urban area. "In addition," said El-Gaaly, "many self-driving vehicles today are equipped with multiple sensors, so fail-safes can be built in using multiple cameras and lidar sensors." A LiDAR sensor uses lasers, bouncing them off reflective surfaces every second to convert information about other vehicles and objects surrounding a car and create constant awareness of surroundings.

Still, those with a mission to kill may not be daunted by AV security systems or even care about them. It may be that AVs will need to be equipped with "black boxes" similar to those on airplanes in an effort to determine the reasons for highly destructive crashes.

The FBI believes that AVs will not only revolutionize high-speed car chases but could be used as "lethal weapons" by bad actors. In a report written by agents in the Strategic Issues Group and obtained by the *Guardian* newspaper in the United Kingdom under a public records request, the FBI predicts that autonomous cars "will have a high impact on transforming what both law enforcement and its adversaries can operationally do with a car." One scenario described suspects shooting at pursuers from getaway cars that drive themselves. In addition, "autonomy . . . will make mobility more efficient, but will also open up greater possibilities for dual-use applications and ways for a car to be more of a potential lethal weapon than it is today." For instance, terrorists might program explosives-packed cars to become self-driving bombs. On the plus side, the report also claimed that tailing suspects would become more efficient with the next generation of robot cars. "Surveillance will be made more effective and easier, with less of a chance that a patrol car will lose sight of a target vehicle."[106]

This is not entirely comforting, knowing that the potential for an AV to be used as a moving bomb, filled with explosives, is there for an extremist of any ideology to exploit. A future Timothy McVeigh or Mohamed Lahouaiej Bouhlel (who drove into the crowd in Nice on Bastille Day) will no longer need to be behind the wheel of a truck intent on killing or running over as many people as possible. An AV could enable such people to place explosives near crowds, or simply use a vehicle as a weapon, from afar. It may be quite difficult for law enforcement to solve physical, violent crimes committed by people who are never at the scene of the crime.

There is a way to make our streets safer using existing and developing technologies, if we plan ahead. Some, but not most, vehicle attacks could be deterred through better street design and existing mechanisms. Indeed, on January 2, 2018, New York City mayor Bill de Blasio announced plans to install 1,500 steel street barriers to prevent vehicle attacks as part of a $50 million investment in security infrastructure.

However, we can't ring every public space with protective infrastructure. Instead, we should focus our energy on the tool used criminally or accidentally to kill and maim people: the motor vehicle itself. Most 2018 car models are computerized, and many are equipped with lane control, automatic braking, GPS, and other features. In just a few years, all cars will be partially or fully autonomous.

We are a short step away from cars that can be programmed not to go the wrong way down a one-way street, travel on a bike lane, or speed through residential areas. Uber is already using some of this technology in Pittsburgh. Researchers are looking at ways to connect smart cars to other smart cars and to link those cars to smart infrastructure. All of these developments present us with an opportunity to prevent cars from doing what they shouldn't be doing. With infrastructure controlling vehicles, along with GPS and mapping, we can achieve a large drop in crashes.

But in light of the terrorist threat, we need to go a step further and have a government override built into new cars. Bern Grush, the AV researcher, points out that the highly automated vehicles that will hit our streets in the next few years will be fitted with communication and override technology that can prevent such criminal use. I propose a protocol that all auto manufacturers would agree to—a protocol ensuring that their vehicles' technology can communicate with that of all other vehicles and with local infrastructures. Speeds would be controlled, along with access to auto-free zones. A central traffic control center would monitor compliance.

If someone figured out a way to override their vehicle's safeguards, an alarm would be triggered notifying law enforcement to take action. The inevitable argument about loss of privacy could be answered by guaranteeing that any such system wouldn't prevent honest people from going places they want or need to go. Important information could be anonymized. Nor would anyone use an individual's travel patterns for unwanted commercial purposes.

A government- or authority-controlled "kill switch" could stop potential attackers from carrying out their crime. That is, when a bad actor with an intent to use a smart vehicle as a weapon enters a city, it could be recognized and shut off via a city network. However, Vivek Krishnamurthy, a clinical instructor in Harvard Law School's Cyberlaw Clinic specializing in the international aspects of internet governance, says that it may not be that easy to implement such a kill switch. "What are the mechanics in having remote control over vehicles? That's a pretty fundamental question because you would be training AI to make decisions," he says.[107] That would require a high level of machine learning and technology that could be beyond the scope of some cities.

"Once you get beyond the issue of having a remote system kill switch," Krishnamurthy points out, "the way you would program the software, the pathway to execute commands in a vehicle, also creates an access point into the vehicle. A clever hacker will find a way in to it too, and say, 'Let's have some fun and crash the response fleet or the entire network.'"

There is something more worrisome than a lone terrorist attack, says Krishnamurthy. "A more relevant risk may not be terrorists wreaking havoc, but in creating a kill switch system you are also creating a piece of vulnerability that any malicious state could use to launch an attack. Think about Russia or another country saying, 'Let's wreak havoc on another government.'" The good news, Krishnamurthy reports, is that "a lot of technology companies are starting to wise up and are enlisting the help of good guys who have strong science and computer backgrounds who want to do the right thing. Many of them come from the open-source community, who are well versed in finding weaknesses in systems and networks and fixing them." To stay one step ahead of hackers of any kind bent on destruction, we need high-level problem-solvers on both the civic and manufacturing sides of AI development.

STEP AWAY FROM THE CAR

> I have two doctors, my left leg and my right.
> —GEORGE MACAULEY TREVELYAN, BRITISH HISTORIAN

ANOTHER POINT FEW are making about safety and AVs is that autonomy may inevitably have a negative effect on personal health by causing a rise in inactivity. Where active transportation reduced individuals' costs for transportation, made them healthier, and fostered a move toward mixed-use communities and city and town centers, AVs could upset this balanced way of living by putting large numbers of these people back into cars and encouraging suburban sprawl even to rural areas. Inactivity has just overtaken smoking worldwide as a leading factor in mortality. More than five million people annually die from diseases caused by inactivity, including cardiovascular disease, stroke, cancer, and diabetes. In other words, four times as many people die from inactivity than from auto crashes. (Worldwide about 1.25 million people die in crashes yearly.) Studies have shown that inactivity is related to miles traveled by car. If AVs increase travel by vehicle substantially, as many experts predict, death by preventable diseases may reduce overall lives saved by a considerable amount.

People who ride mass transit burn 22 percent more calories than those who drive. How can AVs help encourage movement? One way would be to make both transport to transit and walking and biking trails easier and more accessible. How can cities and towns promote movement if AVs eliminate the need to walk even the shortest of distances? City centers, large and small, can ensure that pedestrians and pedestrian life take precedence over cars by not allowing AVs to take over downtown areas and dictate where foot traffic can and cannot go. The health benefits of walkable neighborhoods are clear: people who live in walkable communities weigh six to ten pounds less than those who do not. In addition, every ten minutes spent commuting in a car is ten minutes less time spent on community or other activities.[108]

Noise, especially too much loud noise, can also have an adverse effect on health. High noise levels have been tied to poor health outcomes, including heart disease, possibly because sleep disturbances cause stress and interrupt body cycles. In the United States, it's estimated that 100 million people are exposed to unhealthy levels of noise, typically from automobile and aircraft traffic (although everything from leaf blowers and lawn mowers to loud music can also contribute.)[109] Basic traffic noise is a combination of engine, tire, wind passage, and road noise (different kinds of surfaces have different noise characteristics). Faster vehicles make more noise than slow ones. Will AVs be quieter than conventional cars? If they are predominantly electric vehicles, they may reduce traffic noise and, of course, air pollution. And of course, we can have EVs with or without AVs.

The high-pitched buzz that electric motors create doesn't travel as far as conventional engine noise does.[110] EVs also have lower coefficients of drag, reducing wind passage noise at higher speeds. But this noise advantage may dwindle as batteries get less expensive and more powerful, and so these cars are likely to cause significant noise pollution as well. Offsetting this rise in noise pollution to some extent will be the fact that electric car tires tend to be quieter than others, and indeed, tires overall have become much quieter in the past few decades.[111]

There is also no guarantee that honking will be reduced with AVs, and in fact, it could increase. Because Google has honking algorithms, its self-driving cars are now able to recognize when honking is appropriate and can even modulate how they use the horn. The company stated in a May 2016 report: "As our honking algorithms improved, we've begun broadcasting our car horn to the world. . . . If another vehicle is slowly reversing towards us, we might sound two short, quieter pips as a friendly heads up to let the driver know we're behind. However, if there's a situation that requires more urgency, we'll use one loud sustained honk."[112]

This may seem like a great idea at first glance, but if people are walking in a trajectory toward an AV (think dense pedestrian environments), in certain situations we could hear honking AVs on a near-continual basis.

ENVIRONMENTAL HEALTH

Pollution is another aspect of human health that, for better or worse, will be influenced by AVs. Some researchers and other experts make the case that AVs = EVs. I'm not sure the two kinds of vehicles are so closely linked, and even the cleanest car requires a lot of energy to build and still releases some pollutants (particles from tires, noise pollution, and so on). The disposal of parts and the vehicles themselves will also involve some pollution. The only way to guarantee less pollution, and thus fewer negative health impacts, is to emphasize having fewer vehicles traveling fewer vehicle miles. Nonetheless, I support accelerating the introduction of EVs.

In 2018, carbon emissions from transportation surpassed those from power plants. The impact of AVs on pollution will depend on the total vehicle-miles traveled in the United States, the resultant traffic congestion, fuel efficiency, and continued fossil fuel consumption. Current research on these questions remains limited, and also inconclusive. All we know for certain is that, if people use public transportation less and drive more, we will create more pollution.

"Autonomous vehicles could encourage additional driving, leading to more energy use and more emissions," according to Will Troppe, writing in the *Christian Science Monitor*. "If you're able to work, nap, or read the newspaper on your daily commute, why bother choosing to live near the workplace? Autonomous cars could give rise to an 'exurbia,' a new development layer farther from urban centers that could undo years of progress on smart, sustainable urban growth and transit-oriented development. Further, many people today make transportation decisions by optimizing based on both time and money. Autonomous vehicles could eliminate the need to optimize based on time."[113]

SIX

Makers, Drivers, Passengers, and Pedestrians: Hard Questions and Moral Dilemmas

The car has become an article of dress without which we feel uncertain, unclad, and incomplete in the urban compound.

—MARSHALL MCLUHAN[1]

O N SATURDAY, DECEMBER 15, 1973, A PORTION OF THE West Side Highway in New York collapsed near Little West Twelfth Street. The trigger was the weight of a heavy trailer-truck filled with the more than 30 tons (60,000 pounds) of asphalt needed to repair the forty-year-old highway. The cause was maintenance neglect; the supporting steel had been weakened by severe corrosion. Afterward, the entire West Side Highway was closed to trucks, and a portion of it was closed to the more than 140,000 vehicles accustomed to traveling it each day.[2] Just two years into my career as a traffic engineer in 1973, I was sent down to the site to survey the damage with a few colleagues.

I expected to see maximum gridlock, and in the first few weeks after the collapse, traffic jams did occur around the area. But over time,

I noticed something else: heavy traffic dissipated, and cars weren't backing up on side streets or clogging other roadways. In fact, Manhattan's
grid was proving to be much more effective at maintaining traffic flow
than the elevated highway.

In the 1980s, when I became chief engineer for the city, I was given
the task of deciding what to do with the hunk of highway left. Should
we tear down the rest of the West Side Highway and build a wide,
at-grade road, or should we try to keep some of it elevated or in tunnels? Anyone visiting New York today knows that I went for the former
option.

One of the issues I grappled with was pedestrian safety. With a
boulevard, there is a chance (and over time just about a certainty) that
pedestrians will be killed; with an elevated highway or tunnel, pedestrian deaths almost never happen.

The decision was in part an ethical one. The boulevard, which is
what you see there today, allows people to walk on a wide pathway or
get on a bike and ride to work, both activities that improve health. The
boulevard has trees and foliage on the sides and on a median down
the middle that help mitigate air pollution. Neighborhoods adjacent
to the West Side Highway boomed and then blossomed. Ultimately,
tearing down the highway and replacing it with a boulevard was, I
believe, the right economic, social, *and* ethical decision. But I must say,
I suffer with each pedestrian fatality I hear about. I rationalize each
one by reminding myself that an elevated or tunneled roadway would
have attracted more cars and led to its own share of traffic deaths and,
because it would have increased driving in the city, more crashes else-
where. I see the same analogy with AVs; some new crashes will happen that would not have occurred with conventional cars, but far more
others will not happen.

Most of us believe that vehicle manufacturing guidelines and traffic
laws designed to prevent human error from causing injury and death
are a good and ethical idea. However, the advent of high-level vehicle
autonomy pushes us to grapple with old ethical questions in new ways.
What does the law say about artificial intelligence, or AI-powered AVs?

Does it say anything at all? What should it say? Who should program a car—its owner, maker, or occupant? Who is responsible for an AV's "actions"—the manufacturer, owner, or passenger? How should public-use AVs be programmed for safety?

How should traffic laws change, if at all? Will AVs guided not by human emotions and prejudices but by machines that can learn be more equitable in how they make decisions about passengers? Will police traffic stops become obsolete? How will our privacy be affected and imposed upon by businesses, government, and fellow citizens? These are difficult questions.

THE TROLLEY PROBLEM

The decision I faced with rebuilding the West Side Highway—whether to choose an option that would probably kill a few pedestrians or one that would kill more drivers—was similar to the Trolley Problem, a thought exercise used by ethicists. Here's the situation: Five people are tied up on the tracks ahead, unable to move, and a runaway trolley is headed straight for them. You are standing some distance off in the train yard, next to a lever. If you pull this lever, the trolley will switch to a different set of tracks. However, you notice that there is also one person tied up on the side track. You have two options:

1. Do nothing, and the trolley will kill the five people on the main track.
2. Pull the lever, diverting the trolley onto the side track, and it will kill one person.

Which is the most ethical choice? And what if the one person tied up on the side track is your child?

A programmer at a carmaker, Google, or a similar tech company must conjure up hazardous situations for AVs and then develop algorithms to either reduce the likelihood of a crash or, where a crash is inevitable, minimize its severity. The programmer wrestles with many scenarios in which none of the outcomes are ideal. They are all variations of the Trolley Problem—an ethical problem based on the principle of double effect. According to the principle of double effect, it is sometimes permissible to cause harm as a side effect of bringing about a result that will be better than would otherwise have occurred.[3]

In the classic situation, an AV is moving at 50 miles per hour on a rural or suburban two-lane roadway and a child darts out into the road. It is impossible for the car to stop before hitting the child. However, there is time to swerve left or right. To the left is an oncoming school bus going 50 miles per hour, and to the right is a giant oak tree. Swerving to the right would probably kill the AV driver and anyone else in the vehicle. Swerving to the left might save him and his passengers but cause the bus to go off-road, with possibly disastrous consequences. Not swerving is likely to kill the child.

A programmer must examine his choices. Is his obligation to protect the driver of the car, in which case the child dies? Does he take the risk involved in swerving left and hope the school bus maneuvers safely? Or does he decide that a child's life needs to be protected at all costs, even at the expense of his customer in the AV? Does the programmer let the driver choose in advance and flip a switch that says, "Protect me at the risk of killing others"? How is the programmer going to feel when he later reads about an incident whose outcome was decided by his programming choices? We are asking people to play God in these scenarios. That is not a light assignment.

Most car companies have found that their best course of action is to sidestep the question.[4] It's true that ethical dilemmas on the road precisely like the Trolley Problem are exceedingly rare. Many of my colleagues tell me to just forget about it, saying that such situations "won't happen," but I'm not as sanguine. I agree that these kinds of incidents are quite rare, occurring probably less than once in 10 billion miles traveled worldwide. If 12 trillion miles are driven annually, as some estimates say, such incidents could occur about 1,000 times a year.

As cars become smart and begin to take decision-making out of the hands of humans, we have to think about how cars will behave. When an AV is driving without passengers and is confronted with a Trolley Problem conundrum, will it decide to kill, or will it total itself? You can forgive a sober human who makes an error and harms someone, but less so a drunken human. You may forgive a human who takes the life of another because of bad weather, but will probably be less inclined to do so if he were texting. In these matters, there is a somewhat agreed-upon idea of culpability. If a car's algorithm causes it to kill a person instead of hitting a tree, we might hold the entity that wrote the software responsible if we can show that the car made the lethal selection owing to an error of logic.

Many more far less extreme examples will occur around the world perhaps tens of thousands of times or more annually. In a more probable scenario, the AV car could choose to slow down to 15 or 20 miles per hour before striking the child—speeds at which she might survive an impact. Or there is no tree to the right and so swerving off the road might only injure the occupants of the AV, probably not mortally. Do we give the decisions to the occupants with a switch they can activate saying no matter what, don't kill or injure us? Or one that says, do the utilitarian thing—kill or harm the fewest people?

There are some who consider such thought experiments unnecessary. "These are silly discourses," says Bern Grush. "Are we going to write algorithms that recognize the age and value of a person and the rest of their lives? I know a sixty-nine-year-old widower with two degrees from MIT who is the single father of a four-year old girl. I know a twelve-year-old who has severe mental challenges. Are you willing to judge the algorithm that picked one over the other, even if such an algorithm could detect the inferred 'value' of each life and written provably?" Grush asks. "If humans cannot always pick whom to kill among a set of humans, how can such an algorithm be written in a way that another human can judge its ethics correctly?"

Others dismiss the Trolley Problem because they believe that litigation will challenge whatever decisions are made. But not everyone thinks it's an overstated problem. Nicolas Evans, a philosophy professor at the University of Massachusetts–Lowell, has won a grant from the

National Science Foundation, to the tune of $556,000, to work with two other professional philosophers and a scientist on algorithms to solve the Trolley Problems that AVs raise.

Among the more profound questions are these: While we usually forgive each other for making split-second decisions that turn out badly, can a computer be forgiven for making a wrong decision and should its programmer be held accountable? What happens when an AV is hacked to act in aggressive and lawless ways? Who pays for the consequences? How do we protect ourselves from malicious programming? The artificial intelligence community adds another layer to the ethical question: When computers become sentient (and AI scientists insist that they will), what happens when an AV decides to save itself, the pedestrians and passengers be damned?

In early 2016, Google's self-driving car system was officially recognized as a "driver" in the United States.[5] Google had asked the National Highway Traffic Safety Administration for clarification on its self-driving vehicles. NHTSA responded by classifying Google's artificial intelligence system as the driver of its cars. "NHTSA will interpret 'driver' in the context of Google's described motor vehicle design as referring to the self-driving system, and not to any of the vehicle occupants," the government said in a letter.[6] Does this mean that the car will be liable for its mistakes? Who is sued or held financially responsible when a Google AV does something wrong? In "no contest" states, it doesn't matter who is at fault; if a pedestrian gets hit by a car, he or she can sue the driver.

A researcher in Rome who tests automated transit vehicles in various Italian cities, Adriano Alessandrini, believes that he has a solution that bypasses ethical considerations entirely. "When you ask a car to make a decision, you have an ethical dilemma," he says. "You might see something in your path, and you decide to change lanes, and as you do, something else is in that lane." His vehicles are programmed to simply follow a preprogrammed route from one place to another and back again, with no variation of path between point A and point B, but on regular public roadways. Programmed to brake if something gets in the way, his cars "don't have this [ethical] problem."[7] I don't think the ethical problem disappears, however, since speed will still remain the biggest factor in whether an AV can stop in time. We must still think about what to do when an impact is inevitable. In Germany, for instance, AVs are being programmed to avoid jeopardizing human lives when an impact is unavoidable by running into animals or hitting objects rather than people.

The journal *Science* polled its readers for suggested answers to this conundrum. Not surprisingly, the results were contradictory: "A large majority of our respondents agreed that cars that impartially minimized overall casualties were more ethical and were the type they would like to see on the road. Yet most people also indicated that they would refuse to purchase such a car, expressing a strong preference for buying the self-protective one. In other words, people refused to buy the car they found to be more ethical."[8]

When I was New York City's traffic commissioner, I had a discussion with the emergency department chief at a large Manhattan hospital. This was after SUVs had become so popular in the late 1980s. He said that, in the past, people brought to the ER after being hit by a car had suffered largely lower-extremity trauma. But he was now seeing far more serious chest injuries in pedestrians who were hit. This was no secret to the auto manufacturers, who saw SUV sales soar in the 1990s. The general public believed that the bigger and heavier the car, the safer it was to its occupants. No matter that pedestrians struck by an SUV stood a smaller probability of survival than pedestrians struck by sedans. In essence, people took the view, protect me at the cost of others.

In theory, people say they approve of cars programmed to sacrifice the occupant to save those outside of the car, but they wouldn't want to drive or ride in one of those cars themselves. If humans can't agree on safety programming in cars, how can machines be expected to? "Frankly, my answer would be very different if I were programming it for driving alone versus having my seven-year-old daughter in the car," says Ken Schotts, another Stanford professor studying the ethical aspects of AVs. "If I have her in the car, I would be very, very selfish in my programming."[9]

The good solution would be to create AVs that never have to make a Trolley Problem decision in the rare event that one presents itself. Daniela Rus, head of the MIT's Artificial Intelligence Lab, told the *Washington Post*, "If we have capable perception and planning systems, perhaps aided by sensors that can detect non-line-of-site obstacles, the car should have enough situational awareness and good control. A self-driving car should be able to not hit anybody—avoid the trolley problem altogether!"[10]

AVs could avoid killing anybody at all, however, only if we never allow them to travel faster than, say, 20 miles per hour, because no vehicles can stop on a dime, and speed increases the distance required to stop exponentially. The distance a conventional car travels before coming to a stop is called braking distance. It includes the distance a car travels in the time it takes a driver to perceive a need for an emergency stop, the quality of the vehicle's tires, the weight of the vehicle, and the coefficient of friction of the roadway when it's dry and when it's wet.[11] Let's assume that perception time in an AV approaches zero. According to a University of Pennsylvania analysis published by the National Association of City Transportation Officials, at 60 miles per hour, the distance required to stop a car by braking would be 172 feet, and at 80 miles per hour, it would be 305 feet—the length of an American football field, or even longer if the road is wet.

ARE AVs AN ETHICAL NECESSITY?

Do safety concerns give us an ethical mandate to usher in AVs? Enthusiasts like Elon Musk seem to think so. In a call to reporters in October 2016, he made this astonishing remark:

> One of the things I should mention that frankly has been quite disturbing to me is the degree of media coverage of Autopilot crashes, which are basically almost none relative to the media coverage of the 1.2 million people that die every year in manual crashes. It's something that I think does not reflect well upon the media. It really doesn't.

Because—and you need to think carefully about this—*because if, in writing some article that's negative, you effectively dissuade people from using an autonomous vehicle, you're killing people* [italics mine].[12]

In a way, the same could be said about mass transit. The media harps on every train crash even though, as I mentioned earlier, transit is already 95 percent safer than cars. I only wish someone with the clout of Musk would make this point.

Musk makes it sound as if we have an ethical imperative to make AVs available to consumers as quickly as possible. But ethical questions and road policy are certainly not exclusive to the AV issue, and we shouldn't wait until AVs are everywhere to resolve them. Since existing technologies could prevent more people from getting injured or killed in car crashes, why aren't these systems required on roadways and in cars now? That's the real ethical question. For instance, roundabouts, or traffic circles, reduce fatal crashes by 70 to 90 percent compared to standard intersections, and injuries in crashes by 75 percent, according to the Insurance Institute for Highway Safety. Wouldn't the ethical thing to do be making roundabouts mandatory where appropriate?[13] Why rush AVs and AI technology to market without sufficient testing if we have sufficient means, in both car and roadway design, to prevent more catastrophic crashes now?

Consider the case of thirty-six-year-old Diane Schuler. On July 26, 2009, sometime after she got into her sister-in-law's red minivan to return home after a family camping trip, she drove the wrong way on New York's Taconic State Parkway at a high rate of speed. After traveling less than two miles, Shuler's van slammed into an SUV whose driver was unable to avoid her, instantly killing four of the children in the minivan (her daughter and three nieces), all three people in the SUV, and herself. One child survived, Schuler's son Bryan, who was five at the time.[14]

The Schuler crash was the worst the county had seen in seventy-five years, and because of its horrific nature, it became national news. The investigation that followed, including two toxicology tests, found that Schuler's blood-alcohol content (BAC), at 0.19 percent, was more than twice the legal limit in New York (0.08 percent). The mother of two also had high levels of THC, the active ingredient in marijuana, in her system. A Westchester County medical examiner's findings led to a ruling of homicide, because of Schuler's dangerous driving, very shortly after the crash occurred—the lab findings notwithstanding.[15]

About 350 people die, and thousands more are injured, each year in the United States in devastating crashes caused by wrong-way driving, according to the Turner-Fairbank Highway Research Center, a federally operated research facility associated with the Federal Highway Administration's Office of Research, Development, and Technology.[16] Texas and Florida currently lead the nation in the number of wrong-way crashes. Both states, along with Arizona, California, and Connecticut, are testing and installing technologies such as red lights on wrong way signs on ramps that flash when a wrong-way driver is detected and overhead billboards on roads that warn drivers of oncoming danger. In some cases, a camera instantly sends a picture of the wrong-way vehicle to troopers and DOT dispatchers. However, this technology is not universally in use.

It is arguable that Diane Schuler was entirely responsible for the outcome of her error because of the unethical decision she made to drink and drive. However, the setting in which the crash occurred could also bear some responsibility for the crash. The design of the Taconic State Parkway's ramps allowed her to get on the wrong side of the road. There was no system in her car, on the highway, or on the ramp to stop her from crossing over the median and settling on the wrong side. Do systems designers have an ethical and social obligation to ensure that wrong-way driving (or any roadway) is rendered impossible for drivers (excluding emergency vehicles, which may have to go the wrong way in certain emergencies)?

Vision Zero (VZ) is one program that puts the onus on government planners and communities to make roads safe. Vision Zero originated in Sweden in 1997, when the Swedish parliament adopted it as official road policy. Founded on the ethical conclusion that loss of life is not an acceptable price to pay for mobility, VZ sets a long-term goal of shifting responsibility for traffic safety from individual road users to system designers. Rather than exclusively faulting drivers and other users of the transportation system, Vision Zero places the core responsibility for crashes on the overall system design, addressing infrastructure, vehicle technology, and enforcement. When applied, the approach has resulted in several successes. Sweden has one of the lowest annual rates of road deaths in the world (3 out of 100,000 persons, as compared to 12.3 per 100,000 in the United States), according to *The Economist*.[17] Not only that, but fatalities involving pedestrians have fallen almost 50 percent since 2012. During the same period, pedestrian fatalities have risen 11 percent in the United States, to nearly 6,000 deaths in 2016 alone.[18]

According to Claus Tingvall, one architect of Sweden's Vision Zero policy, system design should take into account that people make mistakes. "If you take a nuclear power station, if you take aviation, if you take a rail system, all of them are based on [the idea that] they are operated by people who can make a mistake," he said.[19] The same understanding should influence roadway design, in which barriers, traffic calming, well-marked crosswalks and protected pedestrian zones, and separated bike lanes can help minimize the consequences of a driver's mistake.

When I read this, it all becomes so obvious. A hundred years ago, we could have taken the approach that cars and roadways had to be safe; instead, with little regulation, we just allowed these new vehicles onto the same old roadways, with devastating results. We then compounded it by making children, the elderly, bike riders, and others the culprits who had to be corralled and even jailed for "bad" behavior around cars. Shame on us if we make the same mistake with AVs!

According to the Vision Zero philosophy, "In every situation, a person might fail. The road system should not."[20] Vision Zero policies have been adopted in Norway and Denmark and are gaining traction in parts of the United States. As of this writing, thirty-eight US state transportation departments have adopted similar initiatives, though in my estimation many have fallen short in implementation. (Otherwise, why would fatality rates be on the rise?) Nevertheless, when taken seriously, Vison Zero has been shown to work in the United States.

Shortly after his inauguration in January 2014, New York City mayor Bill de Blasio announced his own Vision Zero plan to eliminate traffic deaths and injuries in the city. The NYC plan emphasizes "expanded enforcement against dangerous moving violations like speeding and failing to yield to pedestrians, new street designs and configurations to improve safety, broad public outreach and communications, and a sweeping legislative agenda to increase penalties for dangerous drivers and give New York City control over the safety of our own streets."[21] Since instituting Vision Zero, New York has seen the fewest number of pedestrian fatalities since 1910. Successes from several US states that have taken similar approaches to reducing traffic fatalities have had impressive results, including decreases of 43 percent in Minnesota, 40 percent in Washington State, and 48 percent in Utah. Indeed, Provo was one of the largest cities in the United States (population 114, 801) to have zero traffic fatalities in at least one full calendar year, 2011, because of its Vision Zero plan.[22]

There is also a public health concern underpinning Vision Zero plans to make roadways safer: by increasing the safety of our streets, we not only save lives but also make it easier and more enticing for people to engage in regular physical activity such as walking and biking. If you believe, as I do, that government has an ethical obligation to address all public health concerns, a Vision Zero–style plan could stop people from dying by helping to prevent dangerous behavior while also encouraging healthy behavior.

AVs give us a chance to double down on Vision Zero plans. Why wait? While technological advances in cars, including lane assist and backup cameras, have contributed to the success of many Vision Zero plans, autonomous technology is not a requirement to implement and enjoy the benefits of such programs. Such advances could, however, make these plans even more failsafe. As connected vehicles—both V2V (vehicle to vehicle) and V2I (vehicle to infrastructure)—become more advanced, we may be able to prevent wrong-way driving entirely, along with a host of other car-related incidents that lead to personal injuries and property destruction. A V2I could tell the car it is going the wrong way and compel the car to stop. Ostensibly, V2V and V2I technology could prevent wrong-way and other kinds of crashes even without cars being autonomous.

AI AND THE ETHICS OF SMART CARS

Advances in artificial intelligence will effectively make AVs "moving computers" that we can program in various and specific ways. Cars and their networks will have to be in constant communication, absorbing and analyzing a great deal of information from tens of thousands of vehicles at once, and then make decisions in response to smooth traffic flow, fuel use, and road conditions.[23] Carmakers, well aware of new competitors from the technology sector, see the future and are investing heavily in AI and big data management. In February 2017, Ford paid $1 billion for the artificial intelligence start-up Argo AI. Then, in October 2017, Argo AI purchased Princeton Lightwave, based in Cranbury, New Jersey, for its LiDAR technology. This is the second Ford investment in LiDAR: it put $75 million into Velodyne in August 2016. Also in October 2017, GM's cruise automation unit bought Strobe, Inc.[24]

Meanwhile, the German automaker BMW is building a data center in Munich that is ten times the size of its existing data center. "The processing power needed to deal with all this data is orders of magnitude larger than what we are used to," Reinhard Stolle, BMW's vice president in charge of artificial intelligence, told the *New York Times*. "The traditional control engineering techniques are just not able to handle the complexity anymore."[25]

Volkswagen is getting into the esoteric world of quantum computing, which seeks to harness quantum physics and its power to compute at much faster speeds than conventional computing. In the summer of 2017, Volkswagen demonstrated how a D-Wave computer (using quantum computing) could steer the movements of 10,000 taxis in Beijing at once, optimizing their routes and thereby reducing congestion. The D-Wave computer took just seconds to interpret traffic information that would have taken a conventional supercomputer about thirty minutes to figure out, according to Florian Neukart, a scientist at a Volkswagen lab in San Francisco.[26] The question of how effective and fast D-wave computers will ultimately be is controversial; suffice to say here that we are rapidly gaining the power to collect and manipulate information from cars and drivers.

The Gartner Group, a Connecticut-based technology research company, predicts that by the early 2020s there will be a quarter of a billion connected vehicles on the road worldwide, which will expand in-vehicle services and automated driving capabilities.[27] By 2020, AI-based systems could be standard in infotainment systems, with features such as speech and gesture recognition, eye tracking and driver monitoring, and advanced driver assistance systems (ADAS) that include camera-based machine vision, radar-based direction units, driver condition evaluation, and sensor fusion engine control units (Spredict-FECU).[28] That last futuristic-sounding mechanism combines data derived from disparate sources to help a computer draw conclusions and make decisions.[29]

Some AI technology is already available in driven cars and will eventually take over driving systems completely. Ford's Sync now has voice recognition for its voice-activated communication and entertainment system. Ford users with the system can access Amazon's Alexa from inside their car to check the weather, play audiobooks, add items to shopping lists, and control Alexa-enabled smart home devices.[30] Owners of the Ford Focus Electric, Fusion Energi, and C-MAX Energi can use Amazon Echo or Dot at home to do things like lock or start the car remotely by instructing Alexa to do so. Also installed in many cars is AI technology such as computer vision, which can identify objects, scenes, and activities in unconstrained environments. We are already within shouting distance of being able to ask a car to get itself out of the garage and onto the driveway, ready to roll.

AI will soon be the key technology in driver assistance and safety features. AI technology will enable cars to understand our needs better and to react to and learn from us just as our fellow humans do. In the best-case scenario, AI-controlled vehicles will improve on human choices and learn from their mistakes. For instance, machine learning could stop a car from taking a particular road on Tuesdays between 10:00 and 11:00 a.m. because it remembers that sanitation trucks pick up on that street at that time, blocking traffic. By using deep learning and sensor fusion, it's possible to build a complete three-dimensional map of everything that's going on around the vehicle to empower it to make better decisions than a human driver ever could.

As vehicles receive more and more data, they learn more deeply. Adaptive cruise control will allow a car to take the data from its surroundings and continually improve its automated decision-making as more data is collected about the driving experience in similar places and under similar conditions.

Networks outside of vehicles that work with vehicle systems will collect and share information that can mitigate the causes of some crashes. However, this kind of AI learning requires massive computing power to interpret vast amounts of harvested data. Right now, most sensors are "dumb": they merely capture information without interpreting it. For example, a video camera records 30 frames per second. Each frame is an image made up of several color values and thousands of pixels. Quickly determining if the pixels represent a truck, a cyclist, a pedestrian, or a tree branch takes a great deal of finely tuned vision coupled with deep neural-network processing.

All of the preceding could be among the beneficial outcomes of having connected, smart AVs (and even driven vehicles), and of surveillance and data collection in general. These outcomes would offer greater security from crime and terrorism, although perhaps not always. And as already discussed, data collection can help vehicles make better, safer decisions that improve our quality of life. "A sensible system of automated traffic regulation can save money and direct scarce police resources to serious criminals rather than ordinary motorists," says Neil Richards, a privacy law professor at Washington University in St. Louis.[31]

However, the privacy concerns raised by the massive data collection and interpretation that goes along with networked cars are troubling. Surveillance of private citizens as they go about their business outside of their homes and in their vehicles poses many ethical conundrums. Is it acceptable to allow private companies, or the government for that matter, to capture data from private people when they are in public? Should surveillance by privately owned companies or governments be regulated? Shouldn't citizens have a choice about whether or not their movements are recorded and used by businesses and/or government?

One example would be the existing devices that prevent a car from starting if it detects the scent of alcohol. Some require the driver to breathe into a device that measures alcohol levels. A device from QinetiQ doesn't require blowing into a breath-testing device but instead uses sensors placed around the driver's seat that can immediately determine whether a person has been drinking.[32] But if you're traveling in an AV, does it matter if you are over the limit? Whose business is it if you drink and the automated vehicle drives?

Sometimes you don't want people to know where you're going. A friend told me about his elderly aunt who was suspicious of her husband and was able to use his car's GPS data to find that he was visiting an old flame. Perhaps we don't feel a lot of sympathy for this wayward husband, but what if you didn't want your employer to know you are visiting a cancer specialist, or that you're going on a job interview? Today a taxi ride in many cities includes a backseat monitor that knows the location of the cab and projects advertising to passengers from stores nearby. Companies will want to isolate those people who drive past their businesses using this kind of technology, and then target you on your own electronic devices once you get out of the car. Will you mind that? When they detect that your children are in the car and target them, will you mind that?

Ubiquitous public data collection is already a fact of life in places like the United Kingdom, which has some of the most permissive surveillance laws in the world, little judicial oversight, and not much public criticism over privacy issues.[33] Surveillance cameras are everywhere throughout the country, especially in London and other large metropolitan areas, and there are relatively few restrictions on what information can be collected by the government and how it can be used. This has sparked debate over the efficacy and morality of mass surveillance.

Underlying private companies' thirst for data is their desire to monetize it. Should they be allowed to take your data for free and use it to sell you things?

In the public spaces where AVs will operate, there is little expectation of privacy. We don't have high expectations of privacy now when we are driving on public roads or pulling into public parking areas. Commercial fleets of networked AVs will be able to collect all kinds of data about huge groups of people, including the populations of entire cities—where they go and how they get there. All fleet owners have to do is store the information captured by their many sensors and use software to analyze it.[34]

Large-scale capture and analysis of data enabled by AVs could be used to locate Amber or Silver Alert subjects, and the same technology could be used to analyze driving patterns and adjust insurance rates higher or lower. It's also true, however, that government could use it to identify dissidents, and that employees of AV companies (or others who pay for data) could use the technology for stalking purposes or to group people according to certain characteristics that could later be used to discriminate against them.[35] This prospect is chilling.

I have an old friend from Brooklyn whom I'll call Sara. Sara's brother was convicted of pedophilia in Pennsylvania and sentenced to jail time. He briefly escaped from authorities, triggering a national network of vigilantes who wanted to find him. Some of these vigilantes were would-be cops, others may have suffered sexual traumas themselves, and still others may have been unstable people with nothing better to do. The vigilantes used social media to "spread the word." License plate numbers and addresses of family members were shared. Soon the vigilantes began stalking Sara, who had absolutely nothing to do with her brother. Even after her brother was caught, the vigilantes continued, and continue to this day, because no one flipped the "off switch." They followed Sara everywhere, harassing her, and there was little she could do about it. The police, perhaps not feeling compassion for the sister of a pedophile, did virtually nothing. Ironically, she and her brother are children of a retired police officer.

AVs equipped with sensors and connected to all kinds of networks, both public and private, could ramp up current surveillance by logging the physical movements of every person within a network, making it possible to find anyone anywhere—and to know exactly what they are doing when they are in their vehicles. This will be much more exacting data than cell phones and GPS trackers collect from us now. Networked cars will collect data not only on where we are but on how we got there, what we did when we got to our destination, and any communications we had while in our vehicles.

In 2011, some Uber launch-party attendees were shown the company's God View, a program that "sees" all Uber users in a city. Julia Allison, an attendee at one such event in Chicago, says that the company showed the crowd the whereabouts and movements of thirty Uber users in New York, in real time, and also shared a list of those thirty people. Allison recognized half of the people listed, including entrepreneur Peter Sims, whom she texted during the party to inform him that she knew where he was. He wasn't happy. A subsequent blog post in which he wrote about the incident quickly spread on social media.[36]

Governments already buy and borrow private-sector databases. The National Security Agency (NSA) has been building a massive data and supercomputing center in Utah, with the goal of intercepting and storing much of the world's internet communications for decryption and analysis.[37] Data from private vehicles would add another layer to this material, to be used for unknown purposes.

Neil Richards says that an "overlapping and entangled assemblage of government and corporate watchers" menaces intellectual privacy and "threatens the development of individual beliefs in ways that are inconsistent with the basic commitments of democratic societies." He argues that "surveillance distorts the power relationships between the watcher and the watched, enhancing the watcher's ability to blackmail, coerce, and discriminate against the people under its scrutiny."[38]

To mitigate the harmful effects of surveillance, we need to understand when surveillance is problematic, or even dangerous and unacceptable, and then make sure there are laws, regulations, and a course of remediation available to us when companies and governments engage in harmful surveillance behavior. While we work on allowing technology to help improve mobility, we can't lose sight of protecting our privacy.

ASSIGNING BLAME

The legal aspects of ethics are daunting. Germany's Federal Ministry of Transport and Digital Infrastructure, an ethics committee, recently came up with a list of twenty guidelines for automakers developing self-driving cars.[39] Those guidelines stipulate that saving human life must take precedence over all other considerations in the event of a crash. Further, AV software must not distinguish in any way between humans regarding age, sex, handicaps, and so on. The panel's insistence that the only way to determine liability is to have a way to know when a car is autonomous and when it's under human control suggests that a manufacturer could be found culpable for a crash involving a self-driving car. The panel's suggestions are not law yet, but are likely to be codified soon.

Could a buyer choose a moral algorithm that favors his safety? And could he be legally liable if someone else is injured based on the algorithm's decisions? Sometimes it's best for the consumer not to have a choice in matters of safety. Perhaps it's preferable for safety standards to be instituted uniformly at the factory, the way seat belts are.

ETHICS, AVs, AND THE ENVIRONMENT

How many and what kind of vehicles we allow on roads most certainly has an ethical component as well. Legislators and communities have a moral obligation to ensure that AVs don't clog roadways at the expense of pedestrians, cyclists, and others, and that large, house-sized structures aren't choking people, animals, and green spaces in environmentally unsustainable ways. We tend to think that AVs will look like the cars we are familiar with today, and no doubt some will. To be accepted, AVs will have to have familiar reference points: they will look broadly like cars, as least in the early stages. In the future, however, an AV could take many forms and sizes.

"Compare the way the first PCs looked compared to the way a cell phone looks today," says vehicle designer Dan Sturges. Those early PCs and today's cell phones are two very different machines not only functionally but also aesthetically. "AVs will be free from any reference to vehicles we know; they may not look like anything we are familiar with today. We could be driving anything, something that looks like an office, or a small house, or a structure that collapses entirely when no one is in it," he says. "Technology in materials will open up an amazing new world about what mobility looks like."[40] As usual, the possibilities include the good, the bad, and the ugly. The good would be if vehicle design creates mobility solutions that take up less room and make ride-sharing highly desirable and accessible. The bad and the ugly would be mobile McMansions becoming the norm and invading every bit of available green space.

AV proponents argue that driverless cars are inherently more sustainable than their driven counterparts. Enthusiasts like to say that AVs lend themselves to a sharing economy and that once they're widely available most people will opt to use smaller cars in the same way we rent shared bikes in many cities now, using them only when we need them and leaving them to be used by others when we don't. If this happens, it should reduce the number of cars on the road, and thus pollution. Networked vehicles will mitigate inefficient routes and decrease overall driving time, leading to better air quality and lower carbon emissions. However, if ride-sharing does not become the norm and private ownership continues to prevail, more cars on the road means more pollution, worse congestion, and an excellent chance that roads will privilege drivers over walkers and cyclists.

The increase in driverless vehicles should make people outside of cars safer. AVs are likely to be lighter and to require fewer resources to make, reducing their overall environmental impact even further. Striving for optimal efficiency is an important part of ethical stewardship of the environment.

However, this vision is not guaranteed. Chandra Bhat of the Center for Transportation Research at the University of Texas says that AVs will not necessarily be smaller, more fuel-efficient vehicles with a more modest environmental footprint. They could be much larger cars that guzzle more gas because more people, once freed from the restriction of having to operate the vehicle, may want "more comfortable space" that allows them to stretch out, relax, read, text, work, watch movies, and even nap during trips. I imagine that some AVs, if privately owned, could be the size of Winnebagos: who doesn't want to travel with a refrigerator, massage chair, and stationary bike comfortably within reach?

Robert Kirkman, associate professor in the School of Public Policy at the Georgia Institute of Technology and author of *The Ethics of Metropolitan Growth*, says that "some more extreme advocates on one side or the other [of the sprawl issue]—the anti-sprawl movement and their free-market opposition—see what amounts to a conspiracy to trick, cajole, force, or otherwise manipulate people to live one way or another, either driving them out into the dispiriting and unsustainable suburbs, or attempting to herd them back into crowded and dangerous cities."[41] Throwing AVs into this debate makes the management of sprawl, preventing it from using land inefficiently and destroying open land, more difficult. The answer may not lie entirely in urban planning. We have to decide if we have an ethical mandate to keep downtowns viable and to slow the growth of suburbs even as AV technology makes exurban living more appealing to more people.

There is also an environmental issue concerning animals. Once smart cars and AVs are equipped with 360-degree-sensing technology, they would be able, in theory anyway, to brake or swerve in time to avoid killing animals as small as chipmunks or as large as deer, moose, and black bears, according to Patricia Cramer, a wildlife researcher who works with state transportation departments on roadkill issues. "If we don't kill animals with our vehicles anymore, are we willing to live with them in closer proximity to us?" she asked. "Because that's what's going to happen."[42] Or will engineers program cars to always prioritize human comfort and convenience and the vehicle itself over animals, making it perhaps more likely for animals to be killed on roadways? Or will animals on roadways confuse AVs? That's what happened in Australia.

During a trial session in Canberra, the large animal detection system in Volvo's driverless car, which detects animals on the road by using the ground as a reference point to be able to measure how far the animal is from the vehicle, had no problem identifying and dodging deer, elk, and moose on the road. But it did have difficulty identifying the presence of kangaroos because the detection sensors failed to discern the kangaroos' hopping motions.[43]

The *Boston Globe* reported that the biggest obstacle for self-driving technology in that city could be seagulls. The first month of testing a self-driving car by nuTonomy went according to plan, except that it struggled to recognize the flocks of seagulls that congregate on the roads during winter. "One bird is often small enough that the car assumes it can be ignored. But when you have a flock of birds together, it looks like a big object, so we've had to train the car to recognize the birds. It wasn't something really that we've seen before," nuTonomy chief executive Karl Iagnemma told the paper.[44] I still remember my eldest brother, Harold, giving me driving lessons more than a half-century ago. I slowed because birds were flying ahead in my path. He told me they would get out of the way if I hit the gas, and so they did. In fifty-two years of driving, I never hit a bird. What will an AV do when it sees birds in its trajectory? A few days before writing this paragraph, I was driving on the beautiful island of Aruba. An iguana, less than a foot high, was ahead. I slowed, stopped, and waited for him to cross the road. How do we teach AVs to react in kind?

Should AVs always be programmed to avoid animals large and small (and how small?) or to favor humans over nonhumans? Should they be programmed to avoid areas during periods when important mating and migratory activities occur?" "The car could know: 'O.K., this is a hot spot for frogs. It's spring. It's been raining. All the frogs will be moving across the road to find a mate,'" Daniel Smith, a conservation biologist at the University of Central Florida and an expert in road ecology, told the *New York Times*.[45] As Smith suggests, AVs could be programmed to avoid such roads at critical times so as not to kill off frog populations. For this kind of programming to really take hold, however, many people would have to change their mind-set about the value of animals and also understand that roadways are just one part of an overall ecological system.

VEHICLE DESIGNERS AND MAKERS AND ETHICAL STANDARDS

Manufacturers' ethics in designing and making vehicles also come into play where environmental, safety, and other policies are concerned. Makers may say that they'll do something to make their vehicles green and clean, but they don't always follow through on such promises— even when there are laws compelling them to do so. For instance, Volkswagen's installation of software "defeat devices" in 11 million Volkswagen and Audi diesel vehicles sold worldwide has led to a massive vehicle recall in the United States and an official apology from the company's former CEO.[46] The algorithm was installed in the emissions-control module and detected when the cars were undergoing emissions testing. It ran the engine cleanly during tests and switched off emissions control during normal driving conditions, allowing the vehicle to spew up to forty times the EPA's maximum permitted levels of nitrogen oxides (the air pollutants that cause respiratory problems and smog).

In his paper "Professional Ethics for Software Engineers," Yotam Lurie, a professor at the Ben-Gurion University of Negev, points out that software devices lend themselves to "fixing" and that such tampering is harder for outsiders to discover than modifications to hardware.[47] He draws parallels between Volkswagen software engineers and the Enron accountants who collaborated with the corporation to create accounting loopholes and failed to protect the public by not providing proper auditing.

Of course, it wasn't just a few unethical Volkswagen software engineers who decided on their own to install the defeat devices—it was collusion at the highest levels of the company. "We see how widespread among the product line this device was. It would have had to be tested and updated. This is serious, massive corporate maleficence that affects people's health. There's no question that everyone involved knew this was unethical," says Shannon Vallor, chair of the Department of Philosophy at Santa Clara University in California.[48]

It's not just hacking from bad external actors that we have to worry about when it comes to AVs. How do we know makers themselves are not programming cars to behave in one way while telling us they are acting in another way? How do we protect ourselves from the unethical behavior of manufacturers keen to avoid costly regulations?

The Volkswagen case highlights the failures of a compliance mindset, says Vallor. As long as they don't violate the rules set by agencies like the EPA, professionals do whatever they want. "It's just a box you check off on a list of rules," she says. "It implies that as long as you don't get caught violating rules, there's no harm." Vallor suggests that universities and training programs could do a better job of teaching ethics or making it a mandatory part of curricula. Not all engineering institutions have ethics course requirements. Eva Kaplan-Leiserson said in the National Society of Professional Engineers' *PE* magazine that engineers should look at their work not just from a technical point of view but also with an eye to how their developments may affect humanity's future and whether they are working toward societal improvement and the common good.[49]

ETHICS AND PRIVILEGE

One of the most challenging issues raised by the advent of AVs—and a potentially ugly one—is that they could benefit the wealthy and create more burdens for lower-income people. How will AVs affect the balance of power among various socioeconomic groups? Will they empower people on the lower end of the socioeconomic scale, giving them more access to jobs, locations, and resources than they have had in the past? Or will AVs create a cavernous divide between "us" and "them"—throwing the differences between people of different income levels into stark contrast?

If AVs follow typical ownership models, the wealthiest people will be the "early adopters" in the same way that only those who could afford premium cars enjoy the latest safety features in conventional vehicles. It's a familiar pattern: save the rich, damn the poor. Ten to fifteen years ago, many features such as warning systems, backup assist, and built-in GPS systems were standard in luxury cars but available only at an extra cost, or not available at all, in midpriced and budget models. Those safety features are slowly finding their way into more kinds of cars, both high- and middle-end. The NHTSA says only four of twenty automakers as of 2017 had equipped at least half of their US models with standard automatic emergency brakes, which automatically apply brakes when a front collision is about to occur.[50] If the price of AVs goes down—and many predict that it will, since the technology to make them will become increasingly affordable for manufacturers—then more of us will have access to AVs, until the time comes when only AVs are allowed on the road (and users of mopeds, motorized bikes, and motorcycles fear that their vehicles will be outlawed).

If ride-sharing becomes the standard way to access rides, then social equity could benefit from AVs. That's an important "if," however: AV ride-sharing companies may not find it profitable to offer robust services in low-income areas. Today Uber, Lyft, and similar ride-sharing services are concentrated to a significant extent in higher-income areas that already have good existing transport options.[51] Similarly, more people who live in last-mile and rural locations may have access to mobility with widespread ride-sharing and therefore access to jobs, resources, and amenities, but if individual ownership prevails, those not fortunate enough to have an AV will miss out on these potential benefits. Because they will be able to work while commuting, those with AVs will have more choices of places to live. Income inequality could spread even further as those with more limited transportation options are left behind and lack of mobility restricts their opportunities for career advancement.

ETHICS AND SOCIAL AND CRIMINAL JUSTICE INEQUITIES

As AVs become the vehicle of choice for ride-sharing services, minorities may find that ride-sharing remains harder for them to access than it is for the majority. Addressing these inequities can be a daunting task. The economists Yanbo Ge and Don MacKenzie of the University of Washington, along with Christopher Knittel of MIT and Stephen Zoepf of Stanford, came up with an experiment to test how well the most-used ride-hailing apps serve groups that have been marginalized by the taxi industry.[52]

These researchers sent research assistants out as riders in two cities, Seattle and Boston, to hail nearly 1,500 rides using Uber, Lyft, and another service called Flywheel. Riders took screenshots of the apps to chronicle their experience, recording their estimated wait times, whether a driver accepted them, and where and when they were picked up and dropped off. The trials allowed the researchers to gather data on how the services differed in their treatment of people based on gender and race. Ultimately, they found "significant evidence of racial discrimination"—more specifically, black riders faced longer wait times and more frequent cancellations than white riders.

In Seattle, black riders who requested a ride using Uber or Lyft waited about 16 to 28 percent longer than white riders did for a ride. For black Uber riders in particular, wait times in Seattle were 29 to 35 percent longer than for their white counterparts. In the Boston experiment, black Uber riders were much more likely than white riders to have a driver cancel on them after confirming: the cancellation rate for black men was three times as high as it was for white males. People with "black-sounding" names were significantly more likely to be canceled than either white riders or black riders with "white-sounding" names.

This effect was worse in lower-density or last-mile areas, where finding any ride is harder.

The social profiling of ride-share users will only increase as the data stream from them increases. The more we are known by our data, the easier it is for algorithms to discriminate between us if they are allowed to.

AVs are likely to be programmed not to operate if a vehicle has a broken taillight or if other mechanics required to travel on roadways legally are not working correctly. Routine traffic stops for small infractions have long been used to stop people on the road, particularly people of color, which has led to disastrous outcomes for drivers and passengers. This is not to say that people should not be pulled over for traffic violations—they should. However, they should be pulled over equitably and without a suggestion of racial profiling. AVs could help achieve that goal, and existing technology is already helping: today cameras at stop lights and speed monitors are taking care of much mundane traffic enforcement. Along with providing 24/7 traffic enforcement at a fraction of the cost of flesh-and-blood officers, the cameras are capturing video of more serious crimes as they occur—and cameras and data collection technology can be programmed to be color-blind. However, they could also be programmed to be biased against designated groups of people by race, age, gender, and so on.

Also raising ethical concerns is the potential for hail companies to program vehicles only to pick up and drop off people in the areas that are most profitable—and as a result, to deny service to people outside those areas. Traditionally, this has been the de facto mode of discrimination, whether in medical services, access to supermarkets, housing, or transportation. This outcome of the spread of AVs would be ugly indeed. Additional antidiscrimination laws may be necessary to help prevent AV ride-hailing inequity. Because the scale of transformation offered by AVs is so great, the present moment offers us a chance either to advance fairness or to drastically increase inequality. The choice is ours.

SEVEN

A Way Forward

Space isn't remote at all. It's only an hour's drive away if your car could go straight upwards.

—SIR FRED HOYLE, ASTRONOMER[1]

IN THIS BOOK, I'VE OUTLINED MANY OF THE MAJOR CONCERNS and potential outcomes of an AV-dominated world—the good, the bad, and the truly ugly. None of them are inevitable, and the bad and the ugly can be mitigated dramatically if we act quickly, with intelligence and smart planning. There *is* a right way to respond to the inevitable sea change that AVs will bring. What is good about AVs can be promoted and expanded if we prioritize people over vehicles—not the very opposite, as we did last century with the advent of cars. This point is key.

Stakeholders and citizens can and should work together with government to maximize the benefits of this technology while minimizing its downsides. Legislatures large and small should shape laws and regulations related to AVs in ways that promote equity. We should collaborate with global partners when contemplating AV policies that could affect other nations, such as manufacturing standards that could have adverse effects on countries with production facilities, emissions standards for vehicles that will be exported and imported, data collection standards that comply with various countries' laws, and so on. Manufacturers and developers must partner with a range of constituents to ensure safety, fairness, and service.

I remain skeptical, but I am encouraged when I hear Bill Ford, chairman of Ford Motor Company, and Jim Hackett, its CEO, say that they don't want to stay on the path of inundating the world with AVs to the point of immobility.[2] I was delightfully surprised (just a bit) when Uber supported higher fees for its industry in New York City, through congestion pricing.[3]

But one big fear is hard to shake: the fear that governments will let the private sector dictate what happens on public roadways, just as they did in the United States during the last century. My hope is that this book will help create and support a chorus that sings loud and clear about a better way. Here's my formula.

It's so easy to be seduced by AVs, to wish and believe that they will solve just about all our problems with travel. Traffic will speed up, crashes will be almost nonexistent, and the time we spend in our cars will be enjoyable and productive. A little more than a century ago, we first bought the sales pitch—hook, line, and sinker—that cars would speed our travel, increasing our productivity, that cities would be much healthier without all that horse dung, and that our lives would be more enjoyable. We approached cars, I maintain, with not just a laissez-faire attitude but as a society in servitude to the new vehicles. "What's good for GM is good for America" was a version of a not-so-subliminal message we were already receiving; what is good for the car is good for cities, states, and the country. Today when I meet with AV industry representatives, they only want to talk about the good that will come about from AVs for humankind, in the same way early carmakers talked about all the good the horseless carriage would bring.

We know now that our last century's approach to cars led to the hollowing out of cities, the destruction of transit systems, and a vicious cycle of urban populations decreasing and becoming poorer, of city services being cut and crime becoming rampant. From 1899 to 2013,

3,613,732 people died in motor vehicle accidents in the United States, with another 80 million people injured, many of them permanently maimed.[4] I don't think this level of lethality was the outcome Americans were hoping for when they first embraced the car. That was not the promise people were offered.

As a designer of cities starting in the early 1970s, I was one of those traffic engineers who figured out ways to move traffic faster only to soon see traffic growing and speeds returning to their previous slow levels. I "induced traffic": when I increased road capacity, soon drivers filled up that extra road space, in a variation of the concept, "If you build it, they will come." There was a belief that expanding traffic capacity was an improvement, a way of doing something good. By the 1980s, I saw the folly of that type of thinking. The lesson from what has gone before is to seek the simplest and least invasive solutions (which are often also the most cost-effective and efficient).

The current lack of laws governing AVs represents an opportunity to get new laws right and revise existing laws wisely, to set policy that works for everyone and doesn't favor just carmakers. If a state wants to make AV manufacturing guidelines more rigorous than the minimum set by national laws, that should be allowed. Let's not overrule states with a quest for uniform national laws that favor car manufacturers and ease safety standards on AVs. If a community doesn't feel that it's ready for level 5 AVs, it should be able to legislate to that end. We should not stand in the way of a state that wants to prohibit AVs in cities with more than one million people until logistics and networking and other issues like pedestrian safety are sorted out.

In every area of regulation, lawmakers have to ensure that people are privileged over cars, and that in the rush to innovate, unsafe or untested vehicles are not allowed to come on the market. What's the rush if safe cars can be advanced ahead of self-driving cars? We cannot let manufacturers take the lead in creating laws that benefit only them, as they did in the last century, when the first car manufacturers made sure that new laws governing driving pushed pedestrians to the sidelines. We do not want to repeat the mistakes of the past.

The struggle has already begun. Apple's senior legal counsel met with self-driving experts from California's Department of Motor Vehicles in August 2015 to review the DMV's autonomous vehicle regulations.[5] In February 2017, automakers appealed to lawmakers at a subcommittee hearing of the US House Energy and Commerce Committee to ease safety standards that apply to traditional automobiles in order to better accommodate driverless vehicles. The primary issue highlighted by automakers was the possibility that current industry safety regulations could hamper their ability to roll out driverless cars. Under current standards, for example, cars are required to have a steering wheel and floor pedals. Autonomous vehicle makers need to apply for an exemption to this regulation, but federal officials can grant only 2,500 per year, which could become a problem as more companies seek to test and develop the technology. "It is imperative that manufacturers have the ability to test these vehicles in greater numbers to gather the safety data that will be critical to inform large-scale deployment of life-saving self-driving vehicles," said Mike Ableson, vice president of global strategy for General Motors. "One good way to accomplish this goal is to grant the secretary of Transportation authority to grant specific exemptions for highly automated vehicle development."[6]

Lawmakers have acknowledged that raising the cap could be one legislative solution. Across the Capitol, Senators John Thune (R-SD) and Gary Peters (D-MI) have signaled that they are exploring a bill aimed at reducing hurdles for self-driving car manufacturers, an approach encouraged by Volvo's vice president of government affairs, Anders Karrberg. "Congress should encourage NHTSA to update the [federal guidelines] with an explicit request that states refrain from legislation and regulation of [autonomous] vehicles. We believe Congress should consider incentives for states that do not set any vehicle performance requirements or for states that stay within the parameters of the NHTSA model state bill." Here's how I'm afraid Karrberg's request might play out: any state that passes its own more restrictive rules on AVs will face a cutoff of federal funds.

What follows are smart ways in which we can shape legislation to support technological advancements, encourage greater human mobility without sacrificing safety or the environment, and encourage community engagement. These suggestions can be extended beyond US shores and adopted by any nation that wants to create equitable legislation. We have to put people first. Out of everything I have learned working in the "traffic business," that is the most crucial lesson.

DISCOURAGE PRIVATE OWNERSHIP, INCENTIVIZE THE SHIFT TO TRANSPORTATION AS A UTILITY, AND ENCOURAGE OTHER FORMS OF MOBILITY

Those who hype AVs say that they could drastically reduce personal ownership. Private ownership of AVs could be bad and ugly if everyone who can't drive now decides to own a personal vehicle and those who have cars now decide that each individual in the household should have his or her own vehicle. I want to reiterate that I don't recommend banning private ownership of vehicles, which in any event would be impossible politically in the United States. I prefer a pricing strategy that discourages private ownership in urban areas, recognizing that, for people who live in rural areas and remote locations, personal vehicles are a necessity. Even as we discourage private ownership, however, I do think that AVs could be made enticing and accessible to many more people through ride-sharing and transit.

There is absolutely no reason to wait around for AVs to fill the roads to start making changes that encourage more walking and biking and to create more pedestrian-centric communities. If we can start now to discourage personal ownership—and certainly multi-vehicle ownership as well—autonomous technology could help put the ownership model in reverse and usher in a new norm—one in which people usually rent cars and share rides because these are convenient and affordable alternatives to owning a car (or AV), which is expensive and inconvenient. I know that's a big "if." Changing minds and behaviors isn't easy, and when AVs are cheap and widely available, it may be impossible.

It may be easier to convince carmakers to switch to this model than it will be to entice consumers to give up their cars. While the possibility of selling an AV to every single person on the planet is exciting to carmakers, pursuing that goal could end up being too costly. Manufacturers and even those who program vehicle systems will very likely be liable for AV crashes and related personal injuries. Avoiding the cost of such liability could incentivize makers to retain ownership and control over their fleets. In this event, carmakers would be transformed into service companies. As such, they could keep their vehicles in great shape and retire them before their safety features deteriorate.[7] The loss of revenue from producing fewer vehicles could be offset by the money earned from providing various types of rides on demand. Another view on insurance would come to prevail—the idea that all liability should fall on the owner. Indeed, the high cost of liability insurance might be another way to discourage private ownership to some extent.

Will consumers buy into this model? In most of the developed world, people don't use car services as frequently as they drive their own cars because the cost of labor makes even price-competitive services like Uber and Lyft too expensive. By contrast, one of the reasons why car ownership is not as high in places like India and Africa is that labor costs are minimal and human drivers are plentiful. It's easy and cheap to get a driver when you need one, whether you are sharing the car with other passengers or not. With driverless cars greatly reducing the cost of labor, ride-hailing and -sharing will first become more affordable in places like North America.

But we don't just want people to replace driving with ride-hailing. Discouraging ownership has to be accompanied by efforts to increase other kinds of mobility, not just ride-sharing but also biking, walking, and improved transit. We should offer tax and other incentives for cyclists. Unfortunately, in December 2017, a new federal tax bill in the United States did away with a small $20-a-month reimbursement for commuter cyclists that had been on the books since 2009. In contrast, some European countries are expanding such incentives, a model the United States should revisit. In October 2017, Sweden started to reimburse citizens who buy electric bikes for 25 percent of the purchase price. In February 2017, France offered a flat €200 (about $250) subsidy for e-bike purchases through January 2018. Paris also now offers tax incentives for residents who buy e-bikes and cargo bikes or who forgo their cars in favor of cycling and other forms of transportation. Meanwhile, Oslo, Norway, offers residents $1,200 toward the purchase of an electric cargo bike.[8]

Modify Community Planning

For many years, my firm was contacted by big cities, but in the past five years small and midsize cities are hiring us to help them establish ways to keep their downtown core pedestrian-friendly and more livable. We have worked in Des Moines, Iowa; Grand Rapids, Michigan; Fargo, North Dakota; Macon, Georgia; Rochester, New York; Pittsburgh, Pennsylvania; Ashville, North Carolina; Poughkeepsie, New York; West Palm Beach, Florida; and Boise, Idaho, helping all those cities become more walkable and bike-friendly. Adding car lanes doesn't do that—in fact, having more car lanes in cities often destroys the cities, not to mention its walkability, and they don't get anyone anywhere faster.

In Grand Rapids, like other midsize and small cities, it's important to keep young people from migrating to bigger cities. If you want to keep your kids in your city, I say to government clients, you have to give them more walking and biking opportunities, parks, plazas, and better transit—in other words, more options for getting around and more things to do right in their "front yard." When we survey residents of communities like Grand Rapids, one thing we hear again and again is that they want a grocery store within walking distance, a desire that would have warmed my late father's heart.

Something as simple as a grocery store will keep people in downtown areas or nearby. A grocery store needs to have a user base before it moves into an area, so how do we create that user base? Instead of simply increasing density, we can expand the catchment area by creating safer, more walkable streets for residents. We need a more people-centric approach to the streets. We also have to make explicit the difference between accessibility and mobility, concepts that people often confuse. Good accessibility, for example, means that you can walk to a grocery store in ten minutes or less. Good mobility enables you to drive at 50 miles per hour to the supermarket eight miles away in ten minutes.

Changing existing infrastructure, which doesn't have to be expensive, is one way not only to start moving people from cars to other modes of transportation but to accommodate AVs, which will not need wide lanes. The Blake Street Bridge over Thirty-Eighth Street in Denver was a hazardous stretch with three car lanes, no sidewalks, and no bike lanes. That section of Blake Street is an important connector between Denver's Ballpark, RiNo, Five Points, and Cole. In 2015, the Denver City Council passed a $2.5 million building contract that included a plan to make the bridge more attractive to pedestrians and cyclists. The makeover was a small project in the larger scheme of things, but what Denver did could serve as a blueprint for shaping future people- and AV-friendly infrastructure elsewhere. Rather than widening car lanes, the Denver Department of Public Works:

Narrowed the space for traffic
Added eight-foot-wide sidewalks and six-foot-wide striped bike
    lanes in each direction
Reduced motor vehicle lanes from three to two
Flattened the bridge "hump" to increase visibility for drivers[9]

"All told, 4,000 linear feet of sidewalks have been added throughout the neighborhood," Director of Transportation Crissy Fanganello said.[10] Denver has a long way to go to update more of its roadways and sidewalks. In 2017, the City of Denver's $1.9 billion budget allocated just $2.5 million toward the estimated $475 million needed to repair and enhance sidewalks in the city.[11] Meanwhile, the Blake Street Bridge project is a testament to how simple and relatively low-cost changes can have a big impact.

Peoria, Illinois, has also taken on the task of making its city more walkable and discouraging car ownership. In 2015, the city launched its "Complete Streets" program, which revamps roadways by making the same changes Denver brought to its bridge project: widening sidewalks, adding bike paths, and narrowing vehicle lanes. The program isn't confined to Peoria's downtown core either; changes have been made in outer residential areas of the city as well.

Reduce Parking Opportunities

Eliminating parking spaces is another way to discourage car ownership and steer people away from owning multiple AVs. We may not need as much parking with AVs. If you live in a downtown area and do not need a car to make most trips, and there is no place to park a car if you were to have one, you may rethink car ownership, especially if there are other means of getting to and around downtown, including bike lanes, walking paths, mass transit, and ride-sharing options.

Most major US cities grapple with parking requirements for new housing, and not just in downtowns. Parking space has long been a point of discussion in New York City. The Furman Center for Real Estate and Urban Policy at New York University studied the rationale behind parking requirements for housing developments and found that fewer parking spaces per unit brings down housing prices. But fewer parking spaces could also drive down car ownership: if you have no place to put a car and don't need one to get around your city, the chances that you'd want one are reduced. Parking space requirements were changed in New York in the Zoning for Quality and Affordability Act passed in 2015, which mainly exempted affordable housing close to transit zones. For market-rate housing, however, the requirements have largely remained the same.

In 2007, in its effort to discourage car ownership in favor of other more active modes of mobility, Seattle eliminated minimum parking requirements for new housing developments in urban-center commercial zones, and since that time it has steadily expanded the policy. For instance, in 2012 Seattle city planners recommended that the city eliminate parking requirements for new developments within a quarter-mile of frequent transit. The theory is that more people will walk, bike, or take buses and light rail and fewer people will own cars, especially in dense urban neighborhoods like the West Galer neighborhood of Queen Anne Hill in Seattle, if convenient and accessible transit is available.[12]

Children will certainly be the future users of transit, AV cars, and bikes, depending on what modes of transportation we model for them and encourage them to use. For most of my youth, my family did not have a car. We got around by subway or bus, and a taxi was a rare luxury. By the time I was ten, I was exploring the city with my Bensonhurst pals Gerard Soffian and Barry Politick. We had just about the entire stage of New York City only a 15-cent token away. In my twenties, I remember taking my suburban-raised niece Robin and nephew Adam, then about eight and six years old, to Coney Island. We rode roller coasters, go-carts, swings, and Ferris wheels. When we got home, I asked them which ride they liked the best. Without hesitation, they both blurted out, "The subway!"

Using transit should be second nature, and one of the ways we can shift from a nation of drivers to a nation of transit users is to start making it a normal part of childhood. Besides, most kids I know love spending time around big machines like buses and trains. I have a friend who tells me that visiting Manhattan with her ten-year-old son is cheap entertainment. Why? Because he doesn't want to go shopping or visit expensive attractions. "All he wants to do is ride on city buses." If we can engender a love of transit in children, teach them how to use it, and encourage walking or biking to school or to friends' houses, they may not want to own a car when they grow up.

Sell Rides, Not Cars

Expanding mobility-as-a-service (MaaS)—buying rides instead of cars—could also be a way to reduce the dependency on personal ownership now and in the future. MaaS is not a cure-all, and it has to be done right, but it is one of the keys to discouraging ownership when ownership is not necessary. If MaaS can be autonomous and eliminate the cost of human labor, it can be an affordable and flexible way to move people from place to place and forgo personal vehicles. Existing examples demonstrate that MaaS could be a positive and equitable use of autonomous technology.

UbiGo, a project out of Gothenburg, Sweden, combines public transport, car-sharing, rental car services, and taxis in one intermodal, on-demand, monthly subscription mobility service. Accounts can be shared among family members. The service is described as a mobility solution that eliminates the need for a car. In its initial six-month test period, 195 people representing 83 households tested the service. Overall, people used the service frequently and were satisfied with the mobility solutions it offered. The key service attributes they identified were the "transportation smorgasbord" concept, ease of use, improved access and flexibility, convenience, and economy.[13] The project was such a success that in 2018 it was expanded to include Stockholm, and other Swedish cities will probably follow. Subscribers will have access to public transport, car-sharing, car rental, taxis, and the city bike system, as well as 24/7 support.[14] UbiGo is an example of MaaS done right.

Helsinki, the capital of Finland, tried an on-demand ride-sharing service called Kutsuplus ("call plus") that commuters used to summon a shared vehicle through an app. The service was an add-on to Helsinki's metro and bus service; it served a greater area than the metro, which cannot be expanded, and the bus system, which runs in a primarily north-south direction. With Kutsuplus, east-west trips promised to be easier to make.[15]

The service matched passengers going to the same destination with a minibus driver, and they shared the cost of the ride, which was more than a regular city bus fare but less than a private taxi would cost. Passengers would log on to the service's website, select the start and end points for their journey, and then walk to the closest bus stop to wait for the pickup. In 2014, the average fair was about €5—or $5.50. A bus or metro ride in the city is €3, and taxi fares start at €6 and can go much higher depending on distance.[16]

Kutsuplus was technologically feasible, and riders liked it. Ridership grew steadily and met projections (21,000 registered users within the time frame measured). Unfortunately, the program failed and was shut down in late 2015. Kutsuplus didn't convince anyone to give up their cars. Private car usage grew in Helsinki until 2008 and then flattened, but not necessarily because of the minibus service: the decline coincided with a drop in driving throughout much of the developed world and also with the global recession.

At issue was the massive scale necessary to make the ride-sharing program work. Growing the fleet from the original fifteen buses to forty-five vehicles by 2016, to one hundred by 2017, and then into the thousands in the 2020s was the only way to optimize efficiency. With too few buses and users, Kutsuplus buses were frequently empty because it wasn't always easy to match up passengers who were going in the same direction around the same time. Scaling up to just one hundred vehicles would have increased the efficiency of Kutsuplus threefold. It takes money to achieve scale, however, and although the €3 million it cost to run Kutsuplus was less than 1 percent of the Transport Authority's budget, the service was heavily subsidized. A €17 per-trip cost to taxpayers to fund expansion of the system was controversial, especially during an economic downturn.

The Helsinki story is instructive, as it shows that many pieces must fall into place to make innovative transit solutions work—users need to accept them, they have to be scaled for efficiency, and they need to be adequately funded. In the absence of even one of those elements, failure will ensue.

It may also be that a service like UbiGo, which depends on existing transit options, has more hope of winning people over because its financial requirements are not as great as those for an entirely new set of buses. The link with existing transit is critical because, as Bern Grush points out, just "adding another ride-hailing provider means more traffic, trips and congestion. . . . This happens in every city with a significant degree of ride-hailing—Boston, New York, San Francisco."[17] Grush cites research showing that 49 to 61 percent of ride-hailed trips in major US cities—generally provided by Lyft and Uber—would have otherwise been made by transit, walking, or biking or would not have been made at all.[18] Occupying the sweet spot, as discussed next, are app services that increase transit usage.

MAINTAIN AND SUPPORT GOOD TRANSIT SYSTEMS

I have long maintained that transit systems are best funded when they are used by both the well-to-do and the not-doing-so-well. A system viewed as "for the poor" will be poorly maintained.[19] Some of the complaints about mass transit—it takes too long, cuts service during off-hours, has limited last-mile access, and is often dirty or broken down—can be greatly mitigated through better and smarter funding of autonomous technology used for mass transit.[20]

The benefits of public transportation for individuals, communities, and, yes, even states and nations are manifold and worth the investment. For people, well-planned and operated public transportation provides people with more choices, freedom, mobility, and opportunities.[21] It also saves commuters and others money.

Good transit helps revitalize business districts, allows employers to tap into larger workforces, builds economic revenues, and increases property values. Investment in the nation's transportation infrastructure supports and creates more jobs. Transit can reduce dependence on foreign oil, and it provides critical response resources in emergencies.

We want to draw people back into living, working, and playing in our downtowns, but not to bring their cars; neither do we want to encourage more car services. The cities that show a growth in transit use hold the key: a well-maintained and robust transit system. Buses in particular seem to be most effective in many cities, not just for thriving downtowns but for surrounding areas, including their suburbs. The cities that have enjoyed an upswing in transit use have something in common—well-funded buses with robust routes. Here's where AV transit could hit a grand slam as micro-transit services run smaller but more frequent buses matching demand and alter routes based on conditions and ridership needs.

Seattle and Houston have posted 4.1 and 2.3 percent increases in transit use, respectively. In addition to expanding light rail, they have redesigned their bus networks. Houston's redesigned bus network, launched in 2015, increases access to a bus service that has buses arriving at least every fifteen minutes and that now has expanded weekend and nighttime service. Seattle has also expanded its bus routes and light rail routes. Between 2010 and 2017, downtown Seattle added 60,000 jobs. During the same time period, the number of individual car commuters into the city's central business district dropped by 4,500, or 9 percent, according to a new report from *Commute Seattle*.[22]

When Columbus, Ohio, launched its new, expanded bus network, access doubled.[23] Their attention to buses allows Houston and Seattle to stand apart from cities that have just expanded rail transit.

Underwriting a strong bus network makes sense. Buses are one form of mass transit that benefit greatly from autonomous technology. A driverless bus could have expanded service times, since there is no double or triple time to be paid for overnight shifts. It could also reach last-mile outposts, connecting non-urban residents to amenities, eliminating their dependence on cars. Networked buses will rarely if ever have to operate without passengers.

AV transit should not be confused with the hype surrounding "AV road trains." Some proponents of AVs maintain that robo-cars operating in platoons can mimic the performance of bus rapid transit or even a rail line. It isn't true. A single lane of cars today has a capacity, at best, of 2,000 vehicles per hour. With an average occupancy in the United States of 1.1 persons per car, 2,200 people would be moved. Upgrade those cars to AVs and perhaps 3,600 vehicles could traverse the lane each hour. (*Note:* Others have suggested much higher numbers, but I think spacing vehicles traveling at 60 miles per hour with less than one second between them over the course of an hour is risky and not reasonable where there is merging, weaving, and exiting traffic.)

Although 3,600 vehicles per hour is still about an 80 percent increase in lane capacity, the goal should be moving people, not vehicles. Some of those vehicles are likely to be empty as they head to a pickup somewhere or after they drop the occupant off and then go home or to a home base. I'll be generous and say that average car occupancy is 2.0, even though Americans drivers have been going increasingly solo for more than a generation. With an occupancy rate of 2.0 people per car, the AV lane capacity would be 7,200 people moved per hour. A lane full of AV buses at, say, 1,500 conventional-sized buses per hour has the capacity to move 60,000 persons per hour. It's no contest: AV transit is the smarter way to go.

I have yet to see a Congress since the 1960s that has much appetite for investing in transit. This has to change if we are going to go forward with AVs and not backward. The Fords, GMs, Apples, Googles, and their ilk need to support a smarter approach and convey that to elected officials. Cities are stepping up, but I'm afraid the feds are stuck with an early twentieth-century mind-set.

GUARANTEE MOBILITY WITH CONGESTION PRICING

In the late 1970s, I chaired a quarterly meeting on Midtown Manhattan traffic circulation. Attendance was open to the public. A frequent participant was a gray-haired professorial man in a tweed jacket with elbow patches. He was well mannered, but dismissive of most of my ideas for improving traffic flow. He kept harping on the point that the answer was to have fewer vehicles in Manhattan and insisted that the way to accomplish that was to use the capitalist approach to any valuable resource: price it appropriately. In Manhattan, the precious resource is space. He introduced me to the concept of congestion pricing.

William Vickrey was in fact a professor of economics, at Columbia University, and less than twenty years later he would go on to win the Nobel Prize in Economics. I knew Vickrey was right, and in 1980, as New York City's assistant DOT commissioner, I attempted to introduce congestion pricing in Manhattan. I was promptly sued by the Automobile Club of New York (the local AAA) and the Metropolitan Garage Board of Trade (which, ironically, practices geographic and temporal congestion pricing with its customers).

In 2018, I am still working on a pricing plan for New York City. Called MOVE NY, it involves lowering tolls on every bridge outside of Manhattan's core (which is the right thing to do in terms of policy *and* politics) but charging drivers of all vehicles entering the core a user fee. The first part of the MOVE NY plan, charging a fee to Ubers, Lyfts, taxis, and other car services, was approved by New York State in April 2018 and scheduled to go into effect in 2019. I am still pushing for charging *all* vehicles entering Manhattan's Central Business District.

Congestion charging is vital because the risks of gridlock are so great with AVs. First, vehicular capacities on highways feeding into business districts will increase dramatically by 50 to 100 percent (some predict even higher numbers). More cars will try to enter these business zones faster, but the capacity of the streets will change little. Second, as Uber, Lyft, and others have shown us, MaaS leads to more cars, not fewer, in our busiest areas. Think of it this way. The street system is a bathtub, and the faucet is the highways. Widening the faucets will just fill the tub with more water faster, causing it to overflow more quickly. In addition, the standing water already in the tub—Uber, taxis, and other for-hire vehicles (FHVs)—will be higher than ever, allowing even less room for more water.

Uber has recognized this and staunchly supports MOVE NY's congestion pricing as long as all FHVs are treated the same way. Why would Uber support an increase in fees? Let's go back a half-century to when I was driving a taxicab in Manhattan. My goal, as is every driver's, was to get a passenger and then get rid of him as quickly as possible to get the next fare. If I spent an hour with a fare going a few miles because of bumper-to-bumper traffic, I'd be losing money. Uber has seen the traffic deteriorate to walking speed in Midtown, and their drivers are losing money.

I suppose it's not difficult to understand why it's so hard to get congestion pricing passed in New York City—people don't like what they perceive to be new taxes and fees. And in New York, drivers who would pay the fee are skeptical that the money earmarked for transit improvements would actually be used for that purpose.[24] However, congestion pricing is money you pay voluntarily by choosing to bring a car into a downtown core at a busy time. If you don't drive a car into the city, you don't pay the fee. In contrast, since most cities and states use general tax revenue to pay for transit, highways, and bridges, everyone shoulders the burden of these costs, even those who never use them.

Singapore, London, Oslo, Stockholm, and Milan are just some of the major cities that have used congestion pricing for a long time, and to great effect. It's a policy that does what it is supposed to do: reduce congestion and car traffic in downtown areas during busy times, increase economic activity, and raise revenue for needed improvements to mass transit.[25] My plan for New York City would do the same: it would generate $1.5 billion annually for city transportation, provide faster travel inside the downtown core, and help fund improvements to subway and bus lines throughout all five boroughs.

Now is the time for cities, states, provinces, and countries to introduce and pass enabling legislation so that when the day comes—and it will—they will have another tool to maintain adequate mobility for all.

REALLOCATE PARKING AREAS FOR BETTER USES

State and city planners and private developers should rethink how they build accessory parking over the next decade. Even if there's clear demand over the next few years, by 2025 that demand may wane. In fact, with the advent of FHVs, many airport operators are already seeing significant drops in their most profitable revenue source—parking lots and garages. If a garage must be built, it should be designed so that when the day comes—and again, it will—the facility can easily be converted to commercial, retail, or even residential use by using flat plank building methods and exterior ramps that can be removed, as Gensler's Andy Cohen suggests.

Cohen also points out that there is tremendous opportunity for the land currently taken up by gas and service stations and car washes, especially in urban areas. "There are 125,000 gas stations in the US, so think about the opportunity to repurpose that land, to take back that valuable space in cities for other uses, including green spaces, parks, dining. Gas stations in cities represent an immense opportunity."[26]

In addition, if we can control individual car ownership, if vehicle fleets are owned and operated by their makers, and if autonomous buses and other forms of multipassenger transit become a common form of travel, we'll have a lot of empty parking lots ripe for remaking. We already have scores of empty parking lots begging to be reused. Many malls across the United States are dying, and they and their behemoth asphalt surroundings are being abandoned as people change their shopping habits.[27]

Old parking garages have been turned into clubs, galleries, movie theaters, housing, and business and retail spaces.[28] We need to encourage these uses and plan for them when building new parking lots and garages. Keeping alternative future uses in mind, designers of new parking lots could include green areas, steps for exercises, track lines for running and walking, walls for movie screens, and water features to help people cool off on hot days.

PRIORITIZE LIGHTER, SMALLER, LOWER-ENERGY, AND LESS-POLLUTING VEHICLES

Just because a car is autonomous doesn't guarantee that it will be more environmentally friendly.[29] As we've heard from designers, AVs could take on any size, shape, or form. In 1990, I started teaching at Cooper Union, an elite college in New York's East Village. Its oldest structure, the nine-story Foundation Building, then the tallest building in Manhattan, opened in 1858. I was puzzled by its cylindrical elevator. I soon learned the reason for its shape. Peter Cooper, the school's founder, built the shaft in 1853, well before Elisha Otis installed the first public elevator in 1874. Cooper knew that elevators for high-rise buildings would be invented, but he thought that they would be round, not rectangular. Similarly, what we imagine now as the AVs of the future may take completely different forms.

I like to think of an AV as being like an eggshell—small, light but protective, and energy-efficient. But not everyone is going to see things my way. There will be people who want to build and own autonomous RVs, moving houses that keep moving and polluting and stop only for gas. Vehicle manufacturers should be encouraged either through tax incentives, pollution fees, or legislation to focus on making more efficient, greener cars. Just as congestion pricing can reduce traffic, manufacturing and use fees can shift behaviors around making and buying certain kinds of less desirable vehicles.

Another way to discourage car ownership is through levies on ownership, especially ownership of energy-guzzling vehicles and ownership of second and third cars. Luxury taxes—taxing the least expensive and most energy-efficient vehicles at a lower rate than more expensive gas-guzzling vehicles—present another way to discourage ownership of certain vehicles.

Gasoline and other fuel sources could be taxed at rates similar to those in Europe: paying $4 or $5 a gallon for gas nationwide would help people reevaluate their need for multiple vehicles, including AVs, which will still need fuel to operate. I am also in favor of a vehicle-miles-traveled (VMT) charge for most parts of the country. In the densest urban areas, I'd combine that with a vehicle-hours-traveled (VHT) charge, since cars cover very few miles while traveling in congestion. These monies could be earmarked for maintenance of highways, construction of bike lanes, and maintenance and widening of sidewalks. Much higher gas prices would encourage people to use and/or own more efficient vehicles.

DO NO HARM (TO OUR HEALTH)

> I'm walkin' here! I'm walkin' here!
> —RATSO RIZZO, *MIDNIGHT COWBOY* (1969)

THE HIPPOCRATIC OATH should apply whenever we tackle major problems. We run a real risk to our health if we steer ourselves toward a society where functional activity is reduced even further than it already is. Worldwide, inactivity kills more people than smoking does. It would be great if the overall impact of AVs was less time spent in cars, but that's not a given. The biggest battle I see is over the seduction of libertarians and many elected officials on all sides of the political spectrum by the illusion of a glorious future with AVs as long as we leave the private sector free to choose its own paths. I partially agree that the private sector should be taking the lead in development of the technology. If done right, I do see a better future with AVs. But "done right" has to include the private sector's participation in maintaining the infrastructure it will need to be most effective. Neither the general public nor the AV industry can count on local governments alone to properly maintain lane lines, traffic signs, roadway surfaces, bridges, and V2I communications systems on their own.

Let's have a real partnership. Let's entice the private sector to also attend to transit for low-income communities, persons with disabilities, and others. Where the private sector uses the public right of way, the private sector must pay for that. An equally fierce battle will be fought with local governments intent on remaining a certain kind of city or town and determined to protect their environments, lifestyles, and existing transit systems. Here I call for a joint federal government, private industry, and local government entity to agree on how (not whether) to comply with local rules and regulations. I think we can all agree, for instance, that we don't want terrorists to use vehicles as weapons to kill pedestrians and bike riders in car-free zones.

But I am not sure we can all agree on AVs being required to obey speed limits, traffic signs, parking rules, and pavement markings. For this, we need to accept that local governments set rules and AVs must obey those rules. This will require systems integrations, data-sharing, and independent auditing of compliance. In my mind, this would be done through a central traffic control center, which nearly every major city already has, as do many medium-sized cities. The control center would be able to monitor compliance in real time, identify an errant vehicle, and perhaps thwart a crash or a terrorist act. It's the least we can ask for from an industry that will overtake our public ways.

On April 26, 2017, at the invitation of Amazon Prime Minister of Ideas H. B. Siegel (yes, that's how he signed his name), I attended a "Radical Urban Transportation Summit."[30] The thirty or so attendees represented companies that offered everything from app-based flying FHVs to hyperloops to electric highways. Not one innovator focused on what to me was one of the obvious ways to radically transform urban transportation: apply the latest technologies to urban rail systems. From a private-sector viewpoint, however, there's no money there. An attendee who knew little about transportation planning or engineering might have concluded from the various presentations that there are solutions for urban trips based on distances: For going less than a mile, a hovering skateboard. For more than a mile and up to five miles, a robo-taxi. For trips of five to twenty miles, an app-based flying machine. For longer trips, the hyperloop.

I was struck by how little the attendees knew about urban transport, how enamored they were with gadgets, and how much they were complicating things, at every distance, à la Rube Goldberg. When it came my turn to present, the solution I proposed for trips of less than a mile—and more than half of urban trips are this short—was shoes, available since 1600 BC.

MANY TRILLIONS OF dollars are going to be spent on AVs between now and midcentury. We could easily get giddy and lose perspective as we await their arrival; I'm sure we will soon be barraged with ads that convey the wonderful world ahead. But going forward, we need to maintain our sanity as we consider the best uses of AVs, keeping in mind that they should improve the quality of our lives. We can walk short distances, bike medium distances, take transit in cities, and use AVs for longer trips. We need a mix of modes of transport, not reliance on AVs to do it all. President John F. Kennedy got it right over fifty years ago, in his 1962 message to Congress: "Our national welfare therefore requires the provision of good urban transportation, with the properly balanced use of private vehicles and modern mass transport to help shape as well as serve urban growth."

The key word in that exhortation remains just as important as we move forward in this century: "balanced." There's a lot at stake, most importantly the future health of people, economies, cities, and more. My main message, just like Kennedy's, is that only balanced transportation will bring us safely into a future when autonomous vehicles provide benefits to us all.

Levels of Autonomy

WHAT DOES IT MEAN FOR A VEHICLE TO BE AUTONOMOUS? When I discuss the good, the bad, and the ugly of AVs in this book, I am mainly referring to a fully autonomous, or Level 5, vehicle. However, there are many stages between a Level 5 vehicle and the Level 0 to 2 vehicles that are on the road today. The levels are defined in the following descriptions of vehicle operating systems and constitute the frame of reference used in this book, which was developed and adopted by the US Department of Transportation and the National Highway Traffic Safety Administration.

LEVEL 0 (NO AUTOMATION)

The vast majority of cars and trucks today are Level 0 vehicles. The driver handles steering, throttle, and braking (ST&B), monitors the surroundings, navigates, and determines when to use turn signals, change lanes, and turn. Level 0 vehicles can have some warning systems (blind-spot and collision warnings).

LEVEL 1 (DRIVER ASSISTANCE)

Level 1 vehicles can handle S (steering) or T&B (throttle and braking), but not in all circumstances, and the driver must be ready to take over these functions if called upon to do so by the vehicle. Thus, the driver must remain aware of what the car is doing and be ready to step in if needed.

LEVEL 2 (PARTIAL AUTOMATION)

The Level 2 vehicle handles ST&B, but immediately lets the driver take over if he or she detects objects or events to which the vehicle is not responding. Like drivers of Level 0 or 1 cars, the driver of a Level 2 vehicle is responsible for monitoring the surroundings, traffic, weather, and road conditions.

LEVEL 3 (CONDITIONAL AUTOMATION)

The Level 3 vehicle monitors surroundings and takes care of all ST&B in certain environments, such as freeways. But the driver must be ready to intervene if the vehicle requests it.

LEVEL 4 (HIGH AUTOMATION)

The Level 4 vehicle handles ST&B and monitors the surroundings in a wider range of environments, but not all environments, such as severe weather. The driver switches on the automatic driving only when it is safe to do so. In automatic driving mode, the driver is not required.

LEVEL 5 (FULL AUTOMATION)

The driver of a Level 5 vehicle only has to set the destination and start the vehicle, which handles all other tasks and makes the driving decisions based on traffic conditions that a human traditionally makes in a conventional vehicle.

Acknowledgments

KAREN KELLY HAS been my collaborator throughout the writing of this book. She has done a herculean job of keeping up with perhaps the fastest-paced industry the world has ever seen.

I've been fortunate to have a team throughout guiding me as we delved into the good, bad, and ugly possibilities that will unfold with the full-scale adoption of autonomous vehicles. Working with Karen and me have been the "Three Musketeers": the futurist Bern Grush, who first showed me what's behind the AV industry's curtain of hype; Joe Iacobucci, my colleague at Sam Schwartz Transportation Consultants, who leads our "New Mobility" group; and Charlie Houlton-Vinyl, my former student at Hunter College and now part of the Sam Schwartz team. Corey Tam and Jacob Levine, also students, often joined the team.

I am grateful to Jennifer Raab, president of Hunter College, and Harold Holzer, director of Roosevelt House, for naming me in 2017 the inaugural Theodore Kheel Visiting Fellow at the Roosevelt House Public Policy Institute at Hunter College. It was an honor to serve with the support of Ted Kheel's children, Jane Kheel Stanley and Robert Kheel, through the Nurture Nature Foundation. Ted Kheel was well known to longtime New Yorkers as a negotiator, civil rights leader, and transportation authority. He was among the first to recognize the connection between social equity and transport policy. In a 1969 *New York* magazine article, he wrote:"Transportation is as much a civil rights issue as housing and education and jobs." I have lived by that mantra for over a half-century.

My students at Hunter provided great input and focused their energies on congestion pricing, current trends in travel behavior, and, of course, autonomous vehicles. Thank you, Julia Fiore, Corey Tam, Trevor Lovitz, Atara Lindenbaum, and Nicolas Adamo. I was fortunate to have Charles Komanoff, the best transportation economist in the country, assist me during the semester.

Christina Roman has worked side by side with me for years, helping me form and present my findings on AVs at numerous venues. Richard Retting has been my go-to guy on traffic safety for over three decades and provided great input for the book.

Thanks also go to the many professionals who offered their time and insights, including Brett Berk, Dan Sturges, Andy Cohen, Kevin Gillette, Nyambé Séinya Harleston-Blake, Vivek Krishnamurthy, Venkat Sumantran, Oliver Yaros, Marjorie Harris Loeb, Bryant Smith, Jason Levine, Gerard Soffiar, Eileen de Villa, Barbara Gray, Gabe Klein, and Aaron Renn.

I am grateful to Alain Kornhauser at Princeton University, who invites me to his class each year to unveil my latest findings and follows up with a lively discussion. His weekly e-letter, *Smart Driving Cars*, is a must-read for anyone interested in AVs; it has often given us leads on what is happening in the field, and where. His commentaries under "C'mon Man" and "hmmmm . . ." are incisive, unrelenting, and unapologetic.

Thanks also to Clive Priddle, always available to hear my ideas for a book and always challenging me throughout the process; to Athena Bryan for fine-tuning the book; to Sandra Beris and Cynthia Buck, for all their hard work seeing the book through production; to Julie Ford for her legal counsel; and to my publicity team, Josie Urwin, Jaime Leifer, and Miguel Cervantes, marketing coordinator.

Special thanks to my agent, Carol Mann, for her input and guidance throughout.

Notes

THE MANY COMMENTATORS WEIGHING IN—WHETHER THROUGH WEBSITES, blogs, traditional print media, or academic publications—on what the future holds with the advent of automated vehicles are diverse in their archiving practices, some are available only behind paywalls, and a few have proven ephemeral. All are well worth visiting, but as the reader will see, the "road signs" we have provided are often in the form of links only. An encyclopedic notes section comprising detailed notes for the many sources cited would have been not only disproportionately large for a book of this nature but quickly outdated in many instances by the rapidly evolving online conversation.

INTRODUCTION: YOU CAN'T PUT THIS CAR IN REVERSE

1. Norman Bel Geddes, *Magic Motorways* (New York: Random House, 1940), 4.

2. Mike Isaac, "Self-Driving Truck's First Mission: A 120-Mile Beer Run," *New York Times*, October 25, 2016, https://www.nytimes.com/2016/10/26/technology /self-driving-trucks-first-mission-a-beer-run.html?mtrref=www.bing.com.

3. https://www.rita.dot.gov/bts/programs/freight_transportation/html /transportation.html.

4. http://www.businessinsider.com/heres-everywhere-uber-is-banned-around -the-world-2015-4.

5. https://www.bloomberg.com/news/articles/2015-01-08/driverless-car
-global-market-seen-reaching-42-billion-by-2025; see also https://www.market-
researchfuture.com/statistical-reports/europe-autonomous-vehicles-countries
-market-2402.

6. https://www.infoholicresearch.com/global-autonomous-vehicles-market
-to-reach-126-8-billion-by-2027/.

7. http://reports.weforum.org/digital-transformation/reinventing-the-wheel/.

8. https://newsroom.intel.com/newsroom/wp-content/uploads/sites/11/2017
/05/passenger-economy.pdf.

9. Daniel B. Kline, "How Often Does the Average American Replace Her Cell
Phone?" *Motley Fool*, July 15, 2015, https://www.fool.com/investing/general
/2015/07/15/how-often-does-the-average-american-replace-his-or.aspx.

10. Aarian Marshal, "Elon Musk Reveals His Awkward Dislike of Mass Transit," *Wired*, December 12, 2017, https://www.wired.com/story/elon-musk
-awkward-dislike-mass-transit/.

11. http://asirt.org/initiatives/informing-road-users/road-safety-facts
/road-crash-statistics.

ONE: YESTERDAY, TODAY, AND TOMORROW: THE FUTURE IS NOW

1. Roland Barthes, *Mythologies* (New York: Jonathan Cape, 1972), 88.

2. Rossella Lorenzi, "Da Vinci Sketched an Early Car," *ABC Science/News in
Science*, April 26, 2004, http://www.abc.net.au/science/news/stories/s1094767
.htm.

3. https://www.thoughtco.com/history-of-steamboats-4057901.

4. http://www.thedrive.com/vintage/6797/the-untold-history-of-the-first
-driverless-car-crash-part-1; see also http://brettberk.com/wp-content/uploads
/2017/01/JJ-Lynch-11.jpg; and "Magic Car to Demonstrate Safety," *Herald States-
man*, Yonkers, NY, July 28, 1936, front page (no author).

5. http://www.agriculture.com/technology/robotics/autonomous-ag
-equipment-is-here_581-ar52154; https://www.theatlantic.com/magazine
/archive/2013/09/the-killing-machines-how-to-think-about-drones/309434/;
http://www.tomshardware.com/news/amazon-prime-air-drone-delivery,25252
.html; http://www.unmannedsystemstechnology.com/2017/05/new-autonomous
-technology-allows-ugvs-cooperate-drones/.

6. https://www.technologyreview.com/s/408988/prelude-to-a-robot-race/.

7. http://www.dnaindia.com/scitech/report-navia-the-first-driverless-vehicle
-introduced-by-induct-company-1948091.

8. Reema Punjabi, "Navia—The First Driverless Vehicle Introduced by Induct
Company," *DNA*, January 9, 2014, http://www.dnaindia.com/scitech/report
-navia-the-first-driverless-vehicle-introduced-by-induct-company-1948091.

9. http://news.sky.com/story/public-trial-for-driverless-cars-beginning-in-milton-keynes-10613089.

10. http://www.bbc.com/news/uk-england-beds-bucks-herts-24849948.

11. https://sputniknews.com/science/201711281059504905-sweden-driverless-cars/.

12. https://techcrunch.com/2017/03/27/ubers-autonomous-cars-return-to-the-road-in-san-francisco-today/.

13. https://owlcation.com/social-sciences/Cultural-Differences-Between-the-US-and-Japan.

14. https://www.forbes.com/sites/tromero/2018/04/03/what-ubers-crash-tells-us-about-japans-silent-strategy-for-driverless-cars/#102e2f0a3e39.

15. http://www.businessinsider.com/what-bmw-driverless-car-looks-like-2017-3/#the-interior-is-sleek-and-clear-of-any-clutter-if-you-choose-to-drive-it-yourself-a-heads-up-display-will-show-you-useful-information-like-where-you-are-on-your-route-3.

16. Dan Sturges, telephone interview with the author, June 19, 2017.

17. Isaac Asimov, "Sally," first published in *Fantastic*, May-June 1953, available at: http://www.e-reading.club/chapter.php/82060/20/Isaac_Asimovs_Worlds_of_Science_Fiction._Book_9__Robots.html.

18. Carlton Reid, *Roads Were Not Meant for Cars* (Washington, DC: Island Press, 2015), xiii.

19. https://en.wikipedia.org/wiki/Good_Roads_Movement.

20. http://www.kshs.org/kansapedia/good-roads-movement/12067.

21. https://www.kshs.org/p/western-trails-project-advent-of-automobiles/13881. *Bicycles on roads:* www.Bikeforum.net/touring/123478/how-to-find-out-state-interstate-highways-freeways-you-can-bicycle.html

22. http://www.carhistory4u.com/the-last-100-years/car-production.

23. http://www.drivinglessons-cumbernauld.com/history-of-driving.html.

24. "What Shall Be the Cure for Automobile Speed Mania?" *Illustrated World* 34, no. 1 (September 1920), available at: https://books.google.com/books?id=_-3NAAAAMAAJ&pg=PA85&lpg=PA85&dq="What+Shall+Be+the+Cure+for+Automobile+Speed+Mania?"&source=bl&ots=rri4b633M3&sig=-Bp6tXcM-ysIRDOFLuB8khgbEz8&hl=en&sa=X&ei=3OS2VO-hKIG9ggS-6oOgDA&ved=0CCAQ6AEwAA#v=onepage&q="What%20Shall%20Be%20the%20Cure%20for%20Automobile%20Speed%20Mania%3F"&f=false.

25. https://wikivisually.com/wiki/List_of_traffic_collisions.

26. Edward Robb Ellis, *The Epic of New York City* (New York: Old Town Books, 1966), 460–461.

27. https://thedayintech.wordpress.com/2013/05/30/auto-vs-bike-ouch/.

28. http://irishpost.co.uk/mary-ward-irish-scientist-became-worlds-first-car-death-day-1869/.

29. Andrew McFarlane, "How the UK's First Fatal Car Accident Unfolded," *BBC News*, August 17, 2010.

30. Ellis, *The Epic of New York City*, 460–461.

31. http://www.somacon.com/p469.php.

32. http://worldpopulationreview.com/us-cities/new-york-city-population/.

33. https://blog.allstate.com/from-rome-to-detroit-a-history-of-street-signs/.

34. http://www.cabinetmagazine.org/issues/17/blocking.php.

35. Joseph F. Zimmerman, *The Government and Politics of New York State*, 2nd ed. (Albany: State University of New York Press, 2008), 232.

36. http://www.nytimes.com/2008/10/12/automobiles/12LIMP.html?mtrref=undefined&gwh=22D8F93D6EE798B24C56D8EB7B1D061B&gwt=pay.

37. http://www.destination360.com/europe/germany/autobahn.

38. Lloyd Alter, "It's Blame the Victim Week in the War on Pedestrians," *Treehugger*, December 10, 2015, https://www.treehugger.com/walking/cost-war-pedestrians-69750-jaywalking-halifax.html.

39. https://esnpc.blogspot.com/2014/11/jaywalkers-and-jayhawkers-pedestrian.html.

40. Peter Norton, *Fighting Traffic: The Dawn of the Motor Age in the American City*, Kindle ed. (Cambridge, MA: MIT Press, 2008), location 916.

41. http://www.bbc.com/news/magazine-26073797.

42. https://catalog.hathitrust.org/Record/000968627.

43. https://legalbeagle.com/5436948-history-traffic-laws.html.

44. https://www.myparkingsign.com/blog/pedestrian-crossing-signs-history/.

45. https://en.wikipedia.org/wiki/List_of_motor_vehicle_deaths_in_U.S._by_year.

46. http://www.u-s-history.com/pages/h1674.html.

47. https://en.wikipedia.org/wiki/List_of_motor_vehicle_deaths_in_U.S._by_year.

48. "118. Address Opening the President's Second Highway Safety Conference, June 18, 1947," Public Papers, Harry S. Truman, 1945–1953, *Harry S. Truman Presidential Library and Museum*, https://trumanlibrary.org/publicpapers/index.php?pid=2127&st=highway&st1=.

49. https://en.wikipedia.org/wiki/List_of_motor_vehicle_deaths_in_U.S._by_year.

50. "106. Address Before the President's Highway Safety Conference, May 8, 1946," Public Papers, Harry S. Truman, 1945–1953, *Harry S. Truman Presidential Library and Museum*, https://trumanlibrary.org/publicpapers/index.php?pid=1548&st=highway&st1=.

51. https://www.fhwa.dot.gov/infrastructure/safety01.cfm.

52. Richard F. Weingroff, "Highway History: President Dwight D. Eisenhower, and the Federal Role in Highway Safety: Chapter 1: President Harry S. Truman's Highway Safety Conferences," US Department of Transportation, Federal Highway Administration, https://www.fhwa.dot.gov/infrastructure/safety01.cfm.

53. Richard F. Weingroff, "Federal-Aid Highway Act of 1956: Creating the Interstate System," *Public Roads* 60, no. 1 (Summer 1996), https://www.fhwa.dot.gov/publications/publicroads/96summer/p96su10.cfm.

54. https://legalbeagle.com/5436948-history-traffic-laws.html.

55. http://www.unece.org/trans/main/wp29/meeting_docs_wp29.html.

56. "Nils Bohlin: Swedish Engineer," *Encyclopaedia Britannica*, https://www.britannica.com/biography/Nils-Bohlin; "The Story of Volvo Cars," https://www.volvocars.com/intl/about/our-company/heritage/innovations.

57. Seat belts became mandatory in the United States on January 1, 1968, with the passage of 49 US Code, Chapter 301: Motor Vehicle Safety.

58. https://mitpress.mit.edu/sites/default/files/titles/content/9780262015363_sch_0001.pdf.

59. http://chandigarh.gov.in/knowchd_gen_plan.htm.

60. https://aha.confex.com/aha/2017/webprogram/Paper21474.html.

61. http://www.nyrr.org/about-us/history.

62. http://www.bettertransport.org.uk.

63. http://transalt.org/sites/default/files/news/magazine/034Fall/18europe.html.

64. http://newurbanism.org.

65. Wendell Berry, *The Art of the Commonplace: The Agrarian Essays of Wendell Berry* (Berkeley, CA: Counterpoint, 2002). Most of Berry's books make this point, in fact.

66. http://www.telegraph.co.uk/news/worldnews/11414064/How-Europe-is-slowly-dying-despite-an-increasing-world-population.html.

67. International Monetary Fund, "World Economic Update: Cross Currents," January 2015, http://www.imf.org/external/pubs/ft/weo/2015/update/01/; see also Céline Le Prioux, "Youth Unemployment: Europe's Unshakeable Challenge," *AFP*, January 31, 2018, https://www.yahoo.com/news/youth-unemployment-europes-unshakeable-challenge-175646190.html; and Peter S. Goodman, "Europe's Economy, after 8-Year Detour, Is Fitfully Back on Track," *New York Times*, April 29, 2016, https://www.nytimes.com/2016/04/30/business/international/eurozone-economy-q1.html?mtrref=r.search.yahoo.com&gwh=B45938147C0C8B9CD5C69130F1A9E43E&gwt=pay.

68. http://www.pewtrusts.org/en/research-and-analysis/blogs/stateline /2017/11/03/millennials-to-cities-ready-or-not-here-we-come; https://www .nytimes.com/2014/10/20/upshot/where-young-college-graduates-are-choosing -to-live.html; https://www.nytimes.com/2014/10/22/upshot/where-the-graduates -are-going-and-where-they-already-are.html; see also http://www.businessinsider .com/best-housing-markets-2018-millennial-home-buying-2017-12/#9-madison -wisconsin-2.

69. Jane Jacobs, *The Economy of Cities* (New York: Vintage, 1970), 3–4, 6–8.

TWO: INFRASTRUCTURE: LESS IS MORE

1. Lewis Mumford, *The Highway and the City* (New York: New American Library, 1964), 23.

2. https://www.fhwa.dot.gov/publications/publicroads/96summer/p96su2b .cfm.

3. "1916 Democratic Platform, June 14, 1916," *The Patriot Post*, https:// patriotpost.us/documents/473.

4. https://www.fhwa.dot.gov/publications/publicroads/96summer/p96su2 .cfm.

5. Archer Butler Hulbert and others, *The Future of Road-making in America: A Symposium*, vol. 15, *Historic Highways of America* (Cleveland: Arthur H. Clark Co., 1905), available at: http://www.gutenberg.org/files/33706/33706-h/33706 -h.htm.

6. Richard F. Weingroff, "Highway History: Portrait of a General: General Roy Stone: Part 5 of 8: US Office of Road Inquiry," US Department of Transportation, Federal Highway Administration, https://www.fhwa.dot.gov/infrastructure /stone05.cfm.

7. https://www.fhwa.dot.gov/publications/publicroads/96summer/p96su10cfm.

8. https://www.britannica.com/technology/road.

9. http://www.dartfordarchive.org.uk/20th_century/transport_roads.shtml.

10. http://www.german-autobahn.eu/index.asp?page=history.

11. http://www.abs.gov.au/ausstats/abs@.nsf/0/2e904c15091c39a5ca2569de 0028b416.

12. American Society of Civil Engineers, "2017 Infrastructure Report Card," http://www.infrastructurereportcard.org.

13. Jim Kinney, "Massachusetts Secretary of Transportation Richard Davey Wants to Cut Down on Single Occupancy Car Trips," *MassLive*, October 9, 2012, http://www.masslive.com/business-news/index.ssf/2012/10/massachusetts _state_secretary_of_transpo.html.

14. http://blog.cubitplanning.com/2010/02/road-miles-by-state/.

15. http://usa.streetsblog.org/2012/10/10/massdot-secretary-we-will-build-no-more-superhighways/.

16. http://www.dot.ca.gov/hq/LocalPrograms/atp/index.html; http://la.streetsblog.org/2015/03/18/california-says-it-is-committed-to-increasing-biking-walking/.

17. http://www.sun-sentinel.com/news/transportation/fl-reg-doctor-detour-qna-090417-story.html.

18. https://www.theguardian.com/technology/2016/apr/07/convoy-self-driving-trucks-completes-first-european-cross-border-trip.

19. US Government Accountability Office, *Excessive Truck Weight: An Expensive Burden We Can No Longer Support*, CED-79-94, July 16, 1979, https://www.gao.gov/assets/130/127292.pdf.

20. http://www.eupave.eu/documents/news-items/eupave-event-electric-vehicles.xml?lang=en.

21. http://didattica.unibocconi.it/mypage/upload/49430_20111107_060417_PUBLICINVESTMENTREV.PDF.

22. https://www.pwc.com/gx/en/transportation-logistics/pdf/assessing-global-transport-infrastructure-market.pdf.

23. https://www.angloinfo.com/how-to/greece/transport/driving/on-the-road; https://www.acerentacar.gr/rent-a-car-athens-greece/traffic-signs-signals.html; http://www.athensguide.com/driving/greek-driving-rules.htm.

24. http://www.nytimes.com/2007/11/09/world/europe/09athens.html?_r=2&oref=slogin.

25. http://greeklandscapes.com/travel/driving_athens.html.

26. http://www.rediff.com/business/slide-show/slide-show-1-nations-with-the-worlds-best-infrastructure/20110912.htm#8; https://www.rikvin.com/press-releases/singapores-infrastructure-ranked-best-in-the-world/; http://www.nationsencyclopedia.com/economies/Asia-and-the-Pacific/Hong-Kong-INFRASTRUCTURE-POWER-AND-COMMUNICATIONS.html.

27. https://www.autocarindia.com/industry/nitin-gadkari-states-no-autonomous-vehicles-for-india-405503; http://www.bbc.com/news/technology-40716296; see also Samar Harlarnkar, "1.5 Million Dead in a Decade: Just What Is Wrong with India's Roads and Vehicles?" *Quartz India*, September 25, 2017, https://qz.com/1086057/1-5-million-dead-in-a-decade-just-what-is-wrong-with-indias-roads-and-vehicles.

28. http://www.nationmaster.com/country-info/stats/Transport/Roads/Paved/%25-of-total-roads; http://www.mtri.org/unpaved/; https://www.rita.dot.gov/bts/sites/rita.dot.gov.bts/files/publications/national_transportation_statistics/html/table_01_04.html.

29. Venkat Sumantran, telephone interview with the author, November 20, 2017.

30. "Nitin Gadkari Is Right, Driverless Cars Make No Sense in India," *Economic Times*, July 26, 2017, htpps://economictimes.indiatimes.com/articleshow/59769631.cms?utm_source=contentofinterest&utm_medium=text&utm_campaign=cppst.

31. "Plus, many of India's roads are still far too crowded, and marred by potholes to accommodate driverless cars. Even in Indian cities, it is not uncommon to see livestock, rickshaws, scooters and pedestrians zig-zagging precariously beside cars, none paying any heed to traffic signals or driving etiquette in a frenetic competition for their piece of the asphalt. Logistically, it will take years of preparation before we can have self-driving cars here." Leeza Mangaldas, "Why India May Not See Driverless Cars Anytime Soon," *Forbes*, July 25, 2017, https://www.forbes.com/sites/leezamangaldas/2017/07/25/why-india-may-not-see-driverless-cars-anytime-soon/#334dd5b871bd.

32. Amrit Raj, "India Isn't the Best Market for Autonomous Vehicles: WEF's John Moavenzadeh," *LiveMint*, October 24, 2016, http://www.livemint.com/Companies/4kCgewR8wtLYc20WxAeNqN/India-isnt-the-best-market-for-autonomous-vehicles-says-WE.html.

33. Peerzada Abrar, "Driving Autonomous Vehicles in India Is the Ultimate Test," *The Hindu*, July 25, 2016, http://www.thehindu.com/todays-paper/tp-business/Driving-autonomous-vehicles-in-India-is-the-ultimate-test/article14507656.ece.

34. http://www.ibtimes.co.in/tata-elxsi-planning-test-driverless-cars-bengaluru-roads-712714; see also http://trak.in/tags/business/2017/01/19/tata-autonomous-vehicles-1st-self-driving-car-tata/.

35. https://thetechportal.com/2017/06/20/nissan-autonomous-vehicle-patents-india/.

36. http://12.000.scripts.mit.edu/mission2014/solutions/roads-in-sub-saharan-africa.

37. http://www.un.org/africarenewal/magazine/january-2009/laying-africa's-roads-prosperity.

38. Nyambé Séinya Harleston-Blake, telephone interview with the author, January 8, 2018.

39. https://www.forbes.com/sites/mfonobongnsehe/2012/10/25/poor-infrastructure-is-africas-soft-underbelly/#136a15bc632f.

40. https://www.sciencedaily.com/releases/2017/08/170821111517.htm.

41. https://www.engadget.com/2017/09/16/electric-car-built-for-africa/.

42. https://medium.com/@NissanMotor/autonomous-driving-technology-developing-at-a-rapid-pace-c72014d996b0.

43. https://www.investopedia.com/terms/m/mooreslaw.asp.

44. Pew Research Center, "Cell Phones in Africa: Communication Lifeline," April 15, 2015, http://www.pewglobal.org/2015/04/15/cell-phones-in-africa-communication-lifeline/.

45. http://www.vut-research.ac.za/do-self-driving-cars-have-a-future-in
-south-africa/.

46. http://www.itnewsafrica.com/2017/10/interview-how-autonomous
-vehicles-will-impact-africa/.

47. http://www.motherjones.com/environment/2016/01/future-parking
-self-driving-cars/.

48. http://www.reinventingparking.org/2013/10/is-30-of-traffic-actually
-searching-for.html.

49. http://www.telegraph.co.uk/motoring/news/10082461/Motorists
-spend-106-days-looking-for-parking-spots.html.

50. Graham Cookson and Bob Pishue, "The Impact of Parking Pain in the US,
UK, and Germany," *Scribd*, July 2017, https://www.scribd.com/document
/353598656/Parking-pain-INRIX-studies-parking-woes-in-major-U-S-cities.

51. https://www-03.ibm.com/press/us/en/pressrelease/35515.wss.

52. Eran Ben-Joseph, *Rethinking a Lot: The Design and Culture of Parking*
(Cambridge, MA: MIT Press, 2012), xi.

53. Donald Shoup, *The High Cost of Free Parking* (New York: Routledge,
2011), xxxi.

54. https://www.statista.com/statistics/183505/number-of-vehicles-in-the
-united-states-since-1990/.

55. https://www.lta.gov.sg/ltaacademy/doc/J14Nov_p12Rodoulis_AVcities
.pdf.

56. Andy Cohen, telephone interview with the author, January 8, 2018.

57. https://www.citylab.com/transportation/2012/08/lessons-zurichs
-parking-revolution/2874/.

58. Marcus Fairs, "Paris Deputy Mayor Questions London's Approach to Sky-
scrapers and Public Space," *Dezeen*, September 12, 2017, https://www.dezeen
.com/2017/09/12/paris-deputy-mayor-questions-london-approach-skyscrapers
-public-space/.

59. http://edition.cnn.com/travel/article/public-transportation-ridership
-increasing/index.html.

60. http://www.npr.org/2016/02/11/466178523/like-millennials-more
-older-americans-steering-away-from-driving.

61. http://mashable.com/2017/05/25/cars-replaced-by-ride-hailing-poll
/#F9N2OqiHCOqb.

62. Dan Sturges, telephone interview with the author, July 9, 2017.

THREE: TRAFFIC AND THE FUTURE OF LAND USE

1. Jon Winokur, *Return of the Portable Curmudgeon* (New York: Plume, 1995),
14.

2. https//www.nytimes.com/2018/05/23/technology/uber-finds-profits-in -leaving-tough-overseas-markets.html

3. https://tti.tamu.edu.

4. World Atlas, "Cities with the Worst Traffic in the World," https://www .worldatlas.com/articles/cities-with-the-worst-traffic-in-the-world.html.

5. World Atlas, "Cities with the Worst Traffic in the World."

6. https://www.tomtom.com/en_gb/trafficindex/.

7. http://schallerconsult.com/rideservices/unsustainable.htm#overv.

8. American Highway Users Alliance, "Unclogging America's Arteries 2015: Prescriptions for Healthier Highways," http://www.highways.org/wp-content /uploads/2015/11/unclogging-study2015-hi-res.pdf.

9. https://mobility.tamu.edu/ums/.

10. https://www.huffingtonpost.com/2013/05/16/foreclosure-crisis-lost -wealth_n_3287643.html.

11. Jamie Condliffe, "A Single Autonomous Car Has a Huge Impact on Allevi- ating Traffic," *MIT Technology Review,* May 10, 2017, https://www.technologyreview .com/s/607841/a-single-autonomous-car-has-a-huge-impact-on-alleviating-traffic/; Raphael E. Stern et al., "Dissipation of Stop-and-Go Waves via Control of Autono- mous Vehicles: Field Experiments," May 4, 2017, https://arxiv.org/abs/1705.01693.

12. For a video of the experiment, see Lauren Isaac, "Are We Ready for Driver- less Cars?" TEDxSacramento, April 14, 2016, https://www.youtube.com/watch ?v=kSmTF6KoUb8.

13. http://www.insideedition.com/headlines/19301-school-of-gridlock-how -to-drive-smarter-when-theres-traffic.

14. US Department of Transportation, Federal Highway Administration, Of- fice of Operations, "2012 Urban Congestion Trends Operations: The Key to Reli- able Travel," April 2013, https://ops.fhwa.dot.gov/publications/fhwahop13016 /index.htm.

15. https://iotbusinessnews.com/2017/02/28/90147-honda-launches -connected-car-services-european-countries/.

16. https://www.northjersey.com/story/news/bergen/leonia/2018/02/08 /traffic-ban-leonia-bad-business-shop-owners-say/316070002/.

17. http://cvp.nyc.

18. https://www.consumerreports.org/cro/magazine/2014/04/the-road-to -self-driving-cars/index.htm.

19. Alain Kornhauser, interview with the author, Princeton University, Octo- ber 25, 2017.

20. http://inrix.com/blog/2014/03/top-10-worst-traffic-cities-in-the-us-san -jose-ranks-7/.

21. https://www.itf-oecd.org/sites/default/files/docs/15cpb_self-drivingcars .pdf; https://www.itf-oecd.org/urban-mobility-system-upgrade-1.

22. Dana Hull and Carol Hymowitz, "Google Thinks Self-Driving Cars Will Be Great for Stranded Seniors," *Bloomberg BusinessWeek*, March 2, 2016, https://www.bloomberg.com/news/articles/2016-03-02/google-thinks-self-driving-cars-will-be-great-for-stranded-seniors.

23. Michael Sivak, "Has Motorization in the US Peaked?" UMTRI-2013-17, June 2013, https://deepblue.lib.umich.edu/bitstream/handle/2027.42/98098/102947.pdf?sequence=1&isAllowed=y.

24. http://www.umich.edu/~umtriswt/PDF/UMTRI-2016-4_Abstract_English.pdf.

25. Aaron Renn, interview with the author, July 23, 2017, telephone.

26. "Projections and Implications for Housing a Growing Population: Older Households 2015–2035," Harvard University, Joint Center for Housing Studies, http://www.jchs.harvard.edu/sites/jchs.harvard.edu/files/harvard_jchs_housing_growing_population_2016.pdf.

27. https://www.census.gov/newsroom/releases/archives/miscellaneous/cb12-134.html.

28. Dana E. King, Eric Matheson, Svetlana Chirina, et al., "The Status of Baby Boomers' Health in the United States: The Healthiest Generation?" *JAMA Internal Medicine* 173, no. 5 (2013): 385–386, doi:10.1001/jamainternmed.2013.2006; Linda G. Martin and Robert F. Schoeni, "Trends in Disability and Related Chronic Conditions among the Forty-and-Over Population: 1997-2010," paper presented at an interagency conference sponsored by the Administration for Community Living, US Department of Health and Human Services, National Institute on Aging at the National Institutes of Health, National Institute on Disability and Rehabilitation Research, US Department of Education, and the Interagency Committee on Disability Research and organized by the Center for Aging and Policy Studies at Syracuse University and the Michigan Center on the Demography of Aging at the University of Michigan, Ann Arbor, May 17–18, 2012; Vicki A. Freedman et al., "Trends in Late-Life Activity Limitations in the United States: An Update from Five National Surveys," *Demography* 50, no. 2 (2013): 661–671.

29. Tony Dutzik and Phineas Baxandall, "A New Direction: Our Changing Relationship with Driving and the Implications for America's Future," Frontier Group and US PIRG Education Fund, Spring 2013, http://uspirg.org/reports/usp/new-direction.

30. http://www.umich.edu/~umtriswt/PDF/UMTRI-2016-4.pdf, i.

31. https://www.greencarreports.com/news/1106395_european-millennials-will-flock-to-electric-cars-if-survey-results-hold-true; http://www.pewresearch.org/fact-tank/2015/04/16/car-bike-or-motorcycle-depends-on-where-you-live/.

32. http://www.pewresearch.org/fact-tank/2015/04/16/car-bike-or-motorcycle-depends-on-where-you-live/.

33. https://www.theguardian.com/cities/2015/apr/28/end-of-the-car-age
-how-cities-outgrew-the-automobile.

34. https://www.theatlantic.com/international/archive/2012/08/its-official
-western-europeans-have-more-cars-per-person-than-americans/261108/.

35. http://carnegieendowment.org/2012/07/23/in-search-of-global
-middle-class-new-index/cyo2.

36. "Beijing to Cut New Car Registration by Two Thirds," *China Post*, December 24, 2010, www.chinapost.com.tw/china/local-news/beijing/2010/12/24
/284851/Beijing-to.htm.

37. http://daxueconsulting.com/chinese-millennials-spending-behaviors/.

38. http://www.sohu.com/a/119108215_538479.

39. http://carnegieendowment.org/2012/07/23/in-search-of-global
-middle-class-new-index/cyo2.

40. http://www.prb.org/Publications/Articles/2012/india-2011-census.aspx.

41. https://vimeo.com/157768796; https://www.citylab.com/equity/2016
/03/keeping-millennials-in-cities-dowell-myers/473061/.

42. https://www.wsj.com/articles/more-young-adults-stay-put-in-big-cities
-1421697632.

43. http://ec.europa.eu/eurostat/statistics-explained/index.php/Statistics
_on_European_cities.

44. Julia Fiore, interview, New York City, September 30, 2017.

45. http://cityobservatory.org/are-the-young-leaving-cities/.

46. https://www.forbes.com/sites/petesaunders1/2017/01/12/where
-educated-millennials-are-moving/.

47. Kelly Blue Book Research, "What's Driving Gen Z," March 2016, https://
coxautoinc.app.box.com/v/autotrader-kbb-gen-z-research/file/56691606014.
"Gen Z finds self-driving vehicles appealing, but the reason will surprise you: more than half (54 percent) of Generation Z respondents find fully self-driving vehicles appealing. In fact, 47 percent of Generation Z respondents want most cars to drive themselves in the next 10 years. But once again, their safety concerns take the lead. When asked how the road would be impacted by autonomous vehicles, 61 percent of Gen Z teens think the roads will be safer. Forty-five percent of Gen Z teens surveyed think autonomous vehicles would ease concerns about distracted drivers, while 41 percent think these vehicles would lead to fewer accidents on the road."

48. https://www.nytimes.com/2015/03/29/jobs/make-way-for-generation
-z.html?_r=0.

49. http://www.nielsen.com/us/en/insights/news/2015/the-facts-of-life
-generational-views-about-how-we-live.html.

50. https://www.weforum.org/agenda/2015/10/why-is-tech-getting
-cheaper/.

51. https://fee.org/articles/the-iphone-in-your-pocket-is-worth-millions.

52. Nick Lucchesi, "Google's 'Full-Stack' Approach Will Make Autonomous Driving Cheap AF," Inverse Skunkworks, January 8, 2017, https://www.inverse.com/article/26102-waymo-detroit-auto-show.

53. https://blogs.unicef.org/innovation/how-mobile-phones-are-changing-the-developing-world/.

54. Daniel Schwartz, "Self-Driving Cars Confront Urban Traffic Congestion," *CBC News*, July 22, 2015, http://www.cbc.ca/news/technology/self-driving-cars-confront-urban-traffic-congestion-1.3155811.

55. https://www.statista.com/statistics/183505/number-of-vehicles-in-the-united-states-since-1990/.

56. http://carnegieendowment.org/2012/07/23/in-search-of-global-middle-class-new-index-pub-48908.

57. https://people.hofstra.edu/geotrans/eng/ch6en/conc6en/rci_population.html; https://people.hofstra.edu/geotrans/eng/ch6en/conc6en/ch6c4en.html.

58. http://eprints.whiterose.ac.uk/92861/.

59. http://documents.atlantaregional.com/taqc/2017/2017-01-12/Regional_Trails.pdf.

60. http://www.sciencedirect.com/science/article/pii/S0968090X15000042.

61. Eric Jaffe, "How Driverless Cars Could Make Traffic Dramatically Worse," *CityLab*, January 26, 2015, https://www.citylab.com/life/2015/01/how-driverless-cars-could-make-traffic-dramatically-worse/384821/.

62. Jaffe, "How Driverless Cars Could Make Traffic Dramatically Worse."

63. http://usa.streetsblog.org/2017/07/18/honolulu-city-council-wants-tighter-distraction-rules-for-pedestrians-than-for-drivers/.

64. https://systemicfailure.wordpress.com/2017/07/24/the-hysteria-over-distracted-walking/.

65. Jack L. Nasar and Derek Troyer, "Pedestrian Injuries Due to Mobile Phone Use in Public Places," *Accident Analysis and Prevention* 57 (2013): 91–95, https://pdfs.semanticscholar.org/40d4/4805cd7aa72e53355f61c07427d8a71ccff9.pdf.

66. http://www.nytimes.com/2010/01/17/technology/17distracted.html.

67. https://pdfs.semanticscholar.org/40d4/4805cd7aa72e53355f61c07427d8a71ccff9.pdf.

68. http://www.courierpostonline.com/story/opinion/columnists/2016/04/02/criminalizing-pedestrians-step-wrong-direction/82529988/.

69. https://www.6sqft.com/loop-nyc-proposes-driverless-auto-expressways-across-manhattan-and-a-13-mile-pedestrian-park/.

70. https://transitapp.com.

71. https://www.geekwire.com/2017/uber-announces-new-integration-with-transit-app-on-android-to-better-connect-with-public-transportation/.

72. http://www.businessinsider.com/ford-using-chariot-service-to-focus-on-enterprise-2018-1.

73. http://whimapp.com/fi-en/.

74. https://www.csail.mit.edu/news/study-carpooling-apps-could-reduce
-taxi-traffic-75.

FOUR: BUSINESS AND CONSUMERISM

1. Reuters, "Amazon Being Amazon: Strong Sales Gain, but Losing Money,"
Fortune, April 23, 2015, http://fortune.com/2015/04/23/amazon-being-amazon
-strong-sales-gain-but-losing-money/.

2. https://www.nakedcapitalism.com/2016/11/can-uber-ever-deliver-part
-one-understanding-ubers-bleak-operating-economics.html.

3. https://www.bloomberg.com/news/articles/2017-11-29/uber-s-third
-quarter-loss-is-said-to-widen-to-1-46-billion.

4. https://www.bloomberg.com/news/features/2015-06-23/this-is-how
-uber-takes-over-a-city.

5. http://www.jwj.org/how-much-will-uber-spend-to-get-its-way.

6. http://www.nydailynews.com/news/national/uber-spent-1-2m-lobbying
-efforts-2017-article-1.3408470.

7. Matthew Flamm, "Bradley Tusk Made $100 Million Helping Uber Con-
quer New York, and He's Not Apologizing," *Crain's New York Business*, September
12, 2017, http://www.crainsnewyork.com/article/20170912/TECHNOLOGY
/170919983/bradley-tusk-made-100-million-helping-uber-conquer-new-york
-now-hes-helping-other-startups-disrupt-the-status-quo.

8. https://www.forbes.com/sites/joannmuller/2017/11/30/gm-says-self
-driving-car-service-could-add-billions-to-its-bottom-line/#4a45d5963d28.

9. http://www.businessinsider.com/dying-shopping-malls-are-wreaking
-havoc-on-suburban-america-2017-2; https://fee.org/articles/retail-stores-are
-dying-and-we-should-let-them/; http://time.com/4865957/death-and-life
-shopping-mall/.

10. https://www.wired.com/2017/06/impact-of-autonomous-vehicles/.

11. Jenni Bergal, "No More Toll Booth Collectors," *Governing*, July 27, 2015,
http://www.governing.com/topics/mgmt/no-more-toll-booth-collectors.html.

12. Barry Devlin, "Autonomous Vehicles: The Employment Outlook (Part 3
of 4)," *TDWI*, July 13, 2016, https://upside.tdwi.org/articles/2016/07/13
/autonomous-vehicles-and-employment-pt3.aspx.

13. Grayson Brulte, "Autonomous Cars Are Coming, but Not for Your Job,"
future.com, January 10, 2017, https://futurism.com/autonomous-cars-are-coming
-but-not-for-your-job/.

14. http://www.rediff.com/business/slide-show/slide-show-1-nations
-with-the-worlds-best-infrastructure/20110912.htm#8; https://www.rikvin
.com/press-releases/singapores-infrastructure-ranked-best-in-the-world/;

http://www.nationsencyclopedia.com/economies/Asia-and-the-Pacific/Hong
-Kong-INFRASTRUCTURE-POWER-AND-COMMUNICATIONS.html.

15. http://www.businessinsider.com/the-most-high-tech-cities-in-the-world
-2017-8/#20-shenzhen-china-6.

16. http://fortune.com/2016/04/23/china-self-driving-cars/.

17. Peter Drucker, *The Concept of the Corporation* (New York: John Day,
1946), 149.

18. Bern Grush and John Niles, "Public Fleets of Autonomous Vehicles and
How to Manage Them," thinkinghighways.com, http://endofdriving.org/wp
-content/uploads/2017/03/Public-fleets-of-automated-vehicles-and-how-to
-manage-them.pdf.

19. "Reports, Trends & Statistics," American Trucking Associations, http://
www.trucking.org/News_and_Information_Reports_Industry_Data.aspx.

20. http://www.goldmansachs.com/our-thinking/public-policy/narrowing
-the-jobs-gap-report.pdf.

21. Steven Greenhouse, "Autonomous Vehicles Could Cost America 5 Million
Jobs. What Should We Do About It?" *Los Angeles Times*, September 22, 2016,
http://www.latimes.com/opinion/op-ed/la-oe-greenhouse-driverless-job-loss
-20160922-snap-story.html.

22. Greenhouse, "Autonomous Vehicles Could Cost America."

23. http://sanfrancisco.cbslocal.com/2015/01/27/how-ubers-autonomous
-cars-will-destroy-10-million-jobs-and-reshape-the-economy-by-2025-lyft
-google-zack-kanter/.

24. https://www.bls.gov/iag/tgs/iagauto.htm.

25. https://www.ibisworld.com/media/wp-content/uploads/2017/08/Tech
-Takeover-Six-Industries-Affected-by-New-Autonomous-Vehicles.pdf.

26. International Transport Forum, "Managing the Transition to Driverless
Road Freight Transport," https://www.itf-oecd.org/sites/default/files/docs
/managing-transition-driverless-road-freight-transport.pdf.

27. https://www.digitaltrends.com/cool-tech/walmart-floating-warehouse
-drone-delivery/.

28. https://www.bloomberg.com/news/articles/2017-08-18/wal-mart-s
-amazon-war-takes-to-skies-with-floating-warehouses.

29. Kevin Gillette, interview with the author, Shohola, PA, September 17,
2017.

30. http://ebusiness.mit.edu/erik/.

31. http://prospect.org/article/driverless-future.

32. http://www.maciverinstitute.com/2013/01/feds-regulations-hurt-small
-businesses-more-than-big-business/.

33. International Transport Forum, "Managing the Transition to Driverless
Road Freight Transport."

34. https://www.brookings.edu/wp-content/uploads/2016/09/driverless-cars -3-ed.pdf.

35. Vivek Krishnamurthy, telephone interview with the author, November 21, 2017.

36. https://www.theguardian.com/technology/2016/jun/20/britain-leads -europe-technology-unicorns.

37. http://www.iotevolutionworld.com/autonomous-vehicles/articles/432332 -how-europe-help-move-us-autonomous-car-industry.htm.

38. https://techcrunch.com/2016/07/25/audi-setting-up-a-subsidiary -dedicated-to-self-driving-car-tech/.

39. Viknesh Vijayenthiran, "Volvo, Autoliv Establish Zenuity Joint Venture Dedicated to Self-Driving Cars," *MotorAuthority*, January 3, 2017, https://www .motorauthority.com/news/1108100_volvo-autoliv-establish-zenuity-joint-venture -dedicated-to-self-driving-cars.

40. http://www.autonews.com/article/20170627/COPY01/306289999 /volvo-autoliv-deepen-self-driving-ties-with-nvidia.

41. https://www.bloomberg.com/news/articles/2016-06-29/bmw-is-said -to-team-up-with-intel-mobileye-on-self-driving-cars.

42. http://www.driverlesstransportation.com/bosch-getting-autonomous -done-12893.

43. https://www.reuters.com/article/us-continental-driverless/continental-to -invest-in-driverless-mobility-with-easymile-stake-idUSKBN19P1HS.

44. http://www.hindustantimes.com/opinion/the-future-of-jobs-in-india /story-k5IvU9uSGyjlbSybqodzFL.html.

45. Venkat Sumantran, PhD, telephone interview with the author, November 20, 2017.

46. https://spaces.hightail.com/receive/SdhSlwwnDH/fi-4f1a5caa-6300 -440a-8f83-217fde46ef09/fv-24bded86-7040-4521-a652-90cce8d6a768 /GiveAShift_MotorcycleSalesInTheSlowLane_Ebert.pdf.

47. http://www.motorcycle.com/features/featuresgm-cruise-autonomous -car-and-motorcycle-collide-in-san-francisco-html.html.

48. http://www.motorcycle.com/mini-features/yamaha-motorcycle-sales -down-in-u-s-but-up-worldwide.html.

49. http://www.pantagraph.com/business/investment/markets-and-stocks /motorcycle-statistics-that-ll-floor-you/article_77e14488-0518-52a9-86a7 -0ab063e7fefa.html.

50. https://www.businesswire.com/news/home/20160628005102/en /Increasing-Focus-Consumers-Luxury-Ultra-Luxury-Motorcycles-Drive.

51. Shivali Best, "Forget Driverless Cars, Now There's a Riderless Motorcycle," *Daily Mail*, September 13, 2016.

52. http://www.foxnews.com/auto/2018/01/11/autonomous-honda-atv-could-be-workhorse-future.html.

53. Seth Birnbaum, "The Insurance Impact of Self-Driving Cars and Shared Mobility," *TechCrunch*, November 8, 2016, https://techcrunch.com/2016/11/08/the-insurance-impact-of-self-driving-cars-and-shared-mobility/.

54. http://fortune.com/2015/08/03/driverless-cars-insurance/.

55. https://www.consumerreports.org/cro/magazine/2014/04/the-road-to-self-driving-cars/index.htm.

56. http://www.iihs.org.

57. https://www.theguardian.com/business/2016/may/03/driverless-cars-dent-motor-insurers-volvo.

58. Brian Fung, "This Company Just Solved One of the Thorniest Problems for Driverless Cars," *Washington Post*, June 9, 2016, https://www.washingtonpost.com/news/the-switch/wp/2016/06/09/this-company-just-solved-the-biggest-policy-problem-for-driverless-cars/?utm_term=.eb61d5275ae0.

59. https://www.bjs.gov/index.cfm?ty=tp&tid=451.

60. Marcus Fairs, "Driverless Cars Could Spell the End for Domestic Flights, Says Audi Strategist," *Dezeen*, November 25, 2015, https://www.dezeen.com/2015/11/25/self-driving-driverless-cars-disrupt-airline-hotel-industries-sleeping-interview-audi-senior-strategist-sven-schuwirth/.

61. https://www.nbcmiami.com/news/weird/73-Year-Old-Florida-Man-Sues-Bar-For-Giving-Him--103815024.html.

62. https://www.reuters.com/article/us-usa-autos-autonomous/self-driving-cars-could-generate-billions-in-revenue-u-s-study-idUSKBN0M10UF20150305.

63. https://www.insurancejournal.com/news/national/2016/04/26/406449.htm.

64. Chunka Mui, "Driverless Taxis Might Replace Private Cars and Public Transit," *Forbes*, April 17, 2014, https://www.forbes.com/sites/chunkamui/2014/04/17/mit-and-stanford-researchers-show-robotaxis-could-replace-private-cars-and-public-transit/2/#63c3269e2315.

65. Joseph White and Paul Ingrassia, "Who Wins, Loses in a Driverless Car Economy?" *Insurance Journal*, April 26, 2016, https://www.insurancejournal.com/news/national/2016/04/26/406449.htm.

66. https://legalrideshare.com/lr-chicago-tribune/.

67. http://money.cnn.com/2018/03/31/technology/tesla-model-x-crash-autopilot/index.html.

68. https://www.wisbar.org/NewsPublications/InsideTrack/Pages/Article.aspx?Volume=8&Issue=23&ArticleID=25226.

69. Brulte, "Autonomous Cars Are Coming."

70. Tony Seba and James Arbib, "Are We Ready for the End of Individual Car Ownership?" *San Francisco Chronicle*, July 10, 2017, http://www.sfchronicle .com/opinion/openforum/article/Are-we-ready-for-the-end-of-individual-car -11278535.php.

71. Barry Devlin, "Autonomous Vehicles: Impact on Business and Society (Part 4 of 4)," https://tdwi.org/articles/2016/07/14/autonomous-vehicles -business-society-impact-pt4.aspx.

72. Greenhouse, "Autonomous Vehicles Could Cost America."

73. Aarian Marshall, "Robocars Could Add $7 Trillion to the Global Economy," *Wired*, June 3, 2017, https://www.wired.com/2017/06/impact-of -autonomous-vehicles/.

74. Devlin, "Autonomous Vehicles: Impact on Business and Society (Part 4 of 4)."

75. https://www.wired.com/2016/06/chinas-plan-first-country-self -driving-cars/.

76. "China's Roadmap to Self-Driving Cars," *Reuters*, April 23, 2016; "Officials Want to Open Way for Autonomous Driving," *China Daily*, June 22, 2016.

77. Julien Girault, "Chinese Firms Accelerate in Race toward Driverless Future," *Phys.org*, April 23, 2016.

78. https//qz.com/1250731/china-just-made-it-easier-for-self-driving-to-take -place-on-any-road-in-the-country.

79. https://www.techinasia.com/talk/china-win-self-driving; see also http:// energyfuse.org/behind-closed-doors-china-grapples-autonomous-vehicle-policy/.

80. "Baidu Enters the Global Race for Driverless Car Domination," *Bloomberg News*, January 24, 2016, https://www.bloomberg.com/news/articles/2016-01-24 /baidu-enters-the-global-race-to-dominate-era-of-driverless-cars.

81. http://www.fortune.com/2016/06/07/autonomous-car-sales-ihs; "Baidu Enters the Global Race for Driverless Car Domination," *Bloomberg News*, January 24, 2016.

82. https://www.msn.com/en-sg/money/technology/chinas-supercomputers -race-past-us-to-world-dominance/ar-BBEWGVC; https://www.msn.com/en -us/news/technology/chinas-supercomputers-race-past-us-to-world-dominance /ar-BBEXhPS?OCID=ansmsnnews11.

83. http://www.gov.cn/zhengce/content/2017-07/20/content_5211996.htm; http://english.gov.cn/state_council/ministries/2016/05/23/content _281475355720632.htm.

84. http://fticommunications.com/2017/06/global-race-autonomous -vehicles-views-united-states-europe-asia/.

85. "China's Roadmap to Self-Driving Cars," *Reuters*, April 23, 2016.

86. https://www.brookings.edu/wp-content/uploads/2016/09/driverless -cars-3-ed.pdf.

87. Darrell M. West, "Moving Forward: Self-Driving Vehicles in China, Europe, Japan, Korea, and the United States," *Center for Technology Innovation at Brookings* (September 2016): 14.

88. Girault, "Chinese Firms Accelerate in Race toward Driverless Future."

89. https://media.economist.com/news/special-report/21737418-driverless-vehicles-will-change-world-just-cars-did-them-what-went-wrong.

90. Jennifer Lo, "Didi Casts Doubt on China Driverless Car Outlook," *Nikkei Asian Review*, April 8, 2016, https://asia.nikkei.com/Business/AC/Didi-casts-doubt-on-China-driverless-car-outlook.

91. http://www.telegraph.co.uk/technology/news/12044117/BMW-and-Baidu-partner-to-build-driverless-cars-in-China.html.

92. http://www.ecvinternational.com/2018ChinaVehicle/.

93. https://www.eia.gov.

94. Austin Brown et al., "An Analysis of Possible Energy Impacts of Automated Vehicles," in *Road Vehicle Automation: Lecture Notes in Mobility*, ed. Gereon Meyer and Sven Beiker (Cham, Switzerland: Springer, 2014), 137–153.

95. https://vtnews.vt.edu/articles/2013/02/022613-vtti-ecocruisecontrol.html.

96. https://www.energy.gov/management/timeline-events-2016.

97. https://www.bna.com/energy-department-halts-n57982087155/.

98. James Osborne, "Driverless Cars May Drive Down Oil Demand," *Houston Chronicle*, May 27, 2016, http://www.houstonchronicle.com/business/article/Driverless-cars-may-drive-down-oil-demand-7950658.php.

99. Zack Kanter, "How Uber's Autonomous Cars Will Destroy 10 Million Jobs and Reshape the Economy by 2015," *CBS SFBayArea*, January 27, 2015, http://sanfrancisco.cbslocal.com/2015/01/27/how-ubers-autonomous-cars-will-destroy-10-million-jobs-and-reshape-the-economy-by-2025-lyft-google-zack-kanter/.

100. http://www.governing.com/gov-data/gov-how-autonomous-vehicles-could-effect-city-budgets.html.

101. Jeff Mays, "New York City Collects Record $1.9 Billion in Fines and Fees," *DNAInfo*, March 24, 2016, https://www.dnainfo.com/new-york/20160324/civic-center/new-york-city-collects-record-19-billion-fines-fees.

102. Office of the New York City Comptroller, Bureau of Budget, "Fines and Fees in the New York City Budget," *NYC Budget Brief*, March 2016, https://www.scribd.com/doc/305864974/New-York-City-Fines-and-Fees#download&from_embed.

103. https://www.gemut.com/car-rental-europe-basics/3779-driving-in-europe-traffic-tickets.html.

104. https://www.enotrans.org/?s=VMT+fee.

105. Mike Maciag, "How Driverless Cars Could Be a Big Problem for Cities," *Governing*, August 2017, http://www.governing.com/topics/finance/gov-cities-traffic-parking-revenue-driverless-cars.html.

106. https://nhts.ornl.gov.

107. https://www.cbsnews.com/news/strangers-buy-car-for-20-year-old-who-walks-3-miles-to-work-in-texas-heat/.

108. https://www.autotrader.com/car-shopping/hidden-costs-of-buying-a-used-car-maintenance-207358.

109. Barbara Gray, telephone interview with the author, August 21, 2017.

110. Kelly J. Clifton et al., "Consumer Behavior and Travel Mode Choices," draft final report for the Oregon Transportation Research and Education Consortium, November 2012, http://kellyjclifton.com/Research/EconImpactsofBicycling/OTRECReport-ConsBehavTravelChoices_Nov2012.pdf.

111. Emily Badger, "Cyclists and Pedestrians Can End Up Spending More Each Month Than Drivers," *CityLab*, December 5, 2012, https://www.citylab.com/transportation/2012/12/cyclists-and-pedestrians-can-end-spending-more-each-month-drivers/4066/.

112. "Preparing a Nation for Autonomous Vehicles: Opportunities, Barriers, and Policy Recommendations," Eno Center for Transportation, October 2013, https://www.enotrans.org/wp-content/uploads/AV-paper.pdf.

FIVE: SAVING LIVES: ARE AVs GOOD FOR OUR HEALTH AND SAFETY?

1. http://www.telegraph.co.uk/technology/2016/10/20/youre-killing-people-elon-musk-attacks-critics-of-self-driving-c/.

2. NHTSA, "2016 Fatal Motor Vehicle Crashes: Overview."

3. Richard Retting, telephone interview with the author, September 29, 2017.

4. https://www.cdc.gov/motorvehiclesafety/impaired_driving/impaired-drv_factsheet.html.

5. https://www.nytimes.com/2018/03/19/technology/uber-driverless-fatality.html.

6. https://www.caranddriver.com/news/after-crash-arizona-governor-suspends-uber-self-driving-vehicle-testing.

7. http://www.iihs.org/iihs/topics/t/general-statistics/fatalityfacts/overview-of-fatality-facts.

8. http://www.iihs.org/iihs/topics/t/general-statistics/fatalityfacts/overview-of-fatality-facts.

9. National Transportation Safety Board, *Reducing Speeding-Related Crashes Involving Passenger Vehicles*, NTSB Safety Study 17/01, PB2017-102341, July 25, 2017, https://www.ntsb.gov/safety/safety-studies/Documents/SS1701.pdf; see also "'Self-Drive' Bill Passes House by Unanimous Vote," *Urban Transportation*

Monitor 31, no. 6 (August 31, 2017), http://files.constantcontact.com/b56bd94e001/e65ed192-0c6c-4aa3-9497-b049d37c40a5.pdf.

10. https://www.enotrans.org/wp-content/uploads/AV-paper.pdf?x43122.

11. http://www.mckinsey.com/industries/automotive-and-assembly/our-insights/ten-ways-autonomous-driving-could-redefine-the-automotive-world.

12. Alissa Walker, "The Case against Sidewalks," *Curbed*, February 7, 2018, https://www.curbed.com/2018/2/7/16980682/city-sidewalk-repair-future-walking-neighborhood.

13. https://www.nhtsa.gov/press-releases/new-nhtsa-study-shows-motor-vehicle-crashes-have-871-billion-economic-and-societal; see also https://crashstats.nhtsa.dot.gov/Api/Public/ViewPublication/812013.

14. http://repository.cmu.edu/cgi/viewcontent.cgi?article=1095&context=cee.

15. http://www.iihs.org/frontend/iihs/documents/masterfiledocs.ashx?id=2142.

16. https://www.cdc.gov/motorvehiclesafety/pedestrian_safety/index.html.

17. https://www.npr.org/sections/thetwo-way/2016/03/17/470809148/automatic-braking-systems-to-become-standard-on-most-u-s-vehicles.

18. https://www.consumerreports.org/car-safety/automatic-emergency-braking-availability-expands-with-2017-cars/.

19. https://nacto.org/2016/06/23/nacto-releases-policy-recommendations-for-automated-vehicles/; https://nacto.org/member-cities/.

20. http://hal.pratt.duke.edu/sites/hal.pratt.duke.edu/files/u10/Clamann_etal_TRB2016.pdf.

21. https://www1.toronto.ca/City%20Of%20Toronto/Transportation%20Services/TS%20Publications/Reports/Driving%20Changes%20(Ticoll%202015).pdf.

22. https://www.transportation.gov/AV/federal-automated-vehicles-policy-september-2016/.

23. Adam Millard-Ball, "Pedestrians, Autonomous Vehicles, and Cities," *Journal of Planning Education and Research* 38, no. 1 (2018), http://journals.sagepub.com/doi/full/10.1177/0739456X16675674.

24. Rodney Brooks, "Unexpected Consequences of Self-Driving Cars," January 12, 2017, http://rodneybrooks.com/unexpected-consequences-of-self-driving-cars/.

25. Jason Levine, telephone interview with the author, September 5, 2017.

26. Richard Retting, telephone interview with the author, September 29, 2017.

27. Alain Kornhauser, telephone interview with the author, October 3, 2017.

28. Richard Retting, telephone interview with the author, September 29, 2017.

29. https://mobilitylab.org/2017/09/05/5-ways-cities-counties-can-make-sure-autonomous-vehicles-bikes-mix-safely/.

30. https://www.cnbc.com/2016/01/08/driverless-cars-confused-by-cyclists
.html.

31. https://www.nytimes.com/2016/07/02/business/joshua-brown-technology
-enthusiast-tested-the-limits-of-his-tesla.html.

32. https://www.nytimes.com/2017/01/19/business/tesla-model-s-autopilot
-fatal-crash.html?_r=0.

33. https://www.tesla.com/sites/default/files/model_s_owners_manual
_north_america_en_us.pdf.

34. http://www.freep.com/story/money/cars/2016/07/01/tesla-driver
-harry-potter-crash/86596856/.

35. https://www.apta.com/mediacenter/pressreleases/Documents/Fact
%20Sheet%20The%20Hidden%20Traffic%20Safety%20Solution.pdf.

36. American Public Transportation Association, "The Hidden Traffic Safety
Solution: Public Transportation," September 2016, http://www.apta.com
/resources/reportsandpublications/Documents/APTA-Hidden-Traffic
-Safety-Solution-Public-Transportation.pdf.

37. http://apps.dmv.ca.gov/about/profile/rd/r_d_report/Section_6/S6-238
.pdf.

38. https://www.edmunds.com/car-technology/should-i-buy-a-cars-factory
-navigation-system.html.

39. https://www.scientificamerican.com/article/when-it-comes-to-safety
-autonomous-cars-are-still-teen-drivers1/.

40. https://www.transportation.gov/AV/federal-automated-vehicles-policy
-september-2016.

41. https://www.citylab.com/transportation/2016/09/the-us-dot-officially
-puts-a-car-in-the-self-driving-race/500744/.

42. NHTSA, "Automated Driving Systems 2.0: A Vision for Safety," DOT
HS 812 442, US Department of Transportation, September 2017, https://www
.nhtsa.gov/sites/nhtsa.dot.gov/files/documents/13069a-ads2.0_090617_v9a
_tag.pdf.

43. Laura Bliss, "Trump's $1 Trillion Infrastructure Plan Has New Reason for
Skepticism," *CityLab*, July 27, 2017, https://www.citylab.com/transportation
/2017/07/trumps-1-trillion-infrastructure-plan-has-new-reason-for-concern
/534957/.

44. Johana Bhuiyan, US Transportation Secretary Elaine Chao Has Introduced a New Set of Voluntary Guidance for Self-Driving Cars," *Recode*, September 12, 2017, https://www.recode.net/2017/9/12/16296232/self-driving
-regulation-guidance-elaine-chao-department-of-transportation.

45. Bhuiyan, "US Transportation Secretary Elaine Chao Has Introduced."

46. https://www.insurancejournal.com/news/national/2017/07/31/459421.htm.

47. Ashley Halsey, "Senate Committee Approves Driverless Car Bill," *Washington Post*, October 4, 2017, https://www.washingtonpost.com/local/trafficand commuting/senate-committee-approves-driverless-car-bill/2017/10/04/ba10c5ac -a908-11e7-850e-2bdd1236be5d_story.html?utm_term=.9d9ff7fde2db. For a staff working draft of the bill, see https://cei.org/sites/default/files/AV%20START %20Act%20staff%20working%20draft.pdf.

48. http://fticommunications.com/2017/06/global-race-autonomous -vehicles-views-united-states-europe-asia/.

49. http://safecarnews.com/un-amends-vienna-convention-on-road-traffic -to-allow-driverless-cars/.

50. http://www.unece.org/fileadmin/DAM/trans/doc/2014/wp1/ECE -TRANS-WP1-145e.pdf.

51. https://www.popsci.com/cars/article/2012-08/europe-requires -autonomous-braking-technology-all-commercial-vehicles-sold-next-year/.

52. https://www.wired.com/2012/08/eu-autonomous-braking-law/.

53. http://self-driving-future.com/legislation/europe/.

54. https://www.brookings.edu/wp-content/uploads/2016/09/driverless -cars-3-ed.pdf.

55. Oliver Yaros, "Connected and Autonomous Vehicles in Europe: The Challenges with Using the Data They Generate," https://www.mayerbrown.com /files/Publication/d9fa82f6-0cd1-4fdb-beb7-8472ce6e66b3/Presentation /PublicationAttachment/47eb74d6-8e19-4a42-95b4-855d0cf052ab/UPDATE _Connected_and_Autonomous_Vehicles_in_Europe.pdf.

56. https://www.law360.com/articles/9c07/autonomous-vehicles-and -european-data-protection-part-2; https://encryption.eset.com/us/?CMP=knc -genit-Bing-G_S-US-NB-B-GDPR_B&bkw=%2Bgdpr&gcr=81226429116156 &bcp302110246&bag=1299622776191412&utm_source=bing&utm_medium =cpc&utm_campaign=us_b2b_search_nb_gdpr_a_gen_bmm&utm_term= %2Bgdpr&utm_content=gdpr&gclid=CPvcj6eEwdcCFQSMswodRhkDEA &gclsrc=ds.

57. http://www.nytimes.com/2010/05/16/technology/16google.html.

58. http://www.nytimes.com/2013/04/23/technology/germany-fines-google -over-data-collection.html.

59. Claire Cain Miller and Kevin J. O'Brien, "Germany's Complicated Relationship with Google Street View," *New York Times*, April 23, 2013, https://bits .blogs.nytimes.com/2013/04/23/germanys-complicated-relationship-with-google -street-view/.

60. Miller and Kevin O'Brien, "Germany's Complicated Relationship with Google Street View."

61. https://www.gdpr.associates/what-is-gdpr/.

62. https://winbuzzer.com/2017/03/17/facebook-google-twitter-face-eu
-fines-privacy-concerns-xcxwbn/.

63. https://www.wired.com/story/google-big-eu-fine/.

64. Cade Metz, "Artificial Intelligence Is Setting Up the Internet for a Huge
Clash with Europe," *Wired*, July 11, 2016.

65. Oliver Yaros, telephone interview with the author, November 15, 2017.

66. West, "Moving Forward," 18.

67. Oliver Yaros, telephone interview with the author, November 15, 2017.

68. https://www.express.co.uk/news/world/683224/END-OF-THE-EU
-Germany-France-Austria-Hungary-Finland-Netherlands-Europe-Brexit; https://
www.armstrongeconomics.com/international-news/europes-current-economy
/five-more-countries-want-referendums-to-exit-eu/.

69. http://newsroom.aaa.com/2017/03/americans-feel-unsafe-sharing-road
-fully-self-driving-cars/.

70. Patrick Olsen, "Doubts Grow over Fully Autonomous Car Tech, Study
Finds," *Consumer Reports*, May 25, 2017, https://www.consumerreports.org
/autonomous-driving/doubts-grow-over-fully-autonomous-car-tech/.

71. Alain Kornhauser, telephone interview with the author, October 3, 2017.

72. http://t4america.org/2017/09/12/senate-automated-vehicles-legislation
-jeopardize-safety-millions-leave-cities-states-side-road/.

73. http://www.ncsl.org/research/transportation/autonomous-vehicles-self
-driving-vehicles-enacted-legislation.aspt.

74. https://www.recode.net/2016/12/9/13890080/michigan-dot-self-driving
-cars-laws-automakers.

75. https://www.wired.com/2017/03/californias-finally-ready-truly-driverless
-cars/.

76. https://www.washingtonpost.com/local/trafficandcommuting/california
-launches-system-allowing-driverless-cars-to-ditch-their-backup-drivers/2018
/04/02/3217878c-36a5-11e8-8fd2-49fe3c675a89_story.html?utm_term
=.5fc4a0d6a0da.

77. Ryan Randazzo, "Arizona Getting Ahead of Autonomous Vehicle Industry by Stepping Aside," *The Republic*, June 23, 2017, https://www.azcentral.com/
story/money/business/tech/2017/06/23/arizona-getting-ahead-autonomous-ve-
hicle-industry-stepping-aside-waymo-uber-intel-chevy-bolt/405436001/."

78. https://www.rand.org/pubs/research_reports/RR1478.html.

79. Jeremy Hsu, "When It Comes to Safety, Autonomous Cars Are Still 'Teen
Drivers,'" *Scientific American*, January 18, 2018, https://www.scientificamerican
.com/article/when-it-comes-to-safety-autonomous-cars-are-still-teen-drivers1/.

80. Hsu, "When It Comes to Safety."

81. https://www.anwb.nl/binaries/content/assets/anwb/pdf/over-anwb
/persdienst/rapport_inventarisatie_zelfrijdende_auto.pdf.

82. https://www.busworld.org/articles/detail/2691/autonomous-buses
-testing-in-greece-and-switzerland; https://cleantechnica.com/2015/10/12
/autonomous-buses-being-tested-in-greek-city-of-trikala/.

83. https://www.nrso.ntua.gr/investigating-the-acceptance-of-autonomous
-vehicles-by-greek-drivers-2017/.

84. https://www.gov.uk/government/uploads/system/uploads/attachment
_data/file/401562/pathway-driverless-cars-summary.pdf; https://www.gov.uk
/government/uploads/system/uploads/attachment_data/file/446316/pathway
-driverless-cars.pdf.

85. http://self-driving-future.com/legislation/europe/.

86. https://sputniknews.com/science/201711281059504905-sweden
-driverless-cars/; http://www.unece.org/fileadmin/DAM/trans/doc/2014
/wp1/Autonomous_driving_eng_short.pdf.

87. http://www.themalaymailonline.com/drive/article/european-countries
-agree-to-cooperate-on-connected-and-autonomous-cars#EeWIy1krPPrv
5304.99.

88. http://www.greencarcongress.com/2016/04/20160415-amsterdam.html.

89. https://voorlichting.rijksoverheid.nl/documenten/rapporten/2016/04/29
/declaration-of-amsterdam-cooperation-in-the-field-of-connected-and-automated
-driving.

90. "European Countries Agree to Cooperate on Connected and Autonomous
Cars," *The Star*, April 18, 2016, https://www.thestar.com.my/tech/tech-news/2016
/04/18/european-countries-agree-to-cooperate-on-connected-and-autonomous
-cars/.

91. https://publications.parliament.uk/pa/bills/cbill/2016-2017/0143/cbill
_2016-20170143_en_2.htm.

92. https://www.out-law.com/en/articles/2017/february/new-uk-laws
-address-driverless-cars-insurance-and-liability/.

93. Jason Levine, telephone interview with the author, September 5, 2017;
see also Hiroko Tabuchi, "Automakers Still Selling Cars with Defective Takata
Airbags," *New York Times*, June 1, 2016, https://www.nytimes.com/2016/06
/02/business/automakers-still-selling-cars-with-riskiest-takata-airbags.html?
_r=0.

94. https://www.theatlantic.com/technology/archive/2013/10/the-ethics-of
-autonomous-cars/280360/.

95. http://www.cnn.com/2016/07/15/europe/nice-france-truck/index.html.

96. https://www.washingtonpost.com/news/checkpoint/wp/2016/07/15
/how-the-nice-truck-attack-managed-to-kill-so-many-people-so-quickly/?utm
_term=.072dec4c67c0.

97. https://www.nytimes.com/2017/10/31/nyregion/sayfullo-saipov
-manhattan-truck-attack.html?_r=0.

98. https://www.start.umd.edu/gtd/.

99. https://www.counterextremism.com/roundup/eye-extremism-november-8-0.

100. https://www.pressherald.com/2015/07/22/in-rush-to-add-wireless-features-automakers-leaving-cars-open-to-hackers/.

101. https://www.usatoday.com/story/tech/2017/07/28/chinese-group-hacks-tesla-second-year-row/518430001/f.

102. https://www.usatoday.com/story/tech/2017/07/28/chinese-group-hacks-tesla-second-year-row/518430001/.

103. Ivan Evtimov, et al., "Robust Physical-World Attacks on Deep Learning Models," July 27, 2017, https://arxiv.org/abs/1707.08945.

104. http://blog.caranddriver.com/researchers-find-a-malicious-way-to-meddle-with-autonomous-cars/.

105. http://www.computerscijournal.org/vol8no3/context-driving-speed-limit-alert-synchronized-monitoring-system/.

106. Mark Harris, "FBI Warns Driverless Cars Could Be Used as 'Lethal Weapons,'" *The Guardian*, July 16, 2014, https://www.theguardian.com/technology/2014/jul/16/google-fbi-driverless-cars-leathal-weapons-autonomous.

107. Vivek Krishnamurthy, telephone interview with the author, November 21, 2017.

108. https://www.walkscore.com/walkable-neighborhoods.shtml.

109. http://www.reuters.com/article/us-heart-noise-risk/quieting-down-might-save-billions-in-heart-disease-costs-idUSKBN0OL29B20150605?feedType=RSS&feedName=healthNews.

110. https://cleantechnica.com/2016/06/05/will-electric-cars-make-traffic-quieter-yes-no/.

111. https://cleantechnica.com/2016/06/05/will-electric-cars-make-traffic-quieter-yes-no/.

112. "Google Self-Driving Car Project Monthly Report," May 2016, https://static.googleusercontent.com/media/www.google.com/en//selfdrivingcar/files/reports/report-0516.pdf.

113. Will Troppe, "Driverless Cars: Good for the Planet?" *Christian Science Monitor*, September 20, 2014, https://www.csmonitor.com/Environment/Energy-Voices/2014/0910/Driverless-cars-Good-for-the-planet.

SIX: MAKERS, DRIVERS, PASSENGERS, AND PEDESTRIANS: HARD QUESTIONS AND MORAL DILEMMAS

1. Eric McLuhan and Frank Zingrone, eds., *The Essential McLuhan* (New York: Basic Books, 1995), 217.

2. http://www.nytimes.com/1973/12/17/archives/section-of-west-side-highway-closed-to-traffic-indefinitely.html.

3. https://plato.stanford.edu/entries/double-effect/.

4. http://www.nytimes.com/2016/11/06/opinion/sunday/whose-life-should -your-car-save.html?smprod=nytcore-ipad&smid=nytcore-ipad-share.

5. https://www.dezeen.com/2016/02/12/google-self-driving-car-artficial -intelligence-system-recognised-as-driver-usa/.

6. https://isearch.nhtsa.gov/files/Google%20--%20compiled%20response %20to%2012%20Nov%20%2015%20interp%20request%20--%204%20Feb %2016%20final.htm.

7. https://www.technologyreview.com/s/539731/how-to-help-self-driving -cars-make-ethical-decisions/.

8. Jean-Francois Bonnefon, Azim Shariff, and Iyad Rahwan, "The Social Dilemma of Autonomous Vehicles," *Science* 352, no. 6293 (June 24, 2016): 1573–1576.

9. https://www.gsb.stanford.edu/insights/exploring-ethics-behind-self -driving-cars.

10. Joel Achenbach, "Driverless Cars Are Colliding with the Creepy Trolley Problem, *Washington Post*, December 29, 2015, https://www.washingtonpost .com/news/innovations/wp/2015/12/29/will-self-driving-cars-ever-solve-the -famous-and-creepy-trolley-problem/.

11. National Association of City Transportation Officials, "Vehicle Stopping Distance and Time," https://nacto.org/docs/usdg/vehicle_stopping_distance_and _time_upenn.pdf. The published road braking performance tests for virtually all vehicles currently in production indicate that stopping distances at 60 miles per hour are typically 120 to 140 feet, slightly less than half of the projected safety distances.

12. Pete Pachal, "Elon Musk Accuses Press of 'Killing People' for Criticism of Self-Driving Cars," *Mashable*, October 19, 2016, http://mashable.com/2016/10 /19/elon-musk-youre-killing-people/#R7VNOpa1nEqi.

13. https://www.verdenews.com/news/2017/aug/31/studies-say-roundabouts -are-safer-faster-cost-effe/.

14. "2009 Taconic State Parkway Crash," *Wikipedia*, last edited on February 4, 2018, https://en.wikipedia.org/wiki/2009_Taconic_State_Parkway_crash.

15. Selim Algar, "Wrong-Way Family Feud," *New York Post*, July 26, 2011, http://nypost.com/2011/07/26/wrong-way-family-feud/.

16. Janet L. Kaminski Leduc, "Wrong-Way Driving Countermeasures," Re- search Report 2008-R-0491, Connecticut General Assembly, Office of Legislative Research, September 22, 2008, https://www.cga.ct.gov/2008/rpt/2008-R-0491. htm; Mahdi Pour-Rouholamin, Huaguo Zhou, Jeffrey Shaw, and Priscilla Tobias, "Current Practices of Safety Countermeasures for Wrong-Way Driving Crashes," paper presented at the 94th annual meeting of the Transportation Research Board, Washington, DC, January 2015, https://www.researchgate.net/publication /271207228; "Prevention of Wrong-Way Accidents on Freeways," California

Department of Transportation, Division of Traffic Operations, June 1989, http://
www.ce.siue.edu/faculty/hzhou/ww/PREVENTION-OF-WRONGWAY
-ACCIDENTS-ON-FREEWAYS.pdf.

17. https://www.economist.com/blogs/economist-explains/2014/02
/economist-explains-16.

18. http://www.ghsa.org/resources/spotlight-peds17.

19. https://centerforactivedesign.org/visionzero.

20. Vision Zero, "Safety at Every Turn," http://www.visionzeroinitiative.com.

21. City of New York and Mayor Bill de Blasio, "Vision Zero: Action Plan
2014," http://www.nyc.gov/html/visionzero/pdf/nyc-vision-zero-action-plan.pdf.

22. http://www.city-data.com/city/Provo-Utah.html.

23. https://www.nytimes.com/2017/06/22/automobiles/wheels/driverless
-cars-big-data-volkswagen-bmw.html?_r=0.

24. https://www.forbes.com/sites/samabuelsamid/2017/10/27/argo-ai-and
-ford-double-down-on-lidar-acquire-princeton-lightwave/#35b807583410.

25. Jack Ewing, "BMW and Volkswagen Try to Beat Apple and Google at Their
Own Game," *New York Times*, June 22, 2017, https://www.nytimes.com/2017
/06/22/automobiles/wheels/driverless-cars-big-data-volkswagen-bmw.html.

26. https://www.nytimes.com/2017/06/22/automobiles/wheels/driverless
-cars-big-data-volkswagen-bmw.html.

27. https://www.gartner.com/newsroom/id/2970017.

28. https://www.computerworld.com/article/3083426/car-tech/heres-how
-ai-is-about-to-make-your-car-really-smart.html.

29. http://news.ihsmarkit.com/press-release/artificial-intelligence-systems
-autonomous-driving-rise-ihs-says.

30. http://www.businessinsider.com/amazon-alexa-coming-to-ford-cars
-2017-1.

31. Neil M. Richards, "The Dangers of Surveillance," *Harvard Law Review*,
May 20, 2013, https://harvardlawreview.org/2013/05/the-dangers-of
-surveillance/.

32. http://www.dailymail.co.uk/sciencetech/article-1352474/QinetiQ-Cars
-wont-start-youre-drunk-smell-alcohol-breath.html#ixzz51AiD7uRE.

33. https://www.nytimes.com/2017/06/05/world/europe/london-attack
-uk-election.html?_r=0.

34. https://www.usenix.org/system/files/conference/soups2017/soups2017
-bloom.pdf.

35. https://www.usenix.org/system/files/conference/soups2017/soups2017
-bloom.pdf.

36. http://valleywag.gawker.com/uber-used-private-location-data-for-party
-amusement-1640820384.

37. https://harvardlawreview.org/2013/05/the-dangers-of-surveillance/.

38. Richards, "The Dangers of Surveillance."

39. http://www.thecarconnection.com/news/1112329_german-self-driving -car-ethics-humans-above-animals.

40. Dan Sturges, telephone interview with the author, June 19, 2017.

41. Robert Kirkman, "Freedom and Choice: Behavior and Action, Part 2," *The Ethics of Metropolitan Growth* (blog), April 21, 2010, http://www.metroethics .com/2010/04/choice-behavior-and-action.html.

42. Malia Wollan, "The End of Roadkill," in "Full Tilt: When 100% of Cars Are Autonomous" (special issue), *New York Times Magazine*, November 8, 2017, https://www.nytimes.com/interactive/2017/11/08/magazine/tech-design -autonomous-future-cars-100-percent-augmented-reality-policing.html.

43. http://junkee.com/self-driving-cars-kangaroos/110880.

44. Adam Vacarro, "Biggest Challenge for Self-Driving Cars in Boston? Sea Gulls," *Boston Globe*, February 6, 2017, https://www.bostonglobe.com/business /2017/02/06/the-biggest-challenge-for-self-driving-cars-boston-sea-gulls /N5UHSUIyXlar4r60TXupdN/story.html.

45. Wollan, "The End of Roadkill."

46. https://spectrum.ieee.org/cars-that-think/at-work/education/vw -scandal-shocking-but-not-surprising-ethicists-say.

47. https://www.researchgate.net/publication/277817334_Professional _Ethics_of_Software_Engineers_An_Ethical_Framework.

48. Prachi Patel, "Engineers, Ethics, and the Volkswagen Scandal," *IEEE Spectrum*, September 25, 2015, https://spectrum.ieee.org/cars-that-think/at-work /education/vw-scandal-shocking-but-not-surprising-ethicists-say.

49. https://www.nspe.org/resources/pe-magazine/may-2015/designing -future.

50. http://www.consumerwatchdog.org/news-story/car-safety-features-stuck -slow-lane.

51. http://www.schallerconsult.com/rideservices/unsustainable.pdf.

52. https://www.theatlantic.com/business/archive/2016/10/uber-lyft-and -the-false-promise-of-fair-rides/506000/.

SEVEN: A WAY FORWARD

1. Sir Fred Hoyle, "Sayings of the Week," *Observer*, September 9, 1979.

2. https://www.recode.net/2018/1/9/16865384/smart-vehicles-cars-ford -cities-streets-disruption-sharing-smart-ces-ai-mobility.

3. https://www.citylab.com/transportation/2017/03/why-uber-is-promoting -road-pricing/521283/.

4. https://en.wikipedia.org/wiki/List_of_motor_vehicle_deaths_in_U.S. _by_year.

5. https://www.theguardian.com/technology/2015/sep/18/apple-meets
-california-officials-self-driving-car.

6. Melanie Zanona, "House Gets Serious about Driverless Cars," *The Hill*,
February 14, 2017, http://thehill.com/policy/transportation/319450-house
-lawmakers-weigh-driverless-car-laws.

7. https://www.vox.com/2014/5/28/5758560/driverless-cars-will-mean
-the-end-of-car-ownership.

8. https://www.bicycling.com/culture/paris-electric-bikes-cargo-bikes
-subsidies.

9. David Sachs, "Road Diet, New Sidewalks, and Bike Lanes Coming to Blake
Street Bridge," *StreetsBlogDenver*, May 13, 2015, https://denver.streetsblog.org
/2015/05/13/road-diet-new-sidewalks-and-bike-lanes-coming-to-blake-street
-bridge/.

10. https://denver.streetsblog.org/2016/04/07/mayor-hancock-public
-works-open-the-redesigned-blake-street-bridge/.

11. http://www.denverpost.com/2016/11/14/denver-city-council-budget
-vote/.

12. https://seattletransitblog.com/2013/08/19/your-bus-much-more-often
-no-more-money-really/.

13. http://www.sciencedirect.com/science/article/pii/S2352146516302794
?via%3Dihub.

14. http://ubigo.se/wp-content/uploads/2017/10/Press-release-UbiGo
-Fludtime-MaaS-Stockholm.pdf.

15. Olli Sulopuisto, "Why Helsinki's Innovative On-Demand Bus Service
Failed," *Citiscope*, March 4, 2016, http://citiscope.org/story/2016/why-helsinkis
-innovative-demand-bus-service-failed.

16. Sulopuisto, "Why Helsinki's Innovative On-Demand Bus Service Failed."

17. Bern Grush, "The Future of Transit Is Ride Sharing and Driverless Cars,"
Toronto Star, November 20, 2017, https://www.thestar.com/opinion/contributors
/2017/11/20/the-future-of-transit-is-ride-sharing-and-driverless-cars.html.

18. Regina R. Clewlow and Gouri Shankar Mishra, "Disruptive Transportation: The Adoption, Utilization, and Impacts of Ride-Hailing in the United
States," UC Davis Institute of Transportation Studies research report UCD-
ITS-RR-17-07, October 2017, 5, https://www.scribd.com/document
/372432822/Disruptive-Transportation-The-Adoption-Utilization-and-Impacts
-of-Ride-Hailing-in-the-United-States.

19. http://www.princeton.edu/~alaink/Orf467F16/SamSchwartz092616
PrincetonUniversity.pdf.

20. https://www.thespruce.com/public-transportation-reasons-people-hate
-it-1709096.

21. http://www.apta.com/resources/reportsandpublications/Documents/twenty_first_century.pdf.

22. https://commuteseattle.com/wp-content/uploads/2018/02/2017-Commuter-Mode-Split-Survey-Report.pdf.

23. https://usa.streetsblog.org/2017/02/03/columbus-is-about-to-double-access-to-frequent-bus-service/.

24. https://media.ford.com/content/fordmedia/fna/us/en/news/2017/02/10/ford-invests-in-argo-ai-new-artificial-intelligence-company.html; https://www.nytimes.com/2017/10/09/business/general-motors-driverless.html.

25. http://thisbigcity.net/five-cities-with-congestion-pricing/.

26. Andy Cohen, telephone interview with the author, January 8, 2018.

27. https://fee.org/articles/retail-stores-are-dying-and-we-should-let-them/.

28. https:/untappedcities.com/2013/07/23/repurposed-parking-spaces-garages-in-new-york-city-the-exley-antique-garage-barcade-the-park/; https://nypost.com/2017/08/26/i-turned-a-garage-into-a-loft-so-i-could-live-with-my-van/; http://www.seacoastonline.com/news/20170813/committee-shaping-vision-for-reuse-of-parking-lots.

29. https://www.scientificamerican.com/article/self-driving-cars-could-cut-greenhouse-gas-pollution/.

30. https://www.an-onymous.com/news/2017/4/26/iman-ansari-and-marta-nowak-at-amazons-radical-urban-transportation-salon.

Index

Samuel I. Schwartz, aka "Gridlock Sam," is one of the leading transportation experts in the United States today. He served as New York City's traffic commissioner and the New York City Department of Transportation's chief engineer. Schwartz currently runs Sam Schwartz Engineering and is a columnist at the *New York Daily News*. He has been profiled in the *New Yorker*, the *New York Times*, and many other national publications. Schwartz lives in New York City and owns a Volvo that can drive without him.

Karen Kelly is a freelance writer specializing in current events, business, and culture. Visit her at karenkellythewriter.com.